7047

Textual Politics from Slavery to Postcolonialism

Textual Politics from Slavery to Postcolonialism

Race and Identification

Carl Plasa

First published in Great Britain 2000 by
MACMILLAN PRESS LTD
Houndmills, Basingstoke, Hampshire RG21 6XS and London
Companies and representatives throughout the world

A catalogue record for this book is available from the British Library.

ISBN 0–333–68769–8 hardcover
ISBN 0–333–68770–1 paperback

First published in the United States of America 2000 by
ST. MARTIN'S PRESS, INC.,
Scholarly and Reference Division,
175 Fifth Avenue, New York, N.Y. 10010

ISBN 0–312–23003–6 (cloth)
ISBN 0–312–23004–4 (paperback)

Library of Congress Cataloging-in-Publication Data
Plasa, Carl, 1959–
Textual politics from slavery to postcolonialism : race and identification / Carl
Plasa.
    p.   cm.
Includes bibliographical references and index.
ISBN 0–312–23003–6 (cloth) — ISBN 0–312–23004–4 (pbk.)
    1. English fiction—Women authors—History and criticism.   2. Race in literature.
    3. Equiano, Olaudah, b.1745. Interesting narrative of the life of Olaudah Equiano.
    4. Politics and literature—English-speaking countries—History—20th century.
    5. Politics and literature—English-speaking countries—History—19th century.
    6. Women and literature—English-speaking countries—History.
    7. Postcolonialism—English-speaking countries.   8. Decolonization in literature.
    9. Group identity in literature.   10. Slavery in literature.   I. Title.

PR830.R34 P57   1999
823.009'353—dc21

                                                                99–050362

This book is printed on paper suitable for recycling and made from fully managed and sustained
forest sources.

10   9   8   7   6   5   4   3   2   1
09   08   07   06   05   04   03   02   01   00

Printed and bound in Great Britain by Antony Rowe Ltd, Chippenham, Wiltshire

Contents

Acknowledgements

Chapter 3 first appeared, in slightly different form, in *The Discourse of Slavery: Aphra Behn to Toni Morrison*, ed. and intro. Carl Plasa and Betty J. Ring, Foreword by Isobel Armstrong (London and New York: Routledge, 1994), pp. 64–93, and chapter 6 is a substantially revised and expanded version of an article originally published in *Journal of Commonwealth Literature*, 33. 1 (1998), pp. 35–45. I am grateful to Routledge and *JCL* for permission to reprint. Chapter 4 was first published in *Gulliver: Deutsche-Englische Jahrbücher*, 34. 2 (1993), pp. 42–59.

Material from *Wide Sargasso Sea* by Jean Rhys (Penguin Books, 1968) copyright © 1966 by Jean Rhys is reproduced by permission of Penguin Books Ltd. and W. W. Norton & Company Inc. and from *The Bluest Eye* by Toni Morrison (Picador, 1994) by permission of International Creative Management, Inc. copyright © by Toni Morrison, 1994.

Introduction

> every image of the past that is not recognized by the
> present as one of its own concerns threatens to disappear
> irretrievably.
>
> Walter Benjamin[1]

Postcolonialism today

Over the last ten years or so, postcolonialism has established itself
as an important, challenging and exciting form of inquiry within
the humanities, especially for critics and theorists working in the
increasingly interdisciplinary and politicized realm of what was once
called 'English'. Its impact within this realm has been felt most
powerfully in Britain and America – a situation at once ironic and
appropriate, given these two nations' interlocking histories of colonial domination and racialized slavery – and shows every indication
of continuing to develop into the next millennium. Signs of the
astonishing growth of interest in things postcolonial are everywhere
to be seen. Throughout the 1990s, for example, several prestigious
and theoretically informed academic journals devoted special issues
to colonialism and/or postcolonialism[2] and journals exclusively
dedicated to these topics have recently been launched, from *Jouvert*,
on the Internet (1997), to *Interventions*, under the general editorship
of Robert J. C. Young (1998). Anthologies of postcolonial criticism
and theory have been produced, together with introductory guides
to the field, suitable for undergraduate and specialist alike, and
there has been a number of major book-length studies.[3] In response
to these proliferating critical activities, new undergraduate modules
on postcolonialism have entered the curriculum and specialist MA

1

programmes, emanating mainly from university English departments, have emerged, one of the most recent of these being in the Centre for English Studies at the University of London, commencing in 1998.[4]

Like Benjamin's much fêted 'angel of history',[5] the postcolonial critic looks as much back as around. S/he is concerned not only with literature and culture produced in the postwar wake of formal decolonization, but also with colonialism itself, together with the difficult question of the relation between the colonial and the postcolonial. On the whole, postcolonialism strikes a cautionary note with regard to the linear and liberatory promise contained in its 'post'.[6] The discourses which helped to sustain slavery, colonialism, the building of nations and empires and their attendant racial/racist configurations remain, as Isobel Armstrong notes, 'a matter of living debate as well as the object of historical analysis [and] have not disappeared in a grand narrative which charts emancipation'.[7] This book takes such an argument as its guiding assumption and defines itself as a contribution to the ongoing critical and theoretical project outlined above.

Race and identification

The book's specific concern is with questions of race and identification as they are articulated in and across a range of writings from the era of the Enlightenment – a period in which 'racialised reason and white supremacist terror'[8] stand complicit – to the present. While it locates the texts it examines in their particular historical and cultural contexts and provides close readings of their linguistic operations, the book is equally concerned to highlight the intertextual connections and elements of counterpoint between them. Drawing explicitly on postcolonial theory – particularly the work of Homi K. Bhabha and Frantz Fanon, that 'specter haunting [the] postcolonial world'[9] – the book also enlists the insights of feminism, deconstruction and psychoanalysis. The central aim is to illustrate the ways in which the processes of identification examined here are always implicated in a certain textual and/or intertextual politics.

These processes take different forms according to the different texts, and historical and cultural milieux, in which they are inscribed. In Olaudah Equiano's slave narrative, *The Interesting Narrative of the Life of Olaudah Equiano, or Gustavus Vassa, The African. Written by Himself.* (1789), identification occurs in the space between a black male subject and its white other and is a mode of resistance which invites theorization in terms of the destabilizing structures of colonial mimicry outlined by Bhabha. In Jane Austen's *Mansfield Park* (1814) and Charlotte Brontë's *Jane Eyre* (1847), it is specifically textual, operating, problematically, in terms of the figurative doublings of white women with African and creole slaves in the West Indies. In Jean Rhys's *Wide Sargasso Sea* (1966), the process of identification occurs between a white creole woman and a number of black others and is dramatized, equally problematically, as a kind of fantasmatic crossing into the place occupied by those others. Toni Morrison's *The Bluest Eye* (1970) also inscribes identification in terms of fantasy, while reversing the movement from black to white and exposing both the cultural construction of racial difference and the harrowing effects to which it gives rise. In Tsitsi Dangarembga's *Nervous Conditions* (1988), identification with and resistance to the norms of the colonizer are played out across the symptomatology of the black female body.

Together with its historical breadth, the book focuses on texts which are culturally diverse – located, as they are, in British, Caribbean, African American and African contexts. Such breadth and diversity are deliberate, however, for the inscriptions of racial crossing with which the book deals themselves participate in larger networks of transhistorical and cross-cultural dialogue, revision, interchange and contestation. Equiano writes back to an Enlightenment ideology of race as Dangarembga reworks the figurings of the white female body in Charlotte Brontë. Brontë is situated, in her turn, between Austen and Rhys, in a narrative of colonial and postcolonial textual responses. Similarly, Morrison, and Dangarembga again, engage, implicitly and explicitly, with the work of Fanon, while complicating his male-centred critique from their own distinct black feminist perspectives.

Textual politics

The book's first chapter offers a reading of Equiano's *The Interesting Narrative*. Its main arguments can be introduced by considering a brief extract from John Newton's *Thoughts upon the African Slave Trade*, published one year prior to the appearance of Equiano's text. Describing the typical conditions on board a slaver taking captured Africans to the New World, Newton writes: 'The slaves lie in two rows, one above the other, like books upon a shelf. I have known them so close that the shelf could not, easily, contain one more.'[10] One of the effects of Newton's book simile is to take up the oddly textual figure of the black diaspora as a Middle Passage,[11] turning the hold of the slave ship, in a grotesque irony, into a kind of library, symbol of civilization, learning and tradition. At the same time, the simile works to reduce the black subject to the status of a silent object to be read and construed as its interpreter might wish.

Equiano's own book directly reverses such an objectified status. *The Interesting Narrative*, moreover, is a book which engages with other books, rewriting and subverting the white archive of an Enlightenment discourse on race for its own purposes. Throughout *The Interesting Narrative*, the black male subject repeatedly dramatizes itself as embodying the traits which a white racist culture characteristically and exclusively arrogates to itself, while also, at significant junctures, figuring that same culture in the terms which it projects onto blackness. Taking on the features of an idealized Englishness and emerging, variously, as 'black Christian',[12] entrepreneur and even imperialist, Equiano's 'I' engages in a process which can be theorized in terms of Bhabha's notion of colonial mimicry. In Equiano's text, as in Bhabha's theory, 'the look of surveillance returns as the displacing gaze of the disciplined . . . the observer becomes the observed and "partial" representation rearticulates the whole notion of *identity* and alienates it from essence'.[13] This is the subversiveness of Equiano's autobiographical mimicry: unravelling the oppositions which ordinarily sustain and legitimate the hierarchies of race (white/black, civilized/savage, human/subhuman), *The Interesting Narrative* at the same time dissolves the discourses of difference which are slavery's essentializing and essential ground. The abolitionist politics of Equiano's text is inseparable from its autobiographical mode, the techniques by which the black male subject represents itself to a white audience.

The Englishness with which Equiano disruptively aligns himself is extolled and embodied, critics usually agree, in the work of Jane Austen. Ironically, however, it is not until recently that Austen's novels – and particularly *Mansfield Park* (1814) – have received detailed analysis from the perspectives of the colonialism and slavery in which such Englishness is fully entrammelled – in the work of Edward W. Said, Suvendrini Perera and Moira Ferguson, for example. The book's second chapter sets out to supplement and extend the critical decolonization of Austen through a reading of *Mansfield Park*, arguing that questions of colonialism and slavery in Austen's post-abolition novel are fully interwoven with what might be called its textual strategies. Adapting Pierre Macherey's psychoanalytically inspired notion of history as the unconscious of the literary text, the chapter begins by suggesting that the history repressed in Austen's novel is pre-eminently a colonial one. Yet, as Freudian psycho-analysis points out, it is in the nature of the repressed always to return, albeit in disguised or distorted forms. This movement of return, the chapter argues, is traceable in *Mansfield Park*, as the slavery which is the subject of Equiano's text is refigured, in Austen's, in the form of domestic oppressions enacted in the registers of gender, sexuality and class. Such a play of repression and return is only proper to a text itself concerned constantly with inclusion and exclusion, the setting and transgression of boundaries and the possi-bility of various kinds of encroachment. What is important about the uncanny reinscription of the colonial in and as the domestic, however, is the political ironies to which it leads: the identifica-tion of Englishwoman with slave, which Austen's text implies and presupposes, is at the very least dubious. The return of a repressed colonial history, it transpires, is only the hazardous prelude to its reexpulsion by a different path.

Chapter 3 develops recent rereadings of Charlotte Brontë's *Jane Eyre* (1847) which recover precisely those questions of race and colonial slavery marginalized by the text itself as by many of its earlier Anglo-American feminist critics. In so doing, it argues that Brontë's novel implicitly constitutes a broad revision of Austen's, looking back to *Mansfield Park* while at the same time inverting its textual operations. The chapter focuses on the lexicon of mastery and enslavement within the text and seeks to illustrate its politi-cally double-sided nature. On the one hand, this lexicon systematically constructs and empowers the narrative. The eponymous fictional self is thus apparently able to understand its own identity, just as Brontë herself secures an effective means of elaborating a critique of gender- and class-relations within early Victorian England. Yet the very power which the text's figurative structures accord to its heroine and authoress alike is also one that they reappropriate, taking it back across the gap between enslavement as metaphor and the literal experience of colonial oppression obscurely in-scribed in the novel's margins. This is the first major difference between the inscription of slavery in Brontë's text and Austen's: for Brontë, colonial slavery offers a resource through which to figure the socio-sexual dilemmas of middle-class English women, while in Austen it is that which is figured. Yet in so far as both texts mobilize suspect analogies between colonial domination and forms of female oppression at home, they reveal themselves to share a textual politics whose assumptions solicit interrogation. Indeed – in another significant departure from *Mansfield Park* – Brontë's text itself performs such questioning. Co-opting the slave trope for its own ends, *Jane Eyre* simultaneously disputes and dismantles its own rhetorical strategies, offering a complex and pre-emptive critique of the political problems they entail.

Jean Rhys's *Wide Sargasso Sea* (1966) is the subject of chapter 4 and explicitly revises *Jane Eyre*, as *Jane Eyre* covertly rewrites *Mansfield Park*. Yet as much as it reworks its colonial pre-text, Rhys's novel, in two important senses, also repeats it. If metaphor is the trope of identification *par excellence*, it is refashioned, in Rhys, into the shape of what might be called a certain racial fantasmatics: the narrative of a white creole female subjectivity, which Rhys reclaims from the encrypting silences of Brontë's text, is marked, ironically, by the very movement or crossing from white to black which is the leitmotif of Jane Eyre's story. The continuity between colonial and postcolonial representations is underscored in the ways in which Rhys's text, like Brontë's, seems determined to resist the perils of the identificatory logic which it sets in motion.

Chapter 5 considers Toni Morrison's *The Bluest Eye* (1970). While acknowledging the importance of the tensions between Morrison's novel and the black political and aesthetic movements of the historical moment in which it is written, the chapter invokes Paul Gilroy's notion of the black Atlantic as a means of bringing Morrison's text into intertextual dialogue with Fanon's *Black Skin, White Masks* (1952). The chapter argues that *The Bluest Eye* simultaneously takes up and reinflects the insights of Fanon's work from the perspective of an emergent African American feminism. Like Fanon's text, *The Bluest Eye* concerns itself with pathologies of identification, exploring slavery's legacies and critiquing the ideology of race and its effects upon black subjectivity. In Morrison's text – as in Fanon's again – these effects are primarily encountered, by the black subject, at the level of the scopic, where they are played out in terms of images and representations, sight, seeing and being/not being seen. Yet as well as being an enabling text for Morrison's project, *Black Skin, White Masks* presents certain problems. Privileging black male subjectivity, Fanon evidently has little time for 'the woman of color',[14] as he calls her, representing the figure of Mayotte Capécia, in the second chapter of *Black Skin, White Masks*, in disparagingly sexist terms and failing to take into account the extent to which issues of racial oppression are complicated by gender difference. Such a complication is precisely the *métier*, by contrast, of *The Bluest Eye*, which focuses on the ultimately self-destructive yearning of its central character – the 11-year-old Pecola Breedlove – for 'the eyes of a little white girl'.[15] In this way, Morrison's text shows itself to be principally (though by no means exclusively) concerned with charting the pathologies of identification from the perspective of the black female subjectivity which Fanon so resolutely marginalizes. In thus reslanting the Fanonian critique, Morrison is at the same time able to address dangerous and disturbing questions of intraracial oppression – particularly in the form of Pecola's rape by Cholly, her father – that are elided in Fanon. 'I is an other'[16] in Morrison's text not only with regard to the desired identifications dramatized by its narrative, but also in terms of its confabulation with Fanon and the shift which the novel effects from male to female.

The book concludes with a reading of Tsitsi Dangarembga's *Nervous Conditions* (1988), placing it in a twofold revisionary dialogue, with Fanon's *The Wretched of the Earth* (1961), on the one hand, and Charlotte Brontë's *Shirley* (1849), on the other. These seemingly heterogeneous intertextual relations are mediated through the question of female anorexia as it is enigmatically posed by Nyasha, cousin and *alter ego* to Tambudzai, the narrator of Dangarembga's novel. Nyasha's anorexia is a disorder carrying a dual significance. Like the figurings of female hunger in *Shirley*, it serves, first, as a form of protest against the containment and regulation of women by patriarchy (whether African or Western), while operating, secondly, as the symptom of resistance to colonial oppression. In these terms it provides a powerful means by which *Nervous Conditions* appropriates and reinscribes its intertexts. In drawing attention to a case of female colonial pathology, *Nervous Conditions* effects a black feminist recasting of the androcentric emphasis of *The Wretched of the Earth*, which remains as pronounced in this text as in the earlier *Black Skin, White Masks*. Equally, the disruptive figuration of the anorexia of a black female body as a site of colonial resistance extends the meanings of its white Brontëan counterparts in *Shirley*. At the same time, however, *Shirley*'s anorexic bodies carry colonial burdens of their own. Like the starving bodies of the working-class men in the novel, they bear the marks of that catastrophe which constitutes the historical frame for Brontë's novel – the Irish Famine of 1845–51.

In these ways, identification – whether from black to white or white to black – emerges as a complex, highly charged and multifaceted phenomenon, linking a number of major texts and the violent histories of slavery, colonialism and racial oppression by which they are traversed. As much as, in some cases, they are sites of political struggle and friction, the crossings of identification constitute spaces, in others, where psychic and historical realities, the subjective and the ideological, dramatically collide.

1

'Almost an Englishman': Colonial Mimicry in *The Interesting Narrative of the Life of Olaudah Equiano, or Gustavus Vassa, the African. Written by Himself.*

> If one aspect of the project of Western civilization was to make the inferior others, by education and example, as much like the Whites as possible, another aspect was to maintain precisely that difference which justified white authority.
>
> David Murray[1]

'Burn but his books': Caliban, Equiano, Bhabha

In the third act of William Shakespeare's *The Tempest* (1611), Stephano and Caliban conspire together on the question of how best to put an end to Prospero's rule, both over Caliban's island, which Prospero has colonized, and Caliban himself, whom he has enslaved. After protracted debate, Caliban finally advances a programme of insurgency:

> Why, as I told thee, 'tis a custom with him
> I' th' afternoon to sleep: there thou mayst brain him,
> Having first seiz'd his books; or with a log
> Batter his skull, or paunch him with a stake,
> Or cut his wezand with thy knife. Remember
> First to possess his books; for without them
> He's but a sot, as I am, nor hath not
> One spirit to command: they all do hate him
> As rootedly as I. Burn but his books.[2]

9

What is striking here is Caliban's recognition of the importance of the role played by Prospero's 'books' in securing and maintaining his subjection. Even though the master is to be killed while sleeping, it is none the less thought prudent to 'first seiz[e]', 'possess' and finally 'Burn . . . his books' before the projected murder can be carried out. The suggestion, indeed, is that it is the 'books' themselves which construct the white colonizer and his native other as human and monster, master and slave respectively, 'for without them', as Caliban surmises, the differences between the two dissolve into likeness – 'He's but a sot, as I am'. What is radical, in turn, about such a dissolution is that it erodes the legitimating ground on which the exertion of the colonizer's discriminatory power is based.

Caliban's insight into the complicities between forms of representation and knowledge, on the one hand, and the implementation of power, on the other, has become axiomatic for much postcolonial theory and criticism over the last twenty years or so. It is, however, also operative at a much earlier historical juncture, in the context of the slave narrative tradition of the eighteenth and nineteenth centuries, within which Olaudah Equiano's *The Interesting Narrative of the Life of Olaudah Equiano, or Gustavus Vassa, the African. Written by Himself.* (1789) occupies a central position.

As a slave narrative, Equiano's text unfolds as a double inscription. At one level, it is autobiographical in form, a linear charting of the changing states through which its subject passes: from an original freedom in Africa, through the monumental ruptures of the Middle Passage and enslavement in America and the West Indies, to manumission and the eventual recovery of a liberty memorably celebrated by the ex-slave's dancing in 'Georgia superfine blue cloathes'.[3] Such secular progress is itself the allegorical prelude to a spiritual movement which delivers the penitent into the Christian faith as, in another memorable formulation, Equiano describes how 'the Lord was pleased to break in upon [his] soul with . . . bright beams of heavenly light' (*IN*, p. 190). Yet *The Interesting Narrative* is not solely an act of self-representation. It also participates in a far larger political project, specifically designed, as it is, to further the campaign for the abolition of the slave trade, just formally commencing in both public and parliamentary spheres at the time when the text was first published and finally succeeding in 1807, ten years after Equiano's death.

Like the Caliban of *The Tempest*, Equiano is much concerned, throughout his narrative, with 'books' and the nexus of power/ knowledge of which they are a part. This is clearly suggested in a scene which occurs in chapter 3, during the early phases of his enslavement. Here Equiano recalls the contrasting figures of his master, Michael Henry Pascal (a British naval officer with whom he also served during the Seven Years' War of 1756–63) and Richard Baker, a young white boy who functions as 'constant companion and instructor' (*IN*, p. 65):

> I had often seen my master and Dick employed in reading; and I had a great curiosity to talk to the books, as I thought they did; and so to learn how all things had a beginning: for that purpose I have often taken up a book, and have talked to it, and then put my ears to it, when alone, in hopes it would answer me; and I have been very much concerned when I found it remained silent. (*IN*, p. 68)

As Henry Louis Gates, Jr. points out, this passage is marked by a striking shift of tense (from past to present, 'I had' to 'I have'),[4] as an original failure and frustration of reading seems to repeat itself in the moment of a later narration. Such a shift, however, is subtly ironic. For in thus deploying what Gates calls 'the trope of the Talking Book', Equiano implicitly signals a certain conversancy and alignment with other contemporary black writers – from James Gronniosaw and John Marrant to Ottobah Cugoano – in whose work the trope had previously appeared.[5] By repeating and revising the trope for his own purposes, Equiano simultaneously 'names his relation', as Gates puts it, 'to his three antecedent authors as that of [a] chain of narrators, a link, as it were, between links'.[6]

If the motif of the 'Talking Book' is the sign of a self-consciously intertextual relation to an emergent body of black writing – 'The literature of the slave' in Gates's phrase[7] – it points, in the same gesture, in an alternative direction: the 'books' over which Equiano's master and friend labour are, of course, white texts and can be read as a synecdoche for the Enlightenment discourse of race which comes to be elaborated and consolidated during the mid to late eighteenth-century period spanned by Equiano's narrative.

While it is important – as Emmanuel Chukwudi Eze notes – not to reduce this discourse to a 'monolithic or unanimous picture',[8] it is equally possible, he suggests, to discern a dominant pattern to the inscription of racial difference during the Enlightenment, which at once enables, authorizes and perpetuates the contemporary colonial project in general and, in Equiano's case, the slave trade, within that project, in particular. In *Race and the Enlightenment*, Eze usefully collects together some of the cardinal documents which go to establish this pattern, one of which is David Hume's 'Of National Characters' (1748). Hume's famous footnote, added to the 1754 version of his essay, indicates the kind of discursive milieu which Equiano's own 'book' must enter:

> I am apt to suspect the negroes and in general all other species of men ... to be naturally inferior to the whites. There never was a civilized nation of any other complexion than white, nor even any individual eminent either in action or speculation. No ingenious manufactures amongst them, no arts, no sciences. . . . Such a uniform and constant difference could not happen, in so many countries and ages if nature had not made an original distinction between these breeds of men. Not to mention our colonies, there are negroe slaves dispersed all over Europe, of whom none ever discovered any symptoms of ingenuity; though low people without education will start up amongst us and distinguish themselves in every profession. In Jamaica, indeed, they talk of one negroe [Francis Williams] as a man of parts and learning; but it is likely he is admired for slender accomplishments, like a parrot who speaks a few words plainly.[9]

Here racial difference is essentialized and hierarchized, as 'the negroes' are figured and fixed as 'naturally inferior to the whites', inherently incapable of those 'ingenious manufactures', 'arts' and 'sciences' which are deemed to be exclusively the properties of a 'civilized' – that is, white-complexioned – 'nation'.

Hume's vision of an 'original distinction' between 'negroes' and 'whites' finds its echo in Immanuel Kant's *Observations on the Feeling of the Beautiful and Sublime* (1764). Directly citing Hume, Kant argues that the 'difference between these two races of man' is 'fundamental' and 'as great in regard to mental capacities as in color'.[10] The position adopted by both philosophers – seminal figures in Europe's Enlightenment – has its transatlantic reflection in Thomas Jefferson's *Notes on the State of Virginia* (1787), in which the difference between black and white is said, once again, to be 'fixed in nature' and confirmed by Jefferson's dismayed confession: 'But never yet could I find that a black had uttered a thought above the level of plain narration'.[11]

From this brief overview of the Enlightenment writing of race it becomes apparent that the white 'books' with which *The Interesting Narrative* engages in dialogue are themselves a somewhat garrulous corpus, involved in their own confabulation with one another. The point is summarized by Eze:

> In this climate of in- and cross-breeding of citations and cross-references, one writer being quite dependent upon others in the trading of ideas and authorities, there is room, I think, to speak of the Enlightenment as a historical period that provided . . . identifiable scientific and philosophical vocabulary: 'race,' 'progress,' 'civilization,' 'savagery,' 'nature'. . . . This vocabulary belongs to, and reveals, a larger world of analytical categories that exists as a universe of discourse . . . which, in turn, determines (by making possible and constraining at the same time) not only how studies are done, but also what are constituted as objects of scientific, philosophical, or cultural study.[12]

It is equally apparent, however, that *The Interesting Narrative* stands in an acute and disruptive tension with the taxonomies of racial difference outlined above. If the driving concern of Equiano's politicized autobiography is to help bring about the demise of the slave trade, the central strategy through which it seeks to accomplish such an aim entails persuading the 'candid' (*IN*, p. 5) – that is, white[13] – reader of the text that the one who narrates it is fully capable of participating in that reader's humanity, of being, at least metaphorically, white also. In adopting such a strategy, as Susan M. Marren argues, Equiano thus 'manages to counter the ideological tactics which assign racial subjects essentialist identities',[14] ironically exposing the 'original distinction' between those subjects to be less something that is 'made by nature', as Hume *et al.* would have it, than itself an 'ingenious manufacture[ ]' of their own construction – an ideological fiction. The effect of this reconfiguration of white/black relations in terms of sameness rather than difference is to render both the slave trade and slavery itself untenable since – following the logic of Caliban indeed – the discursive system on which they rely has been dismantled.

Equiano's deployment of such a strategy as a means of negotiating and critiquing the Enlightenment construction of race and the systems of oppression which it underpins simultaneously opens up *The Interesting Narrative* to another dialogue – with the work of the postcolonial theorist Homi K. Bhabha and, in particular, Bhabha's theorization of colonial relations in terms of mimicry. The usefulness of Bhabha's work on mimicry for a reading of Equiano's text lies in the association which he makes between 'resemblance and menace'. On the one hand, Bhabha argues that the process of 'colonial mimicry' entails on the part of the colonizer a 'desire for a reformed, recognizable Other'. Yet, on the other hand, far from leading to a reassuring consolidation of colonial power, such a process works only to produce a certain crisis in its authority: the moments in which the colonized subject becomes like the colonizer are also moments of anxiety and threat, revealing the differences between the two parties to be ideologically constructed rather than grounded, for example, in racial origin. It is for this reason that colonial discourse, for Bhabha, as manifested in the troubling shape of mimicry, is ambivalent and produces its 'excess or slippage'.[15] It imposes a double injunction upon the colonized subject to resemble the colonizer and yet to remain safely different, *'almost the same'*, in Bhabha's tersely insistent formulations, *'but not quite'*, *'Almost the same but not white'*.[16]

As a coda to the first section of this chapter, it is perhaps worth returning briefly to the Hume footnote cited above. In the light of Bhabha's theorization of mimicry as a mode of colonial resistance, Hume's comparison of the 'negroe' alleged to be 'a man of parts and learning' to 'a parrot who speaks a few words plainly' becomes somewhat ironic. The simile clearly carries the derogatory implication that the Western-educated black male subject is ultimately little more than a weak copy of his 'authentic' white counterpart. Yet what is Hume's plain-speaking parrot if not a precise figure for the duplicities of colonial mimicry as outlined by Bhabha? Hume's chosen rhetorical figure (which is itself marked by a tension between similarity and difference) appears to function as the sure sign of an essential – and essentialist – distinction between black and white, even as it hints, by the same token, at a potentially unsettling likeness.

The textual politics of mimicry

For the first seven chapters of his narrative, from the instant of capture – together with his 'dear sister' (*IN*, p. 47) – in what is now Nigeria, until the moment when he becomes '[his] own master, and compleatly free' (*IN*, p. 137), Equiano occupies the position of an object of constant appropriation, commodification and exchange.

In Africa itself he passes through 'various hands' in the course of a journey of some 'six or seven months' which culminates in an arrival at the 'sea coast' (*IN*, p. 54). Here he is confronted by the spectacle of a 'slave-ship . . . riding at anchor' and exchanged between the 'black people . . . who brought [him] on board' and the 'white men' (*IN*, p. 55) who form the ship's crew. Following the Middle Passage from Africa to the New World, he is sold and resold from one white master to another. The Virginia planter who is his initial white owner sells him to Pascal who sells him, briefly, to Captain James Doran. Doran sells him, in turn, to Robert King, a Quaker merchant from Philadelphia.

As if to offset these literal/corporeal appropriations, Equiano's text might itself be said to perform a series of figurative counter-appropriations which, for Marren, are the autobiographer's prerogative since, as she puts it, 'In re-creating the self in writing, one can ascribe to oneself traits denied one in the material world'.[17] In Equiano's case, the 'traits' which the narrative 'I' ascribes or appropriates to itself are those which make up an essentialized whiteness – 'civilization, Christianity, nobility, justice, industry, intellect, truth'.[18] This play of appropriation – or, in Bhabha's terms, of mimicry – is supplemented by an opposite strategy as the ex-slave narrator rejects those characteristics said to define an essentialized blackness and shows them, in fact, to belong more properly to the white culture by which he is oppressed. Equiano thus grounds his opposition to the slave trade – described as 'a traffic both cruel and unjust' (*IN*, p. 5) – by setting in motion a textual counter-traffic, in which supposedly essentialized qualities are transported and exchanged across the 'color-line'[19] dividing white and black.

One of the most striking ways in which Equiano harnesses the strategy of an appropriative mimicry to the abolitionist project is in terms of the very act of writing *The Interesting Narrative* in the first place. As Gates has argued, the question of writing is a major concern throughout 'the eighteenth century's debate over slavery'. He offers a broad historical 'thesis' as to why this might be so:

After Descartes, reason was privileged, or valorized, over all other human characteristics. Writing, especially after the printing press became so widespread, was taken to be the visible sign of reason. Blacks were reasonable, and hence 'men,' if – and only if – they demonstrated mastery of 'the arts and sciences,' the eighteenth century's formula for writing. So, while the Enlightenment is

famous for establishing its existence upon man's ability to reason, it simultaneously used the absence and presence of reason
to delimit and circumscribe the very humanity of the cultures
and people of color which Europeans had been 'discovering' since
the Renaissance.[20]

From the perspective of Gates's argument, it is clear that writing
for Equiano is not just a means of self-inscription but a concrete
political act which is also a form of mimicry: by affirming himself
as a writing subject, Equiano suggests that he too possesses those
qualities of 'reason' and 'humanity' which the Enlightenment would
like to preserve as purely white.

There is a certain irony in the Enlightenment's promotion of writing
as the index of an irreducible difference between white and black,
European and African, human and subhuman. Considered precisely
as a 'visible sign', writing customarily consists in black marks –
like these ones – on a white page and might thus be expected, for
the Enlightenment, to connote the absence of the very qualities
of 'reason' and 'humanity' with which it is none the less associated. This disjunction between signifier and signified suggests that
other visible signs of difference – white skin versus black, for
example – are themselves not necessarily to be taken at face value.
As William Eddis, one of Equiano's abolitionist contemporaries, puts
it – in corroboration of this point – *The Interesting Narrative* 'fully
demonstrates that genius and worth are not limited to country or
complexion' (*IN*, p. 11).

Equiano's disclosure of the arbitrary nature of racial difference is
developed, beyond the issue of writing, in terms of the initial juxtaposition which *The Interesting Narrative* establishes between England
and Africa. Prefacing the text with a petition to the British Parliament, Equiano writes:

Permit me with the greatest deference and respect, to lay at your
feet the following genuine Narrative; the chief design of which
is to excite in your august assemblies a sense of compassion for
the miseries which the Slave Trade has entailed on my unfortu-
nate countrymen. By the horrors of that trade I was first torn
away from all the tender connexions that were dear to my heart;
but these, through the mysterious ways of Providence, I ought
to regard as infinitely more than compensated by the introduction I have thence obtained to the knowledge of the Christian

religion, and of a nation which, by its liberal sentiments, its humanity, the glorious freedom of its government, and its proficiency in arts and sciences, has exalted the dignity of human nature. (*IN,* p. 7)

There are a number of tensions and ambiguities in Equiano's language here, which slyly cut against the grain of its overt meaning and disturb its civil surfaces. The first of these occurs in the *fait accompli* of Equiano's opening 'Permit me' formulation, which paradoxically demands of his 'august assemblies' that they allow him to tell his story. Nor is it entirely clear to whom 'the greatest deference and respect' are to be shown: are these the qualities with which Equiano approaches his white audience, or ones which it should accord to him? The flickering inversion of racial hierarchies suggested by the latter possibility is further supported in the ironic gesture of prostration with which Equiano casts his 'genuine Narrative' at the 'feet' of its white readers, since the very writing of the text – as noted earlier – already puts author and readership on a subversively equal footing. This irony is compounded, finally, by another: in claiming that he 'ought to regard' the traumas of the Middle Passage as 'infinitely more than compensated' by exposure to the finest elements of the English 'nation' to which it has led, Equiano suggests that this, in fact, is a view he does not necessarily entertain.

Beyond these textual slippages, the most dramatic effect of Equiano's address is to confront the English with an image of themselves that is hopelessly contradictory, 'exalt[ing] the dignity of human nature', on the one hand, yet continuing in the practice of 'the Slave Trade', on the other. In highlighting the splits internal to the 'nation' that once enslaved him, Equiano suggests that the idea of 'human nature' is not quite as universal and inclusive as it seems to be, but something grounded, rather, in a logic of exclusion. As Robert Young argues:

> the category of the human, however exalted in its conception, [is] too often invoked only in order to put the male before the female, or to classify 'other' races as subhuman, and therefore not subject to the ethical prescriptions applicable to 'humanity' at large.[21]

The classification of '"other" races as subhuman' certainly plays its part in forging the 'immense cultural portrait of Africa and Africans current in England for nearly two centuries in England'[22] at the time when *The Interesting Narrative* originally appeared, and it is this portrait which is directly redrawn in the text's first chapter. Here Equiano's Ibo homeland certainly emerges as vastly different from the contemporary England where he later claims his 'heart had always been' (*IN*, p. 147), including cultural practices ranging from the ritual scarring of elders to polygamy and military conflicts in which 'Even [the] women are warriors' (*IN*, p. 39). Yet at the same time, as Marren notes, the Ibo and the English 'do not differ in ideals'. 'According to Equiano', she observes, the Ibo 'worship one god; prize industry, chastity, and cleanliness; and constitute "a nation of dancers, musicians, and poets"'.[23] In this way, both Africa and the slaves whose labour comes to be absorbed into the project of Enlightenment colonialism are textually figured less as being other to England and the English, than as similar. As an immediate challenge to the slave trade, Equiano's opening textual strategy – his juxtaposition of images of England and Africa, colonizer and colonized – is an effective one: as Peter Childs and Patrick Williams put it, in their analysis of Bhabha's mimetic model, 'Within the differences constructed by colonial discourse, to resemble is to threaten the basis of power and discrimination'.[24]

The 'constructed' nature of such 'differences' is underscored by Equiano's reworking, in chapter 2, of one of the topoi which govern representations of the colonial encounter between white and black. Recalling his arrival on the African 'coast' and the experience of being 'carried on board' the 'slave-ship . . . waiting for its cargo', Equiano comments:

When I looked round the ship . . . and saw a large furnace of copper boiling, and a multitude of black people of every description chained together, every one of their countenances expressing dejection and sorrow, I no longer doubted of my fate, and, quite overpowered with horror and anguish, I fell motionless on the deck and fainted. When I recovered a little, I found some black people about me, who I believed were some of those who brought me on board, and had been receiving their pay; they talked to me in order to cheer me, but all in vain. I asked them if we were not to be eaten by those white men with horrible looks, red faces, and long hair? They told me I was not. (*IN*, p. 55)

While Equiano's fear that he and his fellow slaves are to be 'eaten by . . . white men' proves to be ill-founded, it remains significant. In figuring his white masters as potential man-eaters, Equiano produces a direct reversal of contemporary historical accounts – like that proffered by Bryan Edwards – of the African as cannibal. For Edwards, indeed, it is the Ibo who 'are in fact more truly savage than any nation of the Gold Coast; inasmuch as many tribes among them . . . have been, without doubt, accustomed to the shocking practice of feeding on human flesh'.[25] In this way, colonizer and colonized, in Equiano's text, exchange places with one another, as the former become endowed with the qualities which they themselves attribute to the latter.

This strategic reversal of roles is obliquely developed by other details in Equiano's account of the Middle Passage. It is not just that the white rather than black body is linked – albeit erroneously – to cannibalism here, but that the black body is itself repeatedly dissociated from the act of eating altogether. Thrust 'down under the decks' of the slaver, Equiano at first becomes 'so sick and low that [he is] not able to eat' and 'on . . . [actively] refusing' sustenance is 'flogged . . . severely', just as other 'African prisoners' around him are 'hourly whipped' for the same defiance. Such rejections of food – like the slaves' suicidal attempts to 'leap into the water' (*IN*, p. 56) – clearly function as collective acts of resistance to colonial power: the black body chooses to starve itself rather than become the means of the production of capital for the white master. At the same time, however, they further undo the figure of the African as cannibal: far from displaying a predilection for Edwards's 'human flesh', and so nourishing his anxious fantasies, Equiano's slaves do not eat at all.

For Paul Gilroy, the ship on whose 'deck' Equiano initially falls 'motionless' is instrumental to the emergence and operation of what he calls 'the black Atlantic', a 'transcultural, international formation' linking the histories, cultures and peoples of 'Europe, America, Africa, and the Caribbean'.[26] Following a discussion of J. M. W. Turner's *The Slave Ship* (1840), Gilroy remarks:

> It should be emphasised that ships were the living means by which the points within [the] Atlantic world were joined. They were mobile elements that stood for the shifting spaces in between the fixed places that they connected. Accordingly they need to be thought of as cultural and political units rather than

abstract embodiments of the triangular trade. They were something more – a means to conduct political dissent and possibly
a distinct mode of cultural production. The ship provides a chance
to explore the articulations between the discontinuous histories
of England's ports, its interfaces with the wider world. Ships also
refer us back to the middle passage, to the half-remembered
micro-politics of the slave trade and its relationship to both in-
dustrialisation and modernisation.[27]

The Interesting Narrative certainly conforms to and in large measure
anticipates Gilroy's model of the black Atlantic as a network of
circulation and exchange between cultures.[28] During the course of
chapter 3 alone, Equiano maps a trajectory which takes him from
'the island of Barbadoes' (*IN*, p. 60) to America and then England.
Perhaps the most significant of the locations to which Equiano
voyages in this chapter, however, is the Channel Islands. '[P]laced . . .
to board and lodge' with one of Pascal's 'mates, who had a wife
and family there', Equiano finds himself quite literally embroiled
in his own version of one of those racial and cultural 'interfaces'
to which Gilroy alludes:

> This mate had a little daughter aged about five or six years, with
> whom I used to be much delighted. I had often observed, that
> when her mother washed her face it looked very rosy; but when
> she washed mine it did not look so; I therefore tried oftentimes
> myself if I could not by washing make my face of the same
> colour as my little play-mate . . . but it was all in vain; and I
> now began to be mortified at the difference in our complexions.
> (*IN*, p. 69)

At first glance, this passage would seem to suggest the sort of pathological identification with whiteness outlined by Frantz Fanon in
Black Skin, White Masks (1952), as 'The black man [who] wants to
be white'[29] is indeed 'mortified at the difference in . . . complexions'
between himself and the white other, coming to view his own blackness as a kind of scar. It is not only complexional difference, however,
that needs to be taken into account here but the distinction between narrated and narrating selves also. The ideology of whiteness
which the written self appears to have internalized is precisely what
the later writing self has already unlearned, as, for example, at the
conclusion to chapter 1, where Equiano challenges the opinion that

'God . . . forbore to stamp understanding on certainly his own image, because "carved in ebony[ ]"' (*IN*, p. 45). Yet if the insights of
the writing self with regard to the construction of racial difference
undercut the cosmetic endeavours of its younger textual counterpart, those endeavours serve none the less to allegorize the strategies
of mimicry deployed by Equiano's narrative as a whole: while Equiano
may not literally seek to whiten his face, his text repeatedly demonstrates the ways in which the black subject can do so metaphorically
and is as much entitled to define itself as 'civilized' as the white
culture that would figure it otherwise.

In thus opposing an essentialist ideology of race, Equiano necessarily also raises questions about the status of *The Interesting Narrative*
as a text 'written by an African in English'.[30] This is because, as
Fanon contends: 'To speak means to be in a position to use a certain syntax, to grasp the morphology of this or that language, but
it means above all to assume a culture, to support the weight of a
civilization'.[31] These questions of language prove to be particularly
complex and are addressed at the beginning of chapter 4. Here
Equiano writes:

> It was now between three and four years since I first came to
> England, a great part of which I had spent at sea; so that I be
> came inured to that service, and began to consider myself as
> happily situated; for my master treated me always extremely well;
> and my attachment and gratitude to him were very great. From
> the various scenes I had beheld on ship-board, I soon grew a
> stranger to terror of every kind, and was, in that respect at least,
> almost an Englishman. . . . I could now speak English tolerably
> well, and I perfectly understood every thing that was said. I now
> not only felt myself quite easy with these new countrymen, but
> relished their society and manners. I no longer looked upon them
> as spirits, but as men superior to us; and therefore I had the
> stronger desire to resemble them; to imbibe their spirit, and imitate
> their manners; I therefore embraced every occasion of improve
> ment; and every new thing that I observed I treasured up in my
> memory. (*IN*, pp. 77–8)

From a Fanonian perspective, Equiano's ability to 'speak English
tolerably well' equips him with a skill which also offers certain
dangers. Not the least of these is the internalization of the assumptions regarding racial difference with which the colonizer's language

is burdened – that 'Blackness and Englishness', in Gilroy's words for instance, 'are ... incompatible, mutually exclusive identities' and that 'To speak of the British or English people is to speak of the *white* people.'[32] In the passage in question there are numerous signs that – at this point in his exposure to white culture at least – Equiano has indeed become the victim of such an internalization, as the reader is once again tempted, in Chinosole's phrase, to 'reach ... for [his/her] frazzled copy of *Black Skin, White Masks*'.[33] For example, Equiano feels the 'desire to resemble' and 'imitate' an allegedly 'superior' white other and wishes to 'imbibe [the] spirit' of his 'new countrymen' – a formulation which carries its own ethereal suggestion of whiteness as racial essence. In addition, Equiano's description of himself as 'almost an Englishman' implies a recognition that full Englishness is denied to him on the basis of a blackness signalled, in its turn, by the pronoun 'us', alluding to the community of slaves of which he remains a part. In this way, Equiano would seem to share Bhabha's assertion that 'to be Anglicized is *emphatically* not to be English'.[34]

Yet if the self is remembered here as one who 'could speak English tolerably well' and has gone on to 'embrace[ ] every occasion of improvement', it follows that the self who does the remembering in the present speaks it better still, leavening the text with irony – that most 'English' of tropes. Equiano's strategy here is a kind of linguistic mimicry – repeating the language and ideology of the oppressor with a critical difference. Its effects are close to those formulated by Graham Huggan, in an essay on Derek Walcott and Jean Rhys, which also draws on Bhabha's thinking on mimicry:

> The 'mimic man' takes up the metropolitan desire to hear the strains of its own voice – to witness the duplication of its own authority – but he then rearticulates that desire as parody. ... he mimics His Master's Voice only to mock it: the simulated obedience of mimicry is revealed as a form of camouflaged disobedience, a means by which the totalizing discourses supporting colonial hierarchies of power are made to confront their own partiality.[35]

Discourses of mimicry: Christianity, enterprise, imperialism

One of those 'totalizing discourses' whose 'partiality' Equiano seeks to expose is Christianity. For Richard Dyer, Christianity – together with enterprise and imperialism – is integral to the 'constitution' of white identity. It 'is founded', he argues:

> on the idea – paradoxical, unfathomable, profoundly mysterious – of incarnation, of being that is in the body yet not of it. This provides a compelling cosmology, as well as a vivid imagery and set of narrative tropes, that survive as characteristics of Western culture. All concepts of *race*, emerging out of eighteenth-century materialism, are concepts of bodies, but all along they have had to be reconciled with notions of embodiment and incarnation. The latter become what distinguish white people, giving them a special relation to race. Black people can be reduced (in white culture) to their bodies and thus to race, but white people are something else that is realized in and yet is not reducible to the corporeal, or racial.[36]

The homologies established here – white is to black as Christian to non-Christian and spirit to body – are ones that *The Interesting Narrative* repeatedly overturns in the course of a series of scenes of religious instruction. The first of these scenes occurs towards the end of chapter 4, as Equiano nears the completion of his enslavement to Pascal and falls under the influence of 'one Daniel Queen, about forty years of age [and] very well educated' (*IN*, p. 91). As well as introducing Equiano to the secular arts of how 'to shave and dress hair a little', Queen acts as scriptural mentor:

> He taught me . . . to read in the Bible, explaining many passages to me, which I did not comprehend. I was wonderfully surprised to see the laws and rules of my country written almost exactly here; a circumstance which I believe tended to impress our manners and customs more deeply on my memory. I used to tell him of this resemblance; and many a time we had sat up the whole night together in this employment. In short he was like a father to me; and some even used to call me after his name; they also styled me the black Christian. (*IN*, p. 92)

The collective work of exegesis performed here by adept and protégé has a significance which extends beyond the boundaries of the text they read: Equiano's emergence as 'black Christian' hybridizes and conflates identities that, according to the racial essentialism elaborated by Dyer, should properly remain discrete. The enslaved African body reveals itself as fully able to accommodate the very spirit which supposedly 'distinguish[es] white people' from black. It is as if the earlier 'transmigration of souls' (*IN*, p. 40) to which Equiano alludes as one of 'the laws and rules of [his] country' has been bodied forth, as it were, by the mimetic operations of his text.

It is 'styled' as a 'black Christian' that Equiano also first appears before his white audience. As Vincent Carretta notes, the frontispiece to *The Interesting Narrative* pictures Equiano as the owner of 'an indisputably African body in European dress' (*IN*, p. xvii) and in this way could be said to give visual expression to the processes of mimicry dramatized within the text itself. Yet although the body framed by the frontispiece is black, it also partakes of that 'something else' of whiteness, as the Bible which Equiano is shown holding in his right hand metonymically endows him with a Christian soul. More particularly, the point at which Equiano's Bible is opened – Acts 4. 12 – constitutes an allusion to the moment of spiritual vision that precipitates his official conversion to the Christian faith. This moment is powerfully rendered in chapter 10:

> In the evening of the . . . day, as I was reading and meditating on the fourth chapter of the Acts, twelfth verse, under the solemn apprehensions of eternity, and reflecting on my past actions, I began to think I had lived a moral life, and that I had a proper ground to believe I had an interest in the divine favour; but still meditating on the subject, not knowing whether salvation was to be had partly from our own good deeds, or solely as the sovereign gift of God: – in this deep consternation the Lord was pleased to break in upon my soul with his bright beams of heavenly light; and in an instant, as it were, removing the veil, and letting light into a dark place. . . . I saw clearly, with the eye of faith, the crucified Saviour bleeding on the cross on Mount Calvary: the Scriptures became an unsealed book, I saw myself a condemned criminal under the law. . . . I saw the Lord Jesus Christ in his humiliation, loaded and bearing my reproach, sin, and shame. (*IN*, pp. 189–90)

The divine violation which Equiano undergoes is met by a different kind of infraction, as the very 'soul' into which 'the Lord [is] pleased to break' stands as the sign of a black body, 'not reducible', to recall Dyer, 'to the corporeal, or racial'. Just as 'light' enters 'a dark place' here, the converted black subject trespasses into realms that are not its 'proper ground' since, as Winthrop D. Jordan puts it, 'to be Christian [is] to be civilized rather than barbarous, English rather than African, white rather than black'.[37]

The identification of Christianity with whiteness is perhaps most clearly illustrated in the tradition of Western pictorial representations of Christ himself. As Dyer writes: 'The gentilizing and whitening of Christ was achieved by the end of the Renaissance and by the nineteenth century the image of him as not just fair-skinned but blond and blue-eyed was fully in place.'[38] From this perspective, it is clear that the body of 'the crucified Saviour bleeding on the cross' which Equiano beholds with his newly focused 'eye of faith' is coded as white. Yet in referring to himself as 'a condemned criminal under the law', Equiano subtly validates his 'interest in the divine favour'. Through such a description Equiano effects his own *imitatio Christi*: the phrase he applies to himself at the same time perfectly characterizes the one who is 'loaded' with his 'reproach, sin, and shame' and is, paradigmatically, a 'being that is in the body yet not of it'.

The sense in which the black body is as much the potential site of incarnation as its white other is underscored by the fate of John Annis, recounted shortly before the passage discussed above. Despite Equiano's best efforts and the 1772 Mansfield Judgement (which declared that slaves could not be removed from England against their will),[39] Annis finds himself taken by force from London to the West Indies by his former master in 1774 and tortured to death:

> and when the poor man arrived at St. Kitt's, he was, according to custom, staked to the ground with four pins through a cord, two on his wrists, and two on his ancles, was cut and flogged most unmercifully, and afterwards loaded cruelly with irons about his neck. (*IN*, p. 181)

'[S]taked to the ground' with 'pins' on its 'wrists' and 'ancles', the enslaved body is splayed out as if crucified. Even as Equiano is unable to avert his friend's suffering – and enters a personal crisis because of it – he offers resistance in another form: by symbolically converting Annis into a kind of black Christ, he continues to critique the reduction of the black subject to the corporeality above which a spiritually imbued whiteness elevates itself.

That Equiano's spiritual conversion also involves a racial crossing, 'removing the veil' between white and black – and is thus a highly charged political act – becomes clearer still in chapter 11. Here, in the course of a journey with his 'old friend, the celebrated Dr. Irving' from England to Jamaica, Equiano attempts to reproduce in another the spiritual transformation he himself has undergone. The 'poor sinner' to whom he directs his attentions is a Native American 'of about eighteen years of age' (*IN*, p. 202) who turns out to be an 'Indian prince'. Though at first successful, the project of instruction is eventually wrecked by the bad example of non-believers. Equiano describes how these Satanic 'emissaries' (*IN*, p. 203) erode the faith he has sought to inculcate in his potential convert:

> Some of the true sons of Belial, who did not believe that there was any hereafter, told him never to fear the devil, for there was none existing; and if ever he came to the prince, they desired he might be sent to them. Thus they teazed the poor innocent youth, so that he would not learn his book any more! He would not drink nor carouse with these ungodly actors, nor would he be with me even at prayers. This grieved me very much. I endeavoured to persuade him as well as I could, but he would not come; and entreated him very much to tell me his reasons for acting thus. At last he asked me, 'How comes it that all the white men on board, who can read and write, observe the sun, and know all things, yet swear, lie, and get drunk, only excepting yourself?' (*IN*, p. 204)

This passage neatly encapsulates the conflict between essentialist and constructionist ideologies that marks *The Interesting Narrative* as a whole, raising questions of belief and unbelief not only in relation to 'the doctrines of Christianity' (*IN*, p. 203) but vis-à-vis race as well. The 'he' imagined as perhaps one day visiting the 'prince' refers most obviously to 'the devil', yet in so far as Satan is himself sometimes represented as a princely figure (as in the colloquial 'prince of darkness', for example), the possibility emerges that it is the 'poor innocent youth' who might be the one to initiate their meeting. In this way, the fluid syntax of the first sentence of this passage suggests the kind of fusion or confusion of racial otherness with the demonic which is characteristic of essentialist orthodoxies. At the same time, however, the final sentence could hardly articulate a greater scepticism towards belief in the notion of an essentialized racial subject. Blindly included by his Native American interlocutor among those 'on board, who can read and write, observe the sun, and know all things', Equiano comes to be spectacularly invested, as Marren notes, with the 'salient qualities associated with whiteness in eighteenth-century English culture'.[40]

Equiano's assumption of a figurative whiteness by means of a manipulation of Christian discourse is paralleled by his negotiation of what are the alternative yet none the less related discourses of enterprise and imperialism. Dyer clarifies the role of these discourses in the shaping of white identity as follows:

> At some point, the embodied something else of whiteness took on a dynamic relation to the physical world, something caught by the ambiguous word 'spirit'. The white spirit organises white flesh and in turn non-white flesh and other material matters: it has *enterprise*. Imperialism is the key historical form in which that process has been realised. Imperialism displays both the character of enterprise in the white person, and its exhilaratingly expansive relationship to the environment.[41]

Equiano is nothing if not an enterprising subject. As a freeman, he participates in a number of projects dazzling in their difficulty, risk and global range: he travels to the Bahamas, where he is shipwrecked (chapter 8), and to the Arctic, where he becomes ice-bound (chapter 9), helps Irving in the establishment of a slave plantation in Nicaragua (chapter 11) and acts as commissary to the Sierra Leone expedition for the resettlement of London's black poor (chapter 12). Yet if enterprise is the sign of 'energy, will, ambition, the ability to think and see things through',[42] its most important manifestation, in *The Interesting Narrative*, takes the form of the economic transactions into which Equiano enters in order to achieve the freedom that makes his subsequent adventures possible.

These transactions are described, with 'ledger-like detail', as Houston A. Baker, Jr. puts it,[43] in chapters 5 to 7, a section of the narrative in which Equiano is enslaved first to Doran and then, principally, to King. Backed with 'but a very small capital to begin with', Equiano's attempts to 'try [his] luck and commence merchant' (*IN*, p. 116) are ones that his own master is evidently happy to sponsor:

[King] thought by carrying one little thing or other to different places to sell I might make money.... he also intended to encourage me in this, by crediting me with half a puncheon of rum and half a hogshead of sugar at a time; so that, from being careful, I might have money enough, in some time, to purchase my freedom: and, when that was the case, I might depend upon it he would let me have it for forty pounds sterling money, which was only the same price he gave for me. (*IN*, p. 126)

Despite 'many instances of ill usage' (*IN*, p. 116) – including an attempt on his life – Equiano eventually finds '[him]self master' (*IN*, p. 135) of the sum stipulated by King for the purchase of a freedom originally denied by the 'commercial deportation'[44] of the Middle Passage. This situation is not without its ironies. On the one hand, as Baker comments, Equiano's 'commercial venture' results in 'the transformation of property by property into humanity'.[45] Yet on the other, Equiano's ability to embark upon, control and complete such a scheme is itself a sign that he is already in possession of the very status he is forced to acquire. The sense in which Equiano's entrepreneurial skills mark him out, once again, as figuratively white is suggested by an episode which occurs in chapter 6, while Equiano is trading his wares at Charlestown:

Here I disposed of some goods on my own account; the white men buying them with smooth promises and fair words, giving me, however, but very indifferent payment. There was one gentleman particularly who bought a puncheon of rum of me, which gave me a great deal of trouble... for, being a negro man, I could not oblige him to pay me. This vexed me much, not knowing how to act; and I lost some time in seeking after this Christian.... When I found him, after much entreaty... he at last paid me in dollars, some of them, however, were copper, and of consequence of no value.... Immediately after, as I was trying to pass them in the market amongst other white men, I was abused for offering to pass bad coin; and though I shewed them the man I had got them from, I was within one minute of being tied up and flogged without either judge or jury. (*IN*, pp. 128–9)

This passage is marked – or 'vexed' – by a linguistic slippage similar to that which occurs in Equiano's description of his encounter with the 'Indian prince'. While the 'I' accused of 'offering to pass bad coin' and the 'white men' with whom it deals appear to be quite separate from one another, the syntax of the sentence within which they commonly circulate works to elide them. This cannot, of course, be literally the case: after all, as Equiano reminds the reader, he is 'a negro man' who comes 'within one minute of being tied up and flogged' by his oppressors. Yet if Equiano cannot be considered white in literal or bodily terms, his aptitude as merchant and businessman – as the sign of enterprise – grants him such a status figuratively. It could even be said that, although thwarted, the action Equiano performs in the 'market' – 'pass[ing] . . . coin' – is itself a trope for the project of passing as metaphorically white carried out rather more successfully by his text as a whole.

In chapter 7, Equiano marvels at the fluctuations in the day on which he secures his liberty: '[King] signed the manumission . . . so that, before night, I who had been a slave in the morning, trembling at the will of another, now became my own master, and compleatly free' (*IN*, pp. 136–7). If freedom makes Equiano '[his] own master', there is a sense in which, at several junctures both before and after this moment, he is also his master's mimic. As Baker points out, Equiano's activities as entrepreneur take place within and are 'constrained by the mercantile boundaries of a Caribbean situation',[46] whose most striking feature is, of course, the institution of colonial slavery itself. Even as he is personally oppressed by this institution, Equiano repeatedly exploits its networks, as the destinations along the slave-trading routes between America and the West Indies are co-opted as resources of liberation. Some of these destinations prove more lucrative than others. Crossing from Philadelphia to St. Eustatia (via Monserrat), Equiano writes:

> After we had discharged our cargo there, we took in a live cargo (as we call a cargo of slaves.) Here I sold my goods tolerably well; but not being able to lay out all my money in this small island to as much advantage as in many other places, I laid out only part, and the remainder I brought away with me neat. (*IN*, p. 133)

Equiano's position here is a complex one. At this point in the narrative, he is still a slave and thus himself always running the risk of abduction into the 'live cargo' he helps to buy. Yet the use of the pronoun 'we' aligns him with the colonial master whose idiom he adopts. These contradictory affiliations generate contradictions of their own. While this scene clearly implies a degree of complicity with the very system which *The Interesting Narrative* is designed to oppose, it is also open to a more politically subversive reading: if the slave can take the place of the master – become, as it were, his surrogate – the implication is that neither identity is naturally determined by race.

To use Marion Rust's formulation, the passage discussed above is one instance of the way in which, prior to his emancipation, Equiano 'approximates the elitist ideologies of his white male mentors',[47] and in so doing disrupts the racially coded distinction, to use Rust's terms, between 'subaltern' and 'imperialist'. Such an effect is paralleled by a curious episode which occurs in the years following Equiano's acquisition of freedom, while he is assisting Irving in the cultivation of his South American plantation. Here he is faced with a 'great commotion' (*IN*, p. 207) among neighbouring tribes of 'native Indians' (*IN*, p. 205), instigated by the actions of their drunken 'Governor' (*IN*, p. 207):

> I . . . thought of a stratagem to appease the riot. Recollecting a passage I had read in the life of Columbus, when he was amongst the Indians in Jamaica, where, on some occasion, he frightened them, by telling them of certain events in the heavens, I had recourse to the same expedient, and it succeeded beyond my most sanguine expectations. When I had formed my determination, I went in the midst of them, and taking hold of the governor, I pointed up to the heavens. I menaced him and the rest: I told them God lived there, and that he was angry with them, and they must not quarrel so; that they were all brothers, and if they did not leave off, and go away quietly, I would take the book (pointing to the bible), read, and *tell* God to make them dead. This was something like magic. The clamour immediately ceased, and I gave them some rum, and a few other things; after which they went away peaceably. (*IN*, p. 208; emphasis in original)

The 'stratagem' Equiano invokes to 'appease the riot' constitutes perhaps the most flamboyant moment of mimicry within the text, as the ex-slave models himself on Columbus, colonizer *par excellence*. The specific 'expedient' to which Equiano alludes (and makes 'recourse') is glossed by Carretta:

On his fourth voyage, to frighten the Indians of Jamaica into supplying his men with provisions, Columbus used his knowledge of an impending lunar eclipse to convince them that his God could punish them with a famine if they continued to refuse his requests. (*IN*, p. 293)

In this respect, the doubling which occurs here between Equiano and Columbus appears to support the earlier identification – made by the 'Indian prince' – of Equiano with those 'white men . . . who can read and write, observe the sun, and know all things'. Yet if the Native Americans whom Equiano here confronts are 'menaced' into docility by his Columbian mimicry – as their ancestors had once been 'frightened' by the original deployment of such 'magic' – this scene also harbours a certain threat for its white readers: as a black subaltern who figures himself as a white colonizer/imperialist, Equiano demonstrates – as he has sought to do throughout *The Interesting Narrative* – the inessentiality of race as a marker of difference.

2

'What was done there is not to be told': *Mansfield Park*'s Colonial Unconscious

> it is not a question of introducing a historical explanation which is stuck on to the work from the outside. On the contrary, [there is] a sort of splitting within the work: this division is *its* unconscious, in so far as it possesses one – the unconscious which is history, the play of history beyond its edges, encroaching on those edges: this is why it is possible to trace the path which leads from the haunted work to that which haunts it. Once again it is not a question of redoubling the work with an unconscious, but a question of revealing in the very gestures of expression that which it is not. Then, the reverse side of what is written will be history itself.
>
> The speech of the book comes from a certain silence.
>
> Pierre Macherey[1]

Textual strategies

Given the importance for the world depicted in *Mansfield Park* (1814) of various forms of propriety (social, moral, sexual, linguistic), it should not be surprising to find the textual operations of Jane Austen's novel themselves marked by a certain concern with right conduct. The nature of such textual propriety can be gleaned by considering the point at which it is fleetingly disrupted, during a conversation (in volume 2, chapter 3) between Fanny Price, the novel's heroine, and Edmund Bertram, her cousin and eventual spouse. This dialogue looks back to an earlier interdicted exchange between Fanny and her uncle, Sir Thomas Bertram, 'master at Mansfield Park'.[2] Edmund's wish that Fanny 'talk . . . more' to Sir Thomas precipitates the following discussion:

> 'But I do talk to him more than I used. I am sure I do. Did not you hear me ask him about the slave trade last night?'
> 'I did – and was in hopes the question would be followed up by others. It would have pleased your uncle to be inquired of farther.'
> 'And I longed to do it – but there was such a dead silence! And while my cousins were sitting by without speaking a word, or seeming at all interested in the subject, I did not like – I thought it would appear as if I wanted to set myself off at their expense, by shewing a curiosity and pleasure in his information which he must wish his own daughters to feel.' (*MP*, p. 178)

Edmund's conviction that Fanny's uncle would have been 'pleased' to have been 'inquired of farther' on the 'question' of the 'slave trade' is itself questionable: Sir Thomas is not only a domestic and patriarchal master, but also a colonial one. He possesses slave-worked plantations in Antigua, from which, at this juncture, he has just returned after a lengthy absence occasioned by the need to resolve the economic crisis that 'unsettle[s]' 'a large part of his income' (*MP*, p. 32). What is significant about this particular textual moment is its relation to *Mansfield Park* as a whole. Even as Fanny recalls how her non-pursuit of the 'subject' of slavery had been based on anxieties about breaching social decorum – that she might thereby favourably 'set [her]self off' against Sir Thomas's daughters, Maria and Julia – the text itself appears simultaneously to be breaking its own codes of conduct. Throughout *Mansfield Park* there are recurrent allusions – albeit strikingly sparing ones – to the existence, and importance, of the economic links between the novel's eponymous world and Antigua. Yet at no other point does Austen's text refer overtly to the realities of colonialism and slave oppression, which not only define the early nineteenth-century period in which the novel is set and published but also form the source of the wealth and privilege enjoyed by the inhabitants of Mansfield Park itself. As Fanny's conversation with Edmund by default suggests, proper textual conduct would thus seem, for Austen's text, to consist, typically, in a refusal properly to name the truths of its own historical moment.[3]

Yet while the textual rule *Mansfield Park* establishes for itself is flouted with anomalous explicitness in the passage cited above, it could none the less be said to be more discretely, and systematically, transgressed throughout the novel. That which Austen's text seeks literally to exclude from itself returns and is rendered legible at another level, in the figurative or translated shape of oppressions played out at home in terms of gender- and class-relations. These stand in, as it were, for the otherwise unspeakable or repressed referent. In this sense *Mansfield Park* is less about 'ordination', as Austen somewhat unhelpfully once remarked,[4] than co-ordination, the orchestration and textual doubling of different modalities and contexts of oppression – the colonial with the domestic.

Such procedures are marked, however, by their own improprieties, presupposing the comparability of orders of oppression which, in the end, are radically distinct from one another. This is the paradoxical irony undercutting *Mansfield Park*'s attempted circumvention of its own discursive protocols. The figurative recovery of colonial slavery under the sign of domestic oppression causes it to be re-covered – concealed again. The strategy which seems to facilitate the return of those realities located in the textual margin at the same time effectively banishes them.

Translating colonialism: the return of the oppressed

The textual contradictions of Austen's novel are initially articulated by its title. On the one hand, the title names a text committed to the avoidance of the proper naming of slavery. By the same token, however, it obliquely invokes that which it seeks to avoid via another proper name, that belonging to Lord Mansfield, Lord Chief Justice of England from 1756 to 1788. Mansfield is best known for his 1772 ruling in the case of the slave James Somerset, which made it illegal for slave-masters forcibly to transport slaves back from England to the colonies.[5] Yet it is not only through a legal context that the allusiveness of Austen's title provides an early sign of what Moira Ferguson calls the novel's 'intrinsic engagement with slavery',[6] but also in terms of the complexities of Lord Mansfield's familial and domestic relations. As well as presiding over the Somerset case, Mansfield was uncle to Sir John Lindsay, 'a professional sailor promoted', as James Walvin writes, 'in the last year of his life to Rear Admiral'.[7] Lindsay fathered a child, Elizabeth Dido, by a slave captured on board a Spanish vessel seized by his ship. On her birth,

Lindsay 'passed the infant on to Lord Mansfield's family',[8] in relation to which, in her adult life, she was to hold, as Walvin puts it, a 'curious position'.[9]

The strange biographical circumstances obscurely called up in Austen's text by its title are obliquely rehearsed in the novel's opening two chapters, as the ten-year-old Fanny – like the dislocated slave-child who is her historical counterpart – is separated from her parental home at Portsmouth and taken into another Mansfield household. Yet the fictional reinscription of history at the beginning of *Mansfield Park* extends beyond the anecdotal. The unceremonious removal of Fanny from Portsmouth to Mansfield constitutes a figure for the violent uprootings of the slave trade, the very activity on which Fanny later seeks to question her discretely slave-holding uncle.

Class relations at home (between Portsmouth and Mansfield) thus perform a kind of doubling of colonial relations (between Africa and the British West Indies). This point is underscored by the representation of Portsmouth as Mansfield's 'uncivilized other',[10] a locus of 'poverty and neglect' (*MP*, p. 5) and sexual indiscipline, producing corrupting effects in those who inhabit it. The prospect of Fanny's introduction into Mansfield Park for example causes Sir Thomas to caution that he and his family will 'probably see much to wish altered in her' and must be prepared 'for gross ignorance, meanness of opinions, and very distressing vulgarity of manner' (*MP*, p. 8). The construction of Portsmouth and Fanny in these terms is what enables the act of 'taking her from her family' to be figured as one of 'kindness' rather than 'cruelty' (*MP*, p. 4) by those who contrive it (principally Sir Thomas and Fanny's vindictive aunt, Mrs. Norris), a civilizing and 'benevolent . . . scheme' (*MP*, p. 6). Such sleight of rhetorical hand mirrors the ideological strategies by means of which colonialism characteristically seeks to legitimate its own material and psychic violence.

From the first, Austen's text suggests itself to be strangely attuned to such processes of doubling – the figurative reinscription of the colonial in the domestic. While the removal of Fanny from Portsmouth to Mansfield constitutes *Mansfield Park*'s narrative origin, it is in fact an idea that takes the place of an earlier plan to ease the Prices' economic difficulties. This plan is formulated 'a twelvemonth' before in the letter Mrs. Price sends to Lady Bertram:

> Her eldest was a boy of ten years old, a fine spirited fellow who longed to be out in the world; but what could she do? Was

there any chance of his being hereafter useful to Sir Thomas in the concerns of his West Indian property? No situation would be beneath him – or what did Sir Thomas think of Woolwich? or how could a boy be sent out to the East? (*MP*, p. 3)

Mansfield Park's beginning entails the exclusion of other narrative options, one of which involves the enlistment of Fanny's eldest brother, William, in the unspecified 'concerns' of Sir Thomas's 'West Indian property'. What is interesting here is the language in which such alternative possibilities are couched. If Mrs. Price's allusion to Sir Thomas's Antiguan plantations as 'property' is a tacit reminder of the way in which, under slavery, such a category also embraces the slaves who are made to work them, her subsequent claim that 'No situation would be beneath' her son similarly collapses the differences between William and those he should be positioned above by virtue of his race. Commencing with the substitution of Fanny's story for William's, *Mansfield Park* makes a kind of intratextual acknowledgement of the status and functioning of the former as a stand in for effaced colonial realities.[11] This is so because, in sketching out a potential narrative line, the text hints at those realities in the linguistic slide which places that narrative's protagonist, William, in the position of slave.

The opening chapters of *Mansfield Park* can also be said to dramatize two forms of 'take in' (*MP*, p. 41). For Fanny they entail a movement from Portsmouth to Mansfield where, despite an initial 'consciousness of misery' (*MP*, p. 10) and the enduringly abusive behaviour towards her of Mrs. Norris, she in fact gradually learns 'to transfer in [Mansfield's] favour much of her attachment to her former home' (*MP*, p. 17). For the reader, however, the 'take in' operates in the figurative sense (of 'deception') in which Mary Crawford uses the phrase with regard to the 'transactions' (*MP*, 40) of marriage, following her own arrival at Mansfield from London with Henry, her brother. Such textual deceit is itself twofold. Not only is the economic hierarchizing of Mansfield above Portsmouth ironically inverted by the overall narrative and thematic action which culminates in the regeneration – explicitly through Fanny – of Mansfield's moral order. It also constitutes a reversal of the truth of Mansfield's own condition of economic dependence upon Antigua.

It is not long, however, before such a truth begins to be suggested, through a series of allusions, in chapters 3 and 4 of the novel's first volume, to the instability of Sir Thomas's colonial holdings.

Following the death of Mrs. Norris's husband when Fanny is 'about fifteen' (*MP*, p. 19), it is revealed that Sir Thomas has himself suffered 'some recent losses', though these are financial rather than personal and located 'on his West India Estate' (*MP*, p. 20). Combining with the 'extravagance' (*MP*, p. 19) of the lifestyle of Sir Thomas's eldest son, Tom, the immediate effect of this is to threaten Fanny with another displacement: she is to be removed from the 'little white attic' (*MP*, p. 7) allocated to her on arrival at Mansfield Park to the 'White house' (*MP*, p. 22) occupied by Mrs. Norris in her widowhood, where, Sir Thomas presumes, his niece will subsequently be financially supported. To Fanny's relief, this scheme is rejected by Mrs. Norris, even as she herself comments that 'Sir Thomas's means will be rather straitened, if the Antigua estate is to make such poor returns' (*MP*, p. 26). Indeed it is not Fanny but Sir Thomas who is obliged, the following year, to leave Mansfield, finding it 'expedient to go to Antigua himself, for the better arrangement of his affairs'. As well as being an exercise in economic troubleshooting, the trip to Antigua is undertaken, it transpires, 'in the hope of detaching [Tom] from some bad connections at home' (*MP*, p. 28). Yet the likelihood of Sir Thomas succeeding in this secondary aim is somewhat qualified by the contemporary status of the West Indies, in Ronald Hyam's words, as 'a kind of sexual paradise for young European men'.[12]

While economic troubles are stated to be the original impetus for Sir Thomas's absence from Mansfield, the text suggests that the reasons for and consequences of the delay in his return relate to other factors:

> for when September came, Sir Thomas was still abroad, and without any near prospect of finishing his business. Unfavourable circumstances had suddenly arisen at a moment when he was beginning to turn all his thoughts towards England, and the very great uncertainty in which every thing was then involved, determined him on sending home his son, and waiting the final arrangement by himself. (*MP*, p. 33)

Like the situation to which it refers, Austen's text is 'involved' here in its own 'uncertainty'. It frustrates the kind of 'immediate eclaircissement' (*MP*, p. 173) which, in a later and different context, Maria vainly awaits from the Henry with whom she has become infatuated. Are the 'Unfavourable circumstances' merely economic,

matters of 'business' and 'arrangement' and if so would they demand the 'sending home' of Sir Thomas's heir? Or do they have
other origins, as the obliquely insurrectionary language would suggest,
in sudden slave-uprising, for example? To adapt a phrase from Mary,
there would seem to be 'a something wanted . . . in [the] language'
(*MP*, p. 261) of the text. The effect of this aporia or indeterminacy
is to turn the activity of reading that text into the hermeneutic
equivalent of the game of 'Speculation' undertaken by the group
of card-players into which Fanny is drawn in the novel's second
volume.

It is not only the reader, however, but also Mrs. Norris who becomes a speculator on the question of Sir Thomas's continuing
absence. Even as Tom's safe return to Mansfield brings with it 'an
excellent account of his father's health', the very presence of the
son is antithetically construed by Mrs. Norris as a sign of the father's
'foreboding of evil to himself'. Filled with 'dreadful presentiments'
and 'terribly haunted by these ideas', Mrs. Norris is 'obliged', the
narrator remarks, to leave 'the sad solitariness of her cottage' and
'take daily refuge in the dining room of the park' (*MP*, p. 33). Such
'fears for the absent' (*MP*, p. 30) are, of course, as disingenuous as
the narration of them is ironic and themselves invite an antitheti-
cal reading which exposes their more probable investments. Anxieties
that 'poor Sir Thomas' may be 'fated never to return' (*MP*, p. 33) –
die or be killed in Antigua – perhaps screen wishes for just such an
occurrence. Not the least of the attractions of this event would be
the full-scale elevation of Mrs. Norris to the position of 'absolute
power' (*MP*, p. 254) currently occupied by her brother-in-law and
yet at the same time already covertly challenged by her instrumental role in arranging the marital 'alliance' (*MP*, p. 35) between Maria
and Mr. Rushworth. Mrs. Norris's speculations betoken the way in
which power-relations at home work to figure realities of colonial
discontent which cannot otherwise be articulated.

As if to confirm his arrival in England, Tom would appear symbolically to re-enact it in the form of a visit 'just after [his] return
from the West Indies' to 'Albion place'. Here he is led 'astray' by
the 'daughters' of the house, 'the two Miss Sneyds': he courts the
one in the mistaken belief that she, rather than the other, is '*out*'
(*MP*, p. 45; emphasis in original) – has made, that is, the kind of
formal introduction into society which would legitimate his attentions. At the same time, Tom's confused social encounter subtly
establishes an intertextual dialogue between *Mansfield Park* and

William Blake's *Visions of the Daughters of Albion* (1793). In echoing Blake, Austen's text implicitly alludes to the compounding, under slavery, of racial and sexual oppressions, since in the figure of Bromion, Blake's text features one who is not only a slave-owner like Sir Thomas but also a rapist.[13] Yet if the colonial slave-master – whether Austen's or Blake's – is thus also seen to be a figure of sexual excess and unrestraint he is not entirely dissimilar to Tom himself, whose own life is a libertine vision, conducted with nothing 'but pleasure in view, and his own will to consult' (*MP*, p. 103). The allusion to Blake underlines the workings of *Mansfield Park* as a whole. It provides a perspective from which the implied *modus vivendi* of the son can be seen to double the sexual licence of the colonial slave-master of whom the father is the type.

From the perspective of their covertness and indirection, the textual strategies by which *Mansfield Park* crosses from domestic to colonial spaces might be said, in the text's own terms, to be gendered as feminine. One way in which the link between form and gender, linguistic concealment and the feminine comes into view is through Edmund's response to Mary's comments on the activities of her uncle, Admiral Crawford. The uncle/admiral is explicitly described by the narrator as 'a man of vicious conduct' who, following his wife's death, has recently brought 'his mistress under his own roof' (*MP*, p. 36). Yet Mary's own criticisms of him, whether trivial or serious, related to past or present actions, only provoke disapproval. This occurs, for example, when she describes her uncle as 'not the first favourite in the world' and goes on to recall the 'nuisances' caused by his scheme, 'Three years ago', to make 'improvements *in hand*' (*MP*, p. 51; emphasis in original) to the grounds of the summer cottage in Twickenham at which she and her aunt once stayed. These remarks evidently produce their own disruptions:

> Edmund was sorry to hear Miss Crawford, whom he was much disposed to admire, speak so freely of her uncle. It did not suit his sense of propriety, and he was silenced, till induced by further smiles and liveliness, to put the matter by for the present. (*MP*, p. 51)

Mary compounds the irksome freedom of her speech in responding to Edmund's question about the extent of her 'acquaintance in the navy'. Her knowledge of naval personnel is limited – excluding 'the inferior ranks' – and yet intimate: 'Certainly', she tells him, 'my home at my uncle's brought me acquainted with a circle of admirals. Of *Rears*, and *Vices*, I saw enough. Now do not be suspecting me of a pun, I entreat' (*MP*, p. 54; emphases in original). As a pun, Mary's remark, as Isobel Armstrong notes, is 'a form of concealment, saying one thing under the guise of another and screening meaning'.[14] Yet what causes Edmund again to become 'grave' (*MP*, p. 54) is that Mary's denial of the pun's existence – for which she seems to anticipate punishment – only works to advertise the presence of the (homo)sexual meaning it is supposed to veil.

For Edmund, what is 'not quite right' (*MP*, p. 50) or 'very indecorous' in Mary's language is not so much her views in themselves, as the act of their disclosure: 'I do not censure her *opinions*', he confides to Fanny, 'but there certainly *is* impropriety in making them public' (*MP*, p. 57; emphases in original). In those uncanny linguistic moments when that which should remain hidden comes to light, Mary can be considered 'perfectly feminine' (*MP*, p. 58) no longer. In this respect, she enacts the fate which – with the scandalous exception of the halting exchange in volume 2, chapter 3 – *Mansfield Park* itself evades through its avoidance of the proper naming of slavery. In the end, though, it is not only the act of publicizing her opinions but their content also which renders Mary truly unfeminine. This occurs towards the end of the novel in connection with the 'sad business' (*MP*, p. 414) of Maria's adultery and flight with Henry. While Maria's adultery is sternly – not to say histrionically – troped by both Fanny and Edmund as 'evil' (*MP*, pp. 402, 404), it is described by Mary less punitively as 'folly' (*MP*, p. 414). As Claudia L. Johnson suggests, Mary's language performs its own 'flagrant indiscretion' (*MP*, p. 411) – refusing to name 'folly' as 'evil' – which both parallels Maria's sexual transgression and itself seems to go beyond the capacities of Edmund to represent it.[15] 'Guess what I must have felt', he dares Fanny, 'To hear the woman whom – no harsher name than folly given! – So voluntarily, so freely, so coolly to canvass it! – No reluctance, no horror, no feminine – shall I say? no modest loathings!' (*MP*, p. 415).

Despite the shock it occasions in Edmund and Fanny in particular, Maria's adultery is far from unexpected, constituting, as it does, a literalization of events which both precede and prefigure it. The clearest example of this occurs during the day spent by Maria *et al.* at Sotherton, the family estate owned by Rushworth (volume 1, chapters 8–10). Maria's dilemma is that even as marriage to Rushworth represents an escape from her father and Mansfield, it is at the same time a prison in itself. The figuration of marriage as prison or cage – from which, via Henry, Maria seeks liberation – is most obviously suggested in volume 1, chapter 10. Maria's 'wish of passing through' the 'iron gate' (*MP*, p. 88) which separates the 'wilderness' (*MP*, p. 81) at Sotherton from the park prompts her fiancé to set off in search of the key that would unlock it, in so doing offering Henry the chance to appropriate the future husband's intended role. Ironically commenting on the brightness of Maria's 'prospects' as Mrs. Rushworth – 'You have a very smiling scene before you' (*MP*, p. 89) – Henry prompts, to Fanny's alarm, the following exchange:

> 'Do you mean literally or figuratively? Literally I conclude. Yes, certainly, the sun shines and the park looks very cheerful. But unluckily that iron gate, that ha-ha, give me a feeling of restraint and hardship. I cannot get out, as the starling said.' As she spoke, and it was with expression, she walked to the gate; he followed her. 'Mr. Rushworth is so long fetching this key!'
>
> 'And for the world you would not get out without the key and without Mr. Rushworth's authority and protection, or I think you might with little difficulty pass round the edge of the gate, here, with my assistance; I think it might be done, if you really wished to be more at large, and could allow yourself to think it not prohibited.'
>
> 'Prohibited! nonsense! I certainly can get out that way, and I will.' (*MP*, pp. 89–90)

'[F]eeling all this to be wrong', Fanny strives to 'prevent it'. Her admonitory protests – 'You will hurt yourself Miss Bertram . . . you will certainly hurt yourself against those spikes – you will tear your gown – you will be in danger of slipping into the ha-ha. You had better not go' – come however, like Rushworth, too late. The ironically echoing 'I will' of autonomous female desire cannot be stopped from translating itself into an act – 'Her cousin was safe on the other side, while these words were spoken' (*MP*, p. 90) – whose figurative meaning (adultery) is in turn translated, by the novel's dénouement, into literal form.

If Maria's adultery stands as the literal in relation to the 'gate-scene' at Sotherton, it should at the same time be remembered that acts of patriarchal rebellion, or 'feminine lawlessness' (*MP*, p. 85), are themselves figurings, conversely, of those literalities of colonial rebellion which *Mansfield Park* is anxious to conceal. This is a point confirmed by the way in which the language of the novel works to conflate domestic with colonial contexts. The 'foreboding of evil to himself' which Mrs. Norris imagines Sir Thomas to have experienced in Antigua is realized in the demonizing/barbarizing of female sexuality: Maria's actions, about which Fanny learns while staying once again with her family at Portsmouth, come to constitute 'too gross a complication of evil, for human nature, not in a state of utter barbarism, to be capable of!' (*MP*, p. 402). By the same token, the punishment of Maria is fantasized by Mr. Price – as he reads her story in the newspaper – in a way which obliquely illuminates the status of her actions as a figure for colonial transgression:

> 'I don't know what Sir Thomas may think of such matters; he may be too much of the courtier and fine gentleman to like his daughter the less. But by G – if she belonged to me, I'd give her the rope's end as long as I could stand over her. A little flogging for man and woman too, would be the best way of preventing such things.' (*MP*, p. 401)

Mr. Price's language functions in a way analogous to the 'sun-shine' on which Fanny meditates immediately prior to the passage cited. Just as sunlight appears to Fanny to be 'a totally different thing in a town and in the country. . . . serving but to bring forward stains and dirt that might otherwise have slept' (*MP*, p. 400), so Mr. Price's outburst promotes and arouses sexually charged images of violent colonial subjugation which Austen's novel would prefer to remain dormant. Though himself 'totally different' from Sir Thomas in terms of class, Mr. Price adopts in fantasy the brutal stance with which, as slave-master, the 'courtier and fine gentleman' of Mansfield Park is necessarily identified. Antigua and slavery make up the unspeakable other for Mansfield Park and the text named after it alike and yet are none the less reflected back in the alternative domestic space of Portsmouth.

Together with prefiguring part of the dénouement of the novel, *Mansfield Park*'s representation of the 'day at Sotherton' (*MP*, p. 96) sets up an intertextual link, as several critics have noted, with Shakespeare's *As You Like It*. For Armstrong:

> The most important function of *As You Like It* in the text . . . is to suggest what happens when a group of outsiders enters an

environment of which they know little or regard with relative contempt and establish a temporary settlement there.[16]

As the terms of this observation fairly strongly suggest, one thing that 'happens' on such intrusive occasions, whether at Austen's Sotherton or in Shakespeare's Forest of Arden, is the rehearsal of a colonial paradigm.

As well as repeating the (colonial) pattern of entrance and 'temporary settlement' characterizing *As You Like It*, *Mansfield Park* surreptitiously offers a hint as to the historical context in which such a pattern is located. Just before the 'gate-scene' discussed above, Henry tells Maria how he had been able to amuse her sister during the 'ten miles' drive' to Sotherton with 'ridiculous stories of an old Irish groom of [his] uncle's', flatteringly adding that he 'could not have hoped to entertain' Maria herself with such 'Irish anecdotes' (*MP*, p. 89). Seemingly insignificant in themselves, Henry's comments operate in fact as traces of a colonial history which Austen's text calls up by dint of its rewriting of *As You Like It*. While Shakespeare's Arden is variously recollected in Sotherton, the former is itself a space through which *As You Like It* carries out some complex ideological and fantasmatic operations. These relate to the situation in Ireland around the time of the play's composition (1599–1600). Across a range of discourses from propaganda to poetry, Ireland is powerfully figured, at this time, as an idealized pastoral realm where the younger sons or brothers of 'gentlemen' might come to enjoy the privileges of land and power denied to them by the law of primogeniture in England. On the other hand, however, the representation of Ireland as a site of easeful self-advancement is subverted in its turn by the contingencies of history in the shape of Hugh O'Neill's 1598 rebellion against the Munster settlement in which, according to the account of Edmund Spenser, the Irish 'spoiled and burnt all the English there dwelling' and made 'all plain and waste'.[17] From this perspective, it can be seen that the point at which *Mansfield Park* becomes a kind of replay of *As You Like It* is one where the repetition is doubled: in Arden, Shakespeare's text reproduces or re-enacts lost colonial fantasies. Fashioning a space enabling the dramatic social betterment of Orlando, initially dispossessed younger son of Sir Rowland de Boys, *As You Like It* makes good the promises history cannot keep.[18]

'Home representation': colonialism on stage

Mansfield Park's troping of the colonial in and as the domestic is nowhere more clearly dramatized, following the Sotherton episode, than in the attempted performance by the 'young people' of *Lovers' Vows*, adapted by Elizabeth Inchbald from August von Kotzebue's *Das Kind der Liebe* in 1798. Just as it is while Sir Thomas is resident at Mansfield that serious economic difficulties arise in Antigua, so his departure for the West Indies is the cue for a domestic crisis in which the 'private theatricals' (*MP*, 109) come to play a central role. By the same token, as Edward W. Said observes, the re-establishment of order, on Sir Thomas's unexpected arrival back at Mansfield, implicitly re-enacts the initial resolution of the problems in the colonies. On the first morning of his return, Sir Thomas undertakes a range of measures (extending 'even to the destruction of every unbound copy of "Lovers' Vows"') designed to enable him to resume 'his seat as master of the house'. On these procedures, 'active and methodical' (*MP*, p, 172), Said comments:

> There is nothing in *Mansfield Park* that would contradict us . . . were we to assume that Sir Thomas does exactly the same things – on a larger scale – in his Antigua 'plantations'. Whatever was wrong there – and the internal evidence garnered by Warren Roberts suggests that economic depression, slavery, and competition with France were at issue – Sir Thomas was able to fix, thereby maintaining his control over his colonial domain. More clearly than anywhere else in her fiction, Austen here synchronizes domestic with international authority.[19]

The synchronization arguably goes beyond Sir Thomas's immediate return in 'a moment of absolute horror' (*MP*, p. 157). Domestic order is not properly reinstated – in the wake of Tom's near-fatal illness, Maria's adultery and Julia's elopement – until the conventional ending of the novel in which Fanny marries Edmund and Susan, her sister, is incorporated into *Mansfield Park* as her 'substitute' (*MP*, p. 431). This parallels the pattern of the West Indian sojourn in which the resumption of the status quo is enigmatically delayed beyond the point originally scheduled for it.

Austen's novel seems to register and confirm its own processes of doubling through the deployment of two characteristic rhetorical idioms – a language of pathology, on the one hand, and of eman-

cipation, on the other. Obliged to explain the 'origin' of the theatrical venture to his father, Tom Bertram figures acting in terms
of the disease which he himself will eventually contract: 'My friend
Yates brought the infection from Ecclesford, and it spread as those
things always spread you know, sir' (*MP*, p. 166). Ecclesford is the
provenance of a dramatic 'infection' capable of turning even the
sanctum sanctorum of Sir Thomas's own study into a (perhaps
nauseous) 'green-room' (*MP*, p. 113) as it extends 'all over the house'
(*MP*, p. 152).[20] But the disease-figure itself has a significant discursive aetiology, used, as it is, in the context of contemporary political
debate as a means of representing the economic condition of the
British West Indies around the time of abolition. An instance of
this is to be found in one of the issues of *The Quarterly Review*
alluded to among the 'chit-chat' (*MP*, p. 94) towards the end of
volume 1, chapter 10. In the following passage, the unnamed reviewer adopts a sceptical stance towards the arguments contained
in the 'pamphlets' under consideration by taking up and parody-
ing the pathological idiom (of 'Distresses' and 'Remedy') which marks
their titles:

> If the promises held out in the title-pages had been faithfully
> kept in the body of these pamphlets, we should have been most
> happy to discharge the humble duty of recording the diagnostics
> of Mr. Spence, and of communicating to our readers the pana-
> cea discovered by the anonymous letter-writer; but we are very
> sorry to observe that the disease which the former undertook to
> class, and the latter professed to cure, continues to assume new
> and more alarming symptoms; that the palliative administered
> by the regular practitioners has produced only a short intermis-
> sion; and that the specific proposed by many able empirics is
> rendered useless by the present stage of the disorder. The situation
> of our colonies is apparently become more critical than ever.[21]

Circulating between economic and theatrical contexts, the disease-
figure strengthens the sense in which the one is replayed, in *Mansfield
Park*, in the other.

While economic decline is overtly advertised by Austen's novel
as the original motive for Sir Thomas's visit to Antigua, the reason
for the lag in his return remains strikingly undisclosed, promoting
speculations about its cause in slave-unrest – a constant source of
colonial anxiety. Whether or not this is the case, it is just such

unrest that is re-enacted or figured in events at Mansfield. Throughout the text the most troubling expression of the moral decline with which acting is associated comes in the form of female disruption of patriarchal ideology and the codes by which it defines a regulatory notion of the feminine. As Ferguson puts it:

> gender relations at home parallel and echo traditional relationships of power between the colonialists and colonized peoples: White British women visibly signify the most egregiously and invisibly repressed of the text – African-Caribbeans themselves. They mark silent African-Caribbean rebels as well as their own disenfranchisement and class and gender victimization.[22]

Ordinarily in collusion with patriarchal constructions of the feminine, Fanny is herself drawn into conflict with them through defiance, in the novel's latter stages, of her uncle's desire that she marry Henry. In the earlier context of *Lovers' Vows*, however, the conditions for the onset of female rebellion are produced by the manner in which the parts of the play are distributed. Against the backdrop of her engagement to Rushworth, Maria is cast as Agatha Friburg, an impoverished working-class woman seduced and abandoned, before the play begins, by Baron Wildenhaim (acted by Mr. Yates). The role of Frederick, her illegitimate son, with whom she is reunited at the opening of the play, is given to Henry. This pairing promotes a 'dangerous intimacy' (*MP*, p. 421) of physical contact between Maria and Henry, thus providing another adumbration of Maria's adultery. Mary plays Amelia, the Baron's daughter, to Edmund's Pastor Anhalt whom Amelia wishes to wed, in preference to the rich but foppish Count Cassel (Rushworth). As Mary notes, Amelia is 'a forward young lady [who] may well frighten the men' (*MP*, p. 130). The basis of such a conjecture is Amelia's sexual and linguistic forthrightness, reaching its height in what is effectively a 'declaration of love' (*MP*, p. 150) made to Anhalt in act 3 scene 2 of *Lovers' Vows*. Through Amelia, Mary is able, like Maria, both to adopt a subject-position from which she is otherwise patriarchally excluded and also quite literally to enact a desire (for Edmund) that cannot otherwise be articulated. As Marilyn Butler argues, *Lovers' Vows* provides:

> a licence for what would normally be entirely improper. . . . Lionel Trilling has ingeniously but anachronistically suggested that Jane

Austen objects to the insincerity involved in acting a role. This
is surely near the opposite of the truth. In touching one another
or making love to one another on the stage these four [Maria,
Henry, Mary, Edmund] are not adopting a pose, but are, on
the contrary, expressing their real feelings. The impropriety lies
in the fact that they are *not* acting, but are finding an indirect
means to gratify desires which are illicit and should have been
contained.[23]

Acting is less disease than symptom, cause than effect, not producing but expressing what is deemed to be 'improper'. *Lovers' Vows*
thus also functions as an intratextual allegory for the workings of
the text at large. Just as the characters in the novel manipulate
Kotzebue's play as an 'indirect means to gratify desires which are
illicit and should have been contained', so *Mansfield Park* deploys
domestic events as a way of re-presenting what it must otherwise
exclude. The play within the text repeats the text itself.

The second of the figurative idioms used by the novel as a way
of underscoring its own operations is a language of emancipation.
Gender- and class-relations, to recall Ferguson, not only 'mark' or
figure 'silent African-Caribbean rebels'; they are themselves figured
by dint of a language resonant with what are implicitly colonial
questions of bondage and freedom. Maria and Julia are said to be
'relieved ... from all restraint' by Sir Thomas's Antiguan absence
and feel 'themselves immediately at their own disposal', with 'every
indulgence within their reach' (*MP*, p. 28). Similarly, because she is
unengaged, Julia regards herself as sufficiently 'at liberty' to enter
into the 'cause of pleasure' (*MP*, p. 116) embodied in the initial
project to 'raise a little theatre at Mansfield' (*MP*, p. 111). Maria,
on the other hand, claims to be 'so much more above restraint'
(*MP*, p. 116) precisely because she is engaged. Edmund is in turn
himself driven to participate in the 'Mansfield Theatricals' (*MP*, p. 134)
in order to ward off the threat that Mary will have 'to act Amelia
with a stranger' – a possibility which, he tells Fanny, 'must do
away all restraints' (*MP*, p. 139). The troping of gender-relations
through an idiom linked with slavery and colonialism is perhaps
most striking in volume 2, chapter 3. Henry's failure to declare his
love for Maria augments her sense of domestic oppression. It causes
her recklessly to hasten the marriage to Rushworth (whom she
despises):

Independence was more needful than ever; the want of it at
Mansfield more sensibly felt. She was less and less able to endure
the restraint which her father imposed. The liberty which his
absence had given was now become absolutely necessary. She must
escape from him and Mansfield as soon as possible. (*MP*, p. 182)

If this is the lesser of two evils, it is none the less of the same
metaphorical kind. As *Lovers' Vows* itself has it, a loveless marriage
is a form of slavery, forging 'fetters' that 'gall with their weight the
married pair'.[24] In Maria's case, such duress is dissolved only in the
novel's final chapters through her adulterous liaison with Henry,
conducted 'without any restraint' (*MP*, p. 410).

Constantly alluded to and anticipated but never staged, *Lovers'
Vows* is simultaneously included and excluded within *Mansfield Park*.
Like Austen's text, it can be read as one that doubles colonial realities, especially in terms of the actions of Baron Wildenhaim, whom
the 'bewildered' (*MP*, p. 165) Sir Thomas discovers being rehearsed
by Mr. Yates in the 'Theatre' adjacent to 'his own dear room' (*MP*,
p. 163). As the seducer of Agatha when she was a young chamber-
maid 'twenty years past',[25] Wildenhaim figures the disposition of
an unchecked male sexuality across class boundaries. In so doing,
he also refigures the miscegenation between masters and their female slaves which was daily a part of the colonial regime. The
Baron's sexual profligacies lead to a severing of the links between
mother and child (when the play begins Frederick has been absent
from Agatha, serving as a soldier, for some five years). Additionally, before it is discovered that he is Frederick's father, the Baron
condemns him to death for personal assault, thus displaying a power
that is as 'arbitrary' (*MP*, 269) as that wielded by the 'infamously
tyrannical' Sir Thomas. Fanny's uncle may well want 'to wipe away
every outward memento' (*MP*, p. 172) of *Lovers' Vows* not least
because, as Ferguson remarks, it 'voice[s] and even accentuate[s]
the major topoi of a muzzled colonialist discourse: brutality, frac-
tured families, and the violated bodies and psyches of innocent
people'.[26]

Kotzebue's text not only discloses the true selves of those who
act in it, but offers also a revelatory doubling, in Wildenhaim, of
the nature of the colonial power in which Sir Thomas is implicated. The latter's encounter with Yates/Wildenhaim is an uncanny
one. The familiar and domestic become strange and foreign and
yet the reverse is also the case:

Sir Thomas had been a good deal surprised to find candles burning in his room; and on casting his eye round it, to see other symptoms of recent habitation, and a general air of confusion in the furniture. The removal of the book-case from before the billiard room door struck him especially, but he had scarcely more than time to feel astonished at all this, before there were sounds from the billiard room to astonish him still further. Some one was talking there in a very loud accent – he did not know the voice – *more* than talking – almost hallooing. He stept to the door, rejoicing at that moment in having the means of immediate communication, and opening it, found himself on the stage of a theatre, and opposed to a ranting young man, who appeared likely to knock him down backwards. (*MP*, pp. 163–4; emphasis in original)

Unlike Sir Thomas, what the text exactly lacks is, in that gently oxymoronic phrase, the 'means of immediate communication', resorting instead to complex strategies of reinscription in order to overcome the 'dead silence' in which the 'subject[s]' of slavery and colonialism remain otherwise lost.

The true complexity of such strategies can be gauged by noting that the Wildenhaim who doubles Sir Thomas has his own obscure historical counterpart in another German aristocrat, Baron Albert von Sack. Von Sack was writer/translator of *A Narrative of a Voyage to Surinam; of a Residence there during 1805, 1806, and 1807; and of the Author's Return to Europe, by way of North America* (1810), a text lambasted in *The Quarterly Review* of May 1811 for the casual racism of its anti-abolitionist and pro-slavery stances. What is interesting about the reviewer's comments on the text is the way in which they work to blur the distinction between the Baron's record of historically real experiences and theatrical representation. Embowered in what is his 'favourite spot' for rural contemplation, the Baron recalls one day noticing 'a string of beads, and a broken cane'. These items move him to put together a series of linked and mawkish surmises as to their possible meanings:

What a pleasure to find so delightful a spot is not entirely neglected by our fellow creatures! – perhaps, some aged negroe rested here with his heavy load! – perhaps, a negress, suckling her new-born babe, and enjoying, in this solemn retreat, undisturbed, the tender feelings of a mother![27]

Historical and theatrical registers become conflated in this passage because, according to the reviewer at least, it is imbued with the 'Spirit of the immortal Kotzebue'.[28] Despite the mother–child tableau, however, the Kotzebue invoked here is not that of *Lovers' Vows* but another play, *The Negro Slaves*, whose content, as the title suggests, directly pertains to the concerns of *Mansfield Park*. The play was translated by Kotzebue himself and published in 1796 (though never staged in England).[29] Notwithstanding its own sentimentalism, several passages in *The Negro Slaves* make it clear that the reviewer's identification of the tenor of von Sack's writing with Kotzebue's is heavily ironic. Act 2 scene 2 provides, for example, an explicit inversion of the 'interesting . . . picture'[30] in von Sack's narrative as a 'Negro-Woman' recounts how the dead child she carries in her arms had been suckled in blood rather than milk as the result of a whipping she received at the hands of her overseer. '[T]he tender feelings of a mother' result, she goes on to state, in an infanticide carried out in order to save her three-day-old child from the torments she herself endures.[31] As with the question of Sir Thomas's deferred return from Antigua, the reader can only speculate as to whether Austen was familiar with *The Negro Slaves*, though it seems highly likely that she would have been. Certainly, one of the consequences of this other Kotzebue play – existing in a displaced or metonymic relation to *Lovers' Vows* – is to consolidate Wildenhaim's status as a double to the sexually licentious colonial master, for *The Negro Slaves* itself contains just such a figure. Another is to underline the circuitousness with which *Mansfield Park* addresses those questions of slavery and colonialism buried at its centre none the less.

'A dance at home' and a 'pretty amber cross': slavery and class, incest and miscegenation

If 'Under [Sir Thomas's] government, Mansfield was an altered place' (*MP*, p. 176), part of the change entails a shift in his own perception of Fanny. This shift is conveyed to Fanny via Edmund, in a passage located just before the reference to the 'slave trade':

> 'but the truth is, that your uncle never did admire you till now – and now he does. Your complexion is so improved! – and you have gained so much countenance! – and your figure – Nay, Fanny, do not turn away about it – it is but an uncle. If you

cannot bear an uncle's admiration what is to become of you? You must really begin to harden yourself to the idea of being worth looking at. – You must try not to mind growing up into a pretty woman.' (*MP*, p. 178)

Following Maria's 'very proper wedding' to Rushworth and the couple's departure, with Julia, 'after a few days to Brighton' (*MP*, p. 183), the timeliness of Edmund's advice becomes evident. For much of the rest of the novel, Fanny indeed comes to find that 'it [is] impossible for her not to be more looked at, more thought of and attended to, than she had ever been before' (*MP*, p. 184) – a situation of some embarrassment to one whose 'favourite indulgence' is 'being suffered to sit silent and unattended to' (*MP*, p. 201). Fanny's discomfort is compounded by the fact that it is Henry's gaze rather than Edmund's that she begins to attract at this point in the text (despite that 'turn away' in the passage above, perhaps designed to exhibit another facet of her 'figure' to the one she loves). Noting, like Sir Thomas, 'the wonderful improvement that has taken place in her looks within the last six weeks' (*MP*, 207), Henry resolves, to Mary's surprise, 'to make Fanny Price in love with [him]'. Nor is the direction of Henry's gaze lost on Fanny's uncle, though the initially seductive intent that lies behind it – to make 'a small hole in Fanny Price's heart' (*MP*, p. 206) – is mistaken by Sir Thomas as being rather more matrimonial in nature. Though himself seemingly far 'above scheming or contriving', Sir Thomas's misreading of Henry's motives encourages his 'willing assent' (*MP*, p. 215) to the increasingly frequent invitations Fanny receives from the parsonage, abode of Dr. and Mrs. Grant and the Crawfords. It also forms the basis for the Christmas ball that becomes the next major domestic and narrative focus, following the failure of *Lovers' Vows* to achieve 'representation' (*MP*, p. 109). Though no one tells her, the ball constitutes the moment of Fanny's '*coming out*' (*MP*, p. 241; emphasis in original), socially signalling her marriageability. Equally, it forms the occasion for a coming back of the colonial.

The ball at Mansfield is a lesser version of the 'balls at Northampton' (*MP*, p. 226) at which William imagines himself dancing incognito with Fanny. These in their turn recall, on a correlatively diminished scale, the Portsmouth 'Assembly night' where Fanny's brother this time conjectures that he 'might not get a partner' and 'as well be nothing' due to the fact that he is a 'midshipman' rather than 'lieutenant' (*MP*, p. 225). The pattern of double displacement and contraction recurs also in relation to the colonial realities so densely mediated by Austen's text. On the one hand, the 'dance at home' (*MP*, p. 228) replicates the 'balls of Antigua' (*MP*, p. 227) described by Sir Thomas, with the help of William, who, having 'been . . . in the West Indies' (*MP*, p. 213), is able to 'relate of the different modes of dancing which had fallen within his observation' (*MP*, p. 227). Like the Mansfield ball that doubles them, the Antiguan festivities themselves stand in for, or mask, larger celebrations, the 'slave "assemblies", the slave dances and "plays" which', according to Walvin, 'were the highlight of the slaves' Christmas'.[32] The Mansfield ball reduces and quite literally domesticates gatherings conducted, in the West Indies, on a scale both larger and more anarchic, as described in the journal of Lady Maria Nugent, Governor's wife in Jamaica between 1801 and 1805. Lady Nugent records her first encounter with such a spectacle as follows:

> *25th.* – Christmas Day! All night heard the music of Tom-Toms, &c. Rise early, and the whole town and house bore the appearance of a masquerade. After Church, amuse myself very much with the strange processions, and figures called Johnny Canoes. All dance, leap and play a thousand anticks. Then there are groups of dancing men and women. . . . Then there was a party of actors. . . . What a *mélange*! . . . We dined in the Council Chamber, but went to bed early, but not to rest, for the noise of singing and dancing was incessant during the night. . . .
> *26th.* – The same wild scenes acting over and over again.[33]

This is slavery's carnivalesque. The extravagant and mocking figure of Jon Kanoo presides over a 'world . . . turned upside down, when the lowest [become] superior and . . . the traditional order and conventions [are] suspended'.[34]

The inversion of colonialism's racial hierarchies is refigured, in the Mansfield ball, through the medium of class. Living in the tangential spaces of the 'little white attic' and the 'East Room' (*MP*, p. 136) and seeming largely to have internalized Mrs. Norris's injunction that she 'must be the lowest and last' (*MP*, p. 199), Fanny feels both astonishment and 'horror' (*MP*, p. 249) on discovering that she is to be 'the Queen of the evening' (*MP*, p. 241):

> Mr. Crawford was not far off; Sir Thomas brought him to her, saying something which discovered to Fanny, that *she* was to

lead the way and open the ball; an idea that had never occurred to her before. . . . and she found herself the next moment conducted by Mr. Crawford to the top of the room, and standing there to be joined by the rest of the dancers, couple after couple as they were formed.

She could hardly believe it. To be placed above so many elegant young women! The distinction was too great. It was treating her like her cousins! (*MP*, 249–50; emphasis in original)

Albeit involuntarily, Fanny enters into the 'nonsense and folly of people's stepping out of their rank and trying to appear above themselves' (*MP*, p. 199) against which she is earlier warned by Mrs. Norris. In this way, she reluctantly mimes and repeats the sanctioned power-reversals which mark the colonial Christmas and help slavery to maintain itself.

The masquerading of the colonial as the domestic is confirmed, once again, by the fact that the former simultaneously re-emerges in the text as a metaphor for the latter. In describing the coming-out ball as a 'trade' (*MP*, p. 241), *Mansfield Park* glances back to the overt reference to slavery which makes so singular an appearance in volume 2, chapter 3, thus figuring Fanny as the slave(s) for whom she is herself a kind of living metaphor. The same effect is achieved by the gifts given to Fanny, in the preparations for the ball, to wear with William's 'pretty amber cross' (*MP*, p. 230) around her 'lovely throat' (*MP*, p. 234). One of these is a gold necklace she is 'requested to chuse' from Mary's 'trinket-box' (on behalf of Henry [*MP*, p. 233]) and the other is a 'plain gold chain' (*MP*, p. 237), more gladly received from Edmund. Both are fetishistic tokens for slavery.

As Fanny is reunited with her 'so long absent and dearly loved brother' (*MP*, p. 209), the narrator comments that in relation to 'the earliest years' (*MP*, p. 211) of childhood, 'even the conjugal tie is beneath the fraternal':

Children of the same family, the same blood, with the same first associations and habits, have some means of enjoyment in their power, which no subsequent connections can supply; and it must be by a long and unnatural estrangement, by a divorce which no subsequent connection can justify, if such precious remains of the earliest attachments are ever entirely outlived.

By extension, the text constitutes the fraternal as the conjugal – since the dissolution of such 'attachments' entails a 'divorce'. Here, as elsewhere, the love between 'William and Fanny Price' (*MP*, p. 212) seems thinly to veil an 'enjoyment' quasi-incestuous in its nature.[35] The figuring of the fraternal as the conjugal is symmetrically reversed by the narrative resolution of Fanny's marriage to Edmund. In the wake of the sexual lapses of Maria and Julia, Fanny becomes Edmund's 'only sister – [his] only comfort now' (*MP*, p. 405), finally bestowing a 'warm and sisterly regard' which, he conjectures, 'would be foundation enough for wedded love' (*MP*, p. 429). On the one hand, the novel's ending seems to indicate a forgetting of Sir Thomas's initial anxieties about 'cousins in love, &c.' (*MP*, p. 4). On the other hand, however, the language of the text suggests the status of marriage as a trope for the fulfilment of those incestuous desires already noted, the 'sins in love' subliminally encrypted in the phrase just cited. In this way, the reality of the Mansfield parsonage where Edmund and Fanny come finally to reside offers a distorted fulfilment of William's regressive fantasy of 'the little cottage . . . in which he and Fanny [are] to pass all their middle and latter life together' (*MP*, p. 341).[36]

The incestuous impulses towards which *Mansfield Park* variously gestures are not without colonial import. For in contemporary antislavery rhetoric, it is precisely as brothers that slaves are popularly represented, as on the abolitionist medallion designed by Josiah Wedgwood in 1787, where a half-kneeling, naked and heavily chained slave asks, 'Am I Not a Man and a Brother?'[37] From this perspective, the inscriptions of incest in Austen's novel assume new meaning: just as the slave is a figurative or metaphorical brother, so the incestuous desire for a literal/biological brother comes to constitute a trope for miscegenation. Signifying a love whose representation covertly links it to the 'unspeakable indulgence' (*MP*, p. 254) of incest, Fanny's 'cross' simultaneously marks the point of intersection between intrafamilial and interracial transgressions. The domestic and the colonial are coupled.

Resistance

While Sir Thomas's pretext for the ball is 'William's desire of seeing Fanny dance' (*MP*, 227), his true purpose is to 'recommend [Fanny] as a wife' (*MP*, p. 255) to Henry. This appears, by the end of the second volume, fully to have been achieved, as Henry re-

nounces his 'idle designs' (*MP*, p. 264) and declares himself 'quite
determined to marry Fanny Price' (*MP*, p. 263). Even as it is with
'*twofold motives*' and '*views and wishes more than could be told*' (*MP*,
p. 272; emphases in original) that Henry negotiates with his admiral-
uncle for the promotion of William to the rank of lieutenant, his
proposal to Fanny is offered 'in words so plain as to bear but one
meaning even to *her*' (*MP*, p. 273; emphasis in original). It thus
exists in a mode noticeably at odds with the textual operations of
Austen's novel as a whole, with their euphemistic doublings, maskings
and obliquities.

Fanny's resistance to Henry's desire provides a major source of
narrative tension in the novel's final stages and is itself marked by
these doublings. On the one hand, her refusal of Henry – 'Oh!
never, never, never; he never will succeed with me' (*MP*, p. 315)
she tells Edmund – is also a defiance of Sir Thomas, 'He who had
married a daughter to Mr. Rushworth' (*MP*, p. 300) and the system
of patriarchal exchange he embodies. At the same time, however,
Fanny's assertion of her own autonomy is, in Ferguson's reading,
'describe[d] . . . in language reserved for slave insurrectionists'.[38] The
passage she cites occurs in volume 3, chapter 1, as Sir Thomas har-
angues his recalcitrant niece:

> 'I had thought you peculiarly free from wilfulness of temper,
> self-conceit, and every tendency to that independence of spirit,
> which prevails so much in modern days, even in young women,
> and which in young women is offensive and disgusting beyond
> all common offence. But you have now shewn me that you can
> be wilful and perverse.' (*MP*, p. 288)

Accused of being 'Self-willed, obstinate, selfish, and ungrateful' (*MP*,
p. 289), Fanny comes to be viewed by Sir Thomas as being 'of a
character the very reverse of what [he] had supposed' (*MP*, p. 288).
She no longer resembles the 'Eurocentrically conceived "grateful
negro" in pre-abolition tales who collaborated with kind owners
and discouraged disobedience among rebel slaves'.[39] The conflict
between the gratitude Sir Thomas expects of Fanny and her actual
response is emblematized in the fire that he arranges to be lit for
the first time in Fanny's room immediately after their interview. If
the fire is a kind of visual pun for what Sir Thomas wishes Fanny
to be (grate-ful/1), it also figures rebellion, like the burning candles
he encounters in his room on returning from Antigua.

Together with doubling colonial in patriarchal rebellion, Fanny's defiance of Henry and Sir Thomas suggests a curious overlapping of plots between *Mansfield Park* and *The Negro Slaves*. While the parallels should not be overstated they are perhaps worth noting. First, Kotzebue's text is structured around the refusal of Ada, a female slave, to yield to the sexual coercions of the slave-master, John. Secondly, as with Fanny, the ground of Ada's resistance is love for another – Zameo, the husband with whom she is reunited at the end of the play's second act. In addition to this, both Sir Thomas and Kotzebue's slave-master contrive schemes of subjugation for the noncompliant women with whom they deal. Sir Thomas determines to send Fanny back to Portsmouth in order to 'incline her to a juster estimate' of 'the elegancies and luxuries' both of Mansfield Park and of 'that home of greater permanence . . . of which she had the offer'. John, on the other hand, threatens Ada with the 'cruel death'[40] of her husband if she continue in her chaste defiance. Sir Thomas's methods of persuasion would appear far less drastic than those used in *The Negro Slaves*. Indeed they are intended not to bring about death but rather the restoration of health, constituting – in another outbreak of the text's pathological idiom – a 'medicinal project' carried out upon a female 'understanding' deemed to be 'at present diseased' (*MP*, p. 335). Yet the differences seem far less clear from the perspective of the anxieties voiced by the narrator toward the novel's end:

> After being nursed up at Mansfield, it was too late in the day to be hardened at Portsmouth; and though Sir Thomas, had he known all, might have thought his niece in the most promising way of being starved, both mind and body, into a much juster value for Mr. Crawford's good company and good fortune, he would probably have feared to push his experiment farther, lest she might die under the cure. (*MP*, p. 376)

Despite the contrasts between Portsmouth and Mansfield, Fanny's return to the parental abode, locus of 'noise, disorder, and impropriety' (*MP*, p. 354), is also, in one sense, a textual repetition of her own induction into her uncle's household. At Mansfield, Edmund assists in the 'improvement of [Fanny's] mind' and 'recommend[s] the books which charmed her leisure hours' (*MP*, p. 19). 'Having formed her mind and gained her affections', he establishes 'a good chance of her thinking like him' (*MP*, p. 58). Fanny, similarly, takes on the 'office of authority' with regard to Susan, 'guiding' and 'informing' by means of her 'more favoured education' (*MP*, p. 361) a sister who is eventually to become 'a most attentive, profitable, thankful pupil' (*MP*, p. 381). Even as Fanny is 'amazed at being any thing *in propria persona*' on subscribing to 'a circulating library' (*MP*, p. 363), she would appear simultaneously to be impersonating the very role Edmund had previously assumed in relation to her. In these repetitive ways Edmund and Fanny alike enact – in the domestic context of class-difference – the civilizing labour of the 'missionary into foreign parts' (*MP*, p. 418), one of the vocations projected for Edmund by Mary amid the rancours of their final meeting.

The novel's recollection of its own narrative outset is completed in Fanny's return to Mansfield, accompanied by Susan, her surrogate-in-waiting. This repeats Fanny's arrival at Mansfield with Mrs. Norris at the beginning of volume 1, chapter 2. Susan spends part of the journey 'meditating much upon silver forks, napkins, and finger glasses' (*MP*, p. 407). The concern with 'silver forks', as opposed to the 'silver knife' (*MP*, p. 351) over whose possession Susan squabbles at home with Betsey, her younger sister, underscores the narrative's growing distance from Portsmouth. Perhaps it could even be said that Austen's text indulges in a bifurcation of its own, swerving away from one conclusion and towards another. The dénouement which weds Fanny to Edmund – enabled by the filial melodramas of illness, adultery and elopement – replaces or screens an alternative outcome, in which the heroine is left to die at Portsmouth as punishment for patriarchal transgression. Such a divergence of narrative trajectories suggests in turn a further parallel with *The Negro Slaves*, whose penultimate scene offers the reader, albeit rather more overtly, a choice of finale. Pretending to have capitulated to the designs and desires of the slave-master, Ada, at this point, has persuaded him to allow her a last meeting with the reprieved Zameo – who is to be returned to Africa while she is to become John's mistress. The true purpose of the meeting, however, involves a more radical act of persuasion on Ada's part – that Zameo kill her with the knife procured earlier to this end by Lilli, Ada's fellow-slave and companion. The scene's final moment is one of literal and figurative suspense alike: the knife hangs over Ada in Zameo's hand as she is about to be forced to make good the false promise to the slave-master. The stage direction at this juncture reads as follows: '*She hides her face on his shoulder. He turns his away.*'[41] Yet if Zameo's face is averted from Ada here the text deviates from itself, splitting into generically (and typographically) distinct endings. In one ending, Ada is killed by Zameo's knife, an event followed by Zameo's hallucination of his wife's ghostly presence and his own suicide. Such an ending is implicitly accorded a secondary status within Kotzebue's play, however. It undergoes typographical reduction and is located in the lower part of the page beneath a horizontal line. Above this line, in standard-sized print, is what must be considered the play's primary ending. Here the reunion of Ada and Zameo is achieved not through death but rather via a bargain struck between John and his pro-abolitionist brother, William, in which the latter gives up 'half his fortune'[42] in order to liberate the slaves from their master. The image on which this ending finally fixes marks the generic transformation – from sentimental/tragic to comic: the knife with which Zameo kills Ada and then himself becomes the pen with which William signs the contract facilitating the slaves' release. Truro, described in the dramatis personae as 'an Old Free Negro', takes the emancipatory pen from William and calls it his 'richest possession' which he will relinquish to 'None but the angel of God'.[43]

The pen which delivers the slaves belongs, equally, to the playwright who offers the one ending, above the line, as a comic alternative to the other, below the line. In Austen, the shaping role of the narrator as agent of redemption is of course rendered quite explicit in the famous opening sentence of the novel's last chapter: 'Let other pens dwell on guilt and misery. I quit such odious subjects as soon as I can, impatient to restore every body, not greatly in fault themselves, to tolerable comfort, and to have done with all the rest' (*MP*, p. 420). The allusion here is arguably, and characteristically, a doubled one. Beyond the immediacies of a domestic crisis about to be resolved, the reader is reminded of those other 'odious subjects' – slavery and slaves – on which the text refuses, precisely, to 'dwell', together with the 'guilt and misery' they might induce.

One of those 'other pens' that responds most pertinently – or impertinently – to Austen's invitation, read in these terms, belongs to Mary Prince. Prince's narrative of her slave-experiences, *The History of Mary Prince, A West Indian Slave, Related by Herself*, was published in 1831 and includes an account of a period spent as a slave in Antigua between 1816 and 1828. It provides an uncanny supplement to Austen's fiction, operating – within the ideological constraints of its own genre – to 'fill up the blanks' (*MP*, p. 196) in *Mansfield Park*, particularly with regard to the sexual violence suffered by the black female slave. However, in the case of Austen's text, it is not solely or simply in and through such 'blanks' – the white spaces of non-representation and erasure – that 'the horrors of slavery' remain unknown, as Prince puts it, to 'all the good people in England'.[44] Instead, *Mansfield Park* ironically compounds the production of such ignorance by the manner in which it seeks to transcend its own narrative limits, reinscribing and translating the colonial as the domestic. Because such strategies rest upon analogies between orders of oppression which are incommensurable with one another, they result less in the return of the colonial than its re-effacement in another guise.

3
'Silent Revolt': Slavery and the Politics of Metaphor in *Jane Eyre*

> Metaphor, in fact, is never an innocent figure of speech.
>
> Alain Robbe-Grillet

> There is no private life that has not been determined by a wider public life.

> The happiest women, like the happiest nations, have no history.
>
> George Eliot

> Oh the horrors of slavery! – How the thought of it pains my heart! But the truth ought to be told of it; and what my eyes have seen I think it is my duty to relate; for few people in England know what slavery is. I have been a slave – I have felt what a slave feels, and I know what a slave knows; and I would have all the good people in England to know it too, that they may break our chains, and set us free.
>
> Mary Prince[1]

The metaphorics of slavery

In what is the classic feminist reading of *Jane Eyre* (1847), Sandra M. Gilbert and Susan Gubar argue that Charlotte Brontë's novel is in large measure an expression of a 'rebellious feminism'.[2] For these critics, as for many other Anglo-American feminists, Jane Eyre's story provides 'a pattern for countless others'.[3] It is, they assert:

[one] of enclosure and escape, a distinctively female *Bildungsroman* in which the problems of the protagonist as she struggles from the imprisonment of her childhood to an almost unthinkable goal of mature freedom are symptomatic of difficulties which Everywoman in a patriarchal society must meet and overcome. . . . Most important, her confrontation, not with Rochester but with Rochester's mad wife Bertha, is the book's central confrontation, an encounter . . . not with her own sexuality but with her own imprisoned 'hunger, rebellion, and rage,' a secret dialogue of self and soul on whose outcome . . . the novel's plot, Rochester's fate, and Jane's coming-of-age all depend.[4]

These comments are themselves symptomatic, ironically, of one of the difficulties underlying the analysis in which they occur. The casual troping of Brontë's protagonist as 'Everywoman' performs a kind of racial legerdemain, by which a female experience of oppression and resistance that is in fact distinctively white and English (and for the most part lower middle-class) becomes silently representative of female experience as a whole: to view the eponymous heroine/narrator of Brontë's novel as somehow universally normative is at the same time for criticism to suggest a certain blindness with regard to forms of subjective experience which are racially and culturally other.[5]

In the context of *Jane Eyre*, such forms are most obviously, if ambiguously, associated with Bertha Mason, the creole heiress whom Rochester marries, for financial gain, in Jamaica and subsequently transports (following the onset of her 'madness') to England, imprisoning her in the third-story attic of Thornfield Hall for some ten years. Precisely as a creole, Bertha's presence in the text is intriguingly equivocal. In its nineteenth-century context, the term can refer equally to persons born and naturalized in the West Indies of either European or African descent, having, as the *OED* stresses, 'no connotation of colour'.[6] Yet the inclusion of Bertha within *Jane Eyre* as the unstable signifier of otherness and difference is something which Gilbert and Gubar seem to want to resist. This resistance takes the form of an interpretative strategy which resolutely denies Bertha's literal presence as a character within Brontë's novel and favours, instead, a psycho-feminist emphasis on her role as the metaphorical expression of Jane's own unconscious desires and discontents. Bertha thus becomes 'Jane's truest and darkest double: she is the angry aspect of the orphan child, the ferocious secret self Jane has been trying to repress ever since her days at Gates-head'.[7] While Jane is troped as 'Everywoman', Bertha figures, or is figured, here, as her 'double' or alter ego. In this way, the racial and cultural differences which she embodies are effectively erased, along with their ambiguities.[8]

Gilbert and Gubar's reading of the 'central confrontation' in *Jane Eyre* along these lines is, it is true, one which Brontë's text appears openly to encourage through its fabrication of numerous parallels and correspondences between Jane and Bertha from first to last. Yet, as Laura E. Donaldson has argued, the consequences of such a reading, both methodologically and politically, are highly discon-certing and themselves to be read as the effects of what she calls 'The Miranda Complex'.[9] Donaldson develops this notion from an early exchange in William Shakespeare's *The Tempest* in which Miranda declines Prospero's invitation to visit the enslaved Caliban by saying, "Tis a villain, sir, / I do not love to look on.'[10] For Donaldson, Miranda's aversion of her gaze from Caliban is replicated in the exemplary failure of Gilbert and Gubar to address questions of slavery, colonialism and race in *Jane Eyre*, as in nineteenth-century women's texts in general. Worse still, the very critics who see Bertha as Jane's 'secret self' find themselves simultaneously locked into an ironic repetition of the workings of patriarchal oppression within the text which they read. Just as Rochester literally and figuratively shuts up his first wife at Thornfield so, according to Donaldson: 'Gilbert and Gubar's interpretation of Bertha . . . not only imprisons her within the privatistic cell of Jane's psyche, but also deprives her of any independent textual significance.'[11]

The denial to Bertha of 'independent textual significance' pro-duces another irony, since it is precisely the absence of such autonomy 'which [Gilbert and Gubar] deplore when it oppresses Anglo-Euro-pean women'.[12] This dilemma is compounded when it is recalled that one of the epigraphs introducing Gilbert and Gubar's analysis of *Jane Eyre* is from Jean Rhys, whose *Wide Sargasso Sea* (1966) – standing as revisionary 'prequel'[13] to Brontë's novel – finally ac-cords to Bertha (renamed in Rhys as Antoinette) just that textual independence, as character and narrating subject, which is with-held from her by Brontë's latter-day feminist readers.[14]

In maintaining a silence over issues of slavery and racial oppres-sion, Gilbert and Gubar, like the generality of white feminist critics of *Jane Eyre*, might be said to collude with the text itself and its evasions of a recent colonial memory. For, despite the pivotal and determinant role of the West Indies in *Jane Eyre* in terms of the narrative and economic fortunes of its major characters, Brontë's text nowhere explicitly refers to the institution of British slavery or the colonial project with which, for the early Victorian reader, the West Indies would still, in 1847, be strongly associated and against whose distant horizon Jane conducts her metropolitan life.[15]

Yet even as *Jane Eyre* excludes the subject of British colonial slavery at the level of the literal, it is nevertheless widely present as discourse, in terms, that is, of the language through which Brontë's heroine characteristically organizes and represents her experience – how, in other words, she comes to see and understand herself. While the novel's autobiographical conventions necessarily entail an emphasis on the personal, Brontë's text also offers a powerful analysis of larger socio-cultural structures in England during the first half of the nineteenth century, focusing on the aspirations of lower middle-class women, such as Jane, in particular. This concern with forms of domestic oppression created by gender and class is, paradoxically, the vehicle for the return of the colonial. Like many other nineteenth-century texts (though perhaps more systematically), Brontë's novel formulates its critique of gender- and class-ideology by means of a habitual recourse to a metaphorical language of enslavement and mastery.

In this sense, it becomes evident that the question of the novel's politics is inseparable from that of its rhetorical operations. The deployment of a metaphorics of slavery as a way of representing forms of domestic oppression is, from one perspective, both a rhetorically powerful and politically radical manoeuvre. Yet from another perspective – belonging to those who are or have been enslaved, experienced the metaphor, as it were – such a strategy can only be viewed as deeply problematic. The unease created by the use of slavery as metaphor, together with the need to resist its seductions, is outlined, in the context of antebellum America, by Frederick Douglass, whose own first-hand account of enslavement was published in 1845, two years before the appearance of *Jane Eyre*. In the course of a lecture given to a meeting in Newcastle upon Tyne on 3 August 1846, Douglass defines it as his 'duty to direct . . . attention to the character of slavery, as it is in the United States'. He goes on to inform his British audience of the urgency of the task:

> I am the more anxious to do this, since I find the subject of slavery identified with many other systems, in such a manner,

as in my opinion, to detract to some extent from the horror
with which slavery in the United States is so justly contemplated.
I have been frequently asked, since coming into this country,
'why agitate the question of American slavery in this land; we
have slavery here, we are slaves here.' I have heard intemper-
ance called slavery, I have heard your military system, and a
number of other things called slavery, which were very well calculated to detract from the dreadful horror with which you at a
distance contemplate the institution of American slavery.[16]

With their emphasis on the identification of slavery with 'many
other systems' of oppression and the recognition of how this can
'detract from the dreadful horror' with which slavery is more 'justly'
associated, Douglass's comments illuminate the politically dangerous repercussions ('calculated' or accidental) of the very rhetorical
basis on which *Jane Eyre* articulates its domestic critique.

The logic of Douglass's argument applies as much to British colonial as to American slavery, though there are, of course, important
differences between the two contexts – one of which is historical.
In contrast to the ongoing situation in America, British slavery in
the West Indies had been formally abolished by Act of Parliament
with effect from August 1834, well over a decade before *Jane Eyre*'s
publication (though full emancipation was not achieved until 1838,
following the dissolution of the system of 'apprenticeship' which
replaced slavery).[17] What needs to be borne in mind, though, is
the doubleness or reversibility of the slave metaphor, as it operates
in either context. On the one hand, the articulation of domestic
oppression in terms of slavery is a kind of shock-tactic, designed to
move the reader into dramatic awareness of the severity of particular conditions of disempowerment existing at home. Yet, on the
other hand, the simultaneous counter-effect, as Douglass's observations suggest, is to lessen and disguise the realities of slavery. In
these terms, it becomes clear that one of the corollaries to the
doubleness of the slave-figure is to enmesh the texts in which it
operates – and *Jane Eyre* is the major Victorian example – in a certain duplicity. In the name of effecting domestic change, such texts
not only appeal to analogies between forms of oppression which
cannot, ultimately, be drawn into comparison, but in so doing also
falsify and diminish the true nature of that which is the ground of
their own efficacy.

The silence of much white feminist criticism on the questions of slavery, colonialism and race in *Jane Eyre* is of a piece with the text's refusal directly to negotiate these issues as they are concretized in the exploitation of African and creole blacks in the West Indies. Such exclusions, it now would appear, are in turn compounded by the figurative logic of Brontë's novel. For, at both levels, the literal and the metaphorical, *Jane Eyre* might be said, in Mary Prince's figure, to 'put a cloak about the truth'.[18] If 'few people in England know what slavery is', part of the responsibility for this perhaps lies with the workings of metaphor itself.

For these reasons, *Jane Eyre* is a text in which, to modify the terms of this chapter's first epigraph, the guilt of metaphor is liable to be particularly acute. This proves, indeed, to be the case, as evidenced by the unfolding of Brontë's novel as a double-inscription: not only does it exploit the slave trope but at the same time also comments upon and critiques its own rhetorical procedures, offering in this way a 'silent revolt'[19] against the political problems which those procedures entail.

Metaphors of slaves and masters

The first sign of this critique comes in the shape of an allusion to William Makepeace Thackeray offered in the Preface to the second edition of Brontë's novel. Thackeray, according to the enthusiastic Preface-writer, is 'the very master of that working corps who would restore to rectitude the warped system of things' – the immediate stimulus for such a judgement being Thackeray's *Vanity Fair* (serialized 1847–8). Yet no sooner is Thackeray figured as 'master' than he is implicitly disfigured, since 'no commentator . . . has yet found the comparison that suits him, the terms which rightly characterize his talent' (*JE*, p. 4), a claim that, properly speaking, must embrace the one who makes it, the pseudonymous 'Currer Bell'.

Such a prefatory play of figuration and disfiguration is, in terms of *Jane Eyre* as a whole, a telling one. Positing and then revoking the representation of Thackeray as 'master', Brontë's Preface marks out for itself a subtle distance from the rhetorical idiom – the language of mastery and enslavement – which dominates the novel. This linguistic self-questioning is underscored in more general terms by the problematic status of the address to Thackeray itself. Having dedicated *Jane Eyre*'s second edition to her fellow author, Brontë comes soon to discover the existence of what she ruefully calls an 'unlucky coincidence'[20] between Thackeray's marital circumstances and

Rochester's. The two figures – the real and the fictional – become weirdly compounded. Thus, by a bizarre intersection of fiction and biography, the disfiguring of Thackeray's mastery itself implies a questioning of the figurative status comparably accorded throughout the novel to Rochester (he is Jane's 'master') and hence an unsettling also of that position as 'slave' contrapuntally adopted by Jane herself.

There is one more twist to the doubling of Rochester in Thackeray. In so far as the latter undergoes a kind of textual disfiguration in the ways indicated, his fate might be said to be a metaphorical version of that literally experienced by Rochester in the form of the physical mutilation – the loss of a hand and the blindness – which he incurs as a result of Bertha's incineration of Thornfield Hall towards the end of the novel. Placed before the narrative but written after it, the Preface thus re-enacts the text in the same way that the text contains parallels with the life of the writer to whom it is so unhappily dedicated.

The Thackeray/Rochester relation leads on to the narrative itself. Having 'drawn parallels in silence', the ten-year-old Jane is subsequently provoked into hyperbolic utterance of them, at the end of the novel's first chapter, by the physical violence of John Reed: '"Wicked and cruel boy!" I said. "You are like a murderer – you are like a slave-driver – you are like the Roman emperors!"' (*JE*, p. 11). The significance of this moment lies not only in the fleeting parallels that it advances between domestic oppression and slavery, but also in its linkage of the very creation of such parallels (even in the lesser mode of simile, as opposed to metaphor) with transgression – Jane's outburst being, as it is, part of that 'moment's mutiny' (*JE*, p. 12) which leads to her incarceration in the red-room in the next chapter. At a narrative or thematic level, the red-room functions as punishment for female defiance of patriarchy: Mrs. Reed offers to 'liberate' Jane from its terrors 'only on condition of perfect submission and stillness' (*JE*, p. 18). Yet at the same time, Jane's punishment works to dramatize the text's recognition of the transgressiveness of its own linguistic actions. It is almost as if the speaking ten-year-old were a kind of preliminary 'scape-goat' (*JE*, p. 16) for her later writing self.

These linguistic actions can be seen as particularly problematic in terms of what Thomas Babington Macaulay refers to as the 'aristocracy of skin'.[21] During her sojourn in the red-room, the young Jane is represented by her older narratorial self as a 'rebel slave'

(*JE*, p. 12) and, again, as a 'slave' who has 'revolted' (*JE*, p. 15). The effect of such self-figurations is to mystify or occult, through language, those hierarchies of difference – in the form of race or colour – on which slavery is predicated. Perhaps this is why the 'looking-glass' (*JE*, p. 14) scene in the red-room is also a scene of failed self-recognition? For the young Jane to grasp 'the strange little figure there gazing at [her], with a white face and arms specking the gloom' (*JE*, p. 15) as her own reflection would also be for the narrative to expose the ways in which its rhetoric works to slight the differences of race.

Yet even as such an exposure is symbolically avoided by Jane's nonself-recognition in the mirror, it is effected in another way, since the divisions between oppressor and oppressed – the Reeds and Jane – are indeed mapped in terms of racial difference: 'I was a discord in Gateshead Hall: I was like nobody there; I had nothing in harmony with Mrs. Reed or her children,' Jane comments. She is 'a heterogeneous thing . . . a useless thing' (*JE*, p. 16) and forced, consequently, to concede the improbability of gaining affection from Mrs. Reed, who could not, Jane comes to recognize, 'really like an interloper, not of her race . . . an uncongenial alien permanently intruded upon her own family group' (*JE*, p. 17).[22]

By means of the identification of slavery with racial otherness, these reflections reinscribe the differences which *Jane Eyre*'s use of slavery as metaphor implicitly works to obscure. They function, that is, to bring to light, and into question, the political implications of the novel's central rhetorical devices and are thus part of the critique to which the text subjects itself. This is seen also in Jane's self-description as a 'thing' – a linguistic turn giving rise to what might be called a high-friction paradox. On the one hand, the reified status which Jane ascribes to herself is one literally experienced by the enslaved black subject through the fact of his or her body being defined as the property of another, the white slavemaster. Yet the very condition which is synonymous with the negation of black subjectivity precisely affords the figurative materials out of which the novel's white narrator comes into possession of her own identity. As female autobiography, *Jane Eyre* constitutes a form of fictional self-empowerment, enabling Jane to assume that position as subject traditionally denied to women by the codes of Victorian patriarchy. The text's enablements remain problematic, however, because of the rhetorical strategies in which they are implicated.

This is a point borne out in another respect, as can be seen by considering the issue of the structure of metaphor. For Eric Cheyfitz, the Aristotelian definition is 'still basic'.[23] According to this definition: 'Metaphor consists in giving the thing a name that belongs to something else; the transference being either from genus to species, or from species to genus, or from species to species, or on grounds of analogy.'[24] Metaphor becomes a scene of redistribution wherein a word that is conventionally the 'property' of one thing is assigned to 'something else'. From this perspective, the very form of metaphor recapitulates the material relations of colonial history as they are articulated in the transference of the enslaved body from Africa to the New World and from its rightful owner to the slave-master. The historically specific referent from which *Jane Eyre* holds back in literal terms is thus not only alluded to by the text's figurative language but also appears to inhabit its structures.

The transferences of metaphor (translated by Quintilian as *translatio* or 'carrying over'),[25] constitute a re-enactment of history in another way which is illuminated by means of Paul Ricœur's observation, extending Aristotle, that metaphor is 'doubly alien'.[26] It is, in Patricia Parker's glossing of Ricœur, 'a name that belongs elsewhere and one which takes the place of the word which "belongs"'.[27] In *Jane Eyre* the transferences are from the colonial to the domestic, West Indian slavery to oppression within the metropolis – a movement scrupulously figured, or logged, by the text in Rochester's narrative of his return to Thornfield from Jamaica with the 'mad' Bertha: 'To England, then, I conveyed her: a fearful voyage I had with such a monster in the vessel' (*JE*, p. 326). Nevertheless, the above description of metaphor (a word whose origins are 'elsewhere' which 'takes the place' of one that 'belongs') suggests once again how linguistic structure can rehearse colonial history – with *its* usurpations of the native by the foreign.

The notion of metaphor as place-taking provides an apposite perspective from which to view *Jane Eyre* because the events which occur in the novel seem themselves to be largely ordered in terms of a logic of substitution. Mrs. Reed 'must stand in the stead of a parent' (*JE*, p. 17) to the orphaned Jane at Gateshead who, given her status as heterogeneous 'interloper' or intrusive 'alien', herself begins to seem like a strangely metaphorical figure. This impression is one confirmed in the novel's second phase at Lowood school. At the end of volume 1, chapter 5, Jane's companion at the school, Helen Burns, is unfairly 'dismissed in disgrace ... from a history class, and sent to stand in the middle of the large school-room' (*JE*, p. 54). Two chapters later, her place has been quite literally taken by Jane, publicly punished by Mr Brocklehurst – equally arbitrarily – for her alleged compulsion to lie by being made to stand upon a stool in 'the middle of the room ... exposed to general view on a pedestal of infamy'. Though the narrator claims that 'no language can describe' the 'sensations' that this incident instils in her, it is not long before the text resumes its familiar idiom, sliding from simile to metaphor:

> just as they all rose, stifling my breath and constricting my throat, a girl came up and passed me: in passing, she lifted her eyes. What a strange light inspired them! What an extraordinary sensation that ray sent through me! How the new feeling bore me up! It was as if a martyr, a hero, had passed a slave or victim, and imparted strength in the transit. I mastered the rising hysteria, lifted my head, and took a firm stand on the stool. (*JE*, p. 70)

While Helen's otherworldly gaze eventually stabilizes Jane, it is not before it has also revealed, *en passant*, how something as apparently personal and localized as the self's relation to its own body is typically to be rendered, throughout *Jane Eyre*, in terms of a shifting rhetoric of colonial struggle: the body threatens to make the self the 'slave' to a 'rising hysteria' and must be 'mastered'.

The hystericized body can either enslave the self through rage, or be enslaved by it, through spiritual repression. Though it is not only the female but also the male body (St. John Rivers's) that is prone to the latter effect,[28] the suggestion of the text – in figuring control over the body as 'mastery' – is that to lose such control, becoming enslaved to the somatic, is also to be 'feminized', occupying what patriarchal ideology defines as the place of a woman. Similarly, the extended burden of *Jane Eyre* is that to be a woman under patriarchy – whether governess, lover, mistress or wife – is to have the place of a slave. Of the numerous passages which illustrate this point one that is particularly relevant to the concerns of this reading occurs during the period of the lovers' engagement. Here Jane's evasions of Rochester's sexuality cause him to remind her of its imminent marital assertion:

> 'it is your time now, little tyrant, but it will be mine presently; and when once I have fairly seized you, to have and to hold, I'll

just – figuratively speaking – attach you to a chain like this'
(touching his watch-guard). (*JE*, pp. 283–4)

Like Rochester, the text speaks 'figuratively', using the slave idiom
as a polemical means by which to mark out the limits of possibility
for nineteenth-century women. Rochester's linguistic self-consciousness
is momentary and bland however, while that of Brontë's text is
sustained and critical, a constant underlining of limits and problems.

The way in which relations between the figures at the narrative
level of Brontë's novel enact the metaphorical play within it becomes particularly noticeable during the long central section at
Thornfield. Here, for example, Grace Poole recurrently figures, in
Jane's bewildered view, as a stand-in for Bertha as the agent of
domestic violence.[29]

Correlatively, the role adopted by Blanche Ingram, particularly
with regard to the charade sequence where she acts out the 'pantomime of a marriage' (*JE*, p. 192) with Rochester as pretend-groom,
has the effect of making her a double stand-in with respect to Bertha
and Jane alike. For both of the latter figures, in their different ways,
are drawn into weddings with Rochester which are themselves mere
mockeries (Bertha in Spanish Town, Jamaica, and Jane at Thornfield,
fifteen years later). By the same token, Blanche stands in for herself
because her position as mock-bride in the charades is a duplication
of her status in what passes for the reality beyond them.

The most important example of the workings of the character-
ological relations in the text as a figuring of metaphor is that between
Jane and Bertha. This relation can be defined as a play of reversible
substitution. For Gilbert and Gubar, Bertha's function is to assume
the tasks of a kind of psychic and ultimately suicidal stunt-woman:

> Jane's profound desire to destroy Thornfield, the symbol of
> Rochester's mastery and of her own servitude, will be acted out
> by Bertha, who burns down the house and destroys *herself* in
> the process as if she were an agent of Jane's desire as well as her
> own.[30]

Equally, however, Brontë's novel can be viewed as the drive, finally achieved in the last chapter, to put Jane in Bertha's place as
wife to Rochester. Yet the plot-resolution is anti-climactic, a 'quiet
wedding' indeed, which not even the narratorial nudge of 'Reader,
I married him' (*JE*, p. 473) can much enliven. The eventual marital

place-taking comes to be displaced, ironically marginalized by the earlier scene of its not taking place, at the end of volume 2.

As the substitution of one woman for another, Rochester's attempted marriage to Jane at this point is evidently arranged on the basis of her differences from Bertha. These, in Rochester's estimation, are considerable. Jane, he declares, is 'something at least human', while Bertha constitutes a 'bad, mad, and embruted partner!' (*JE*, p. 306). He drives the point home a little later:

> 'That is *my wife*,' said he. . . . 'And *this* is what I wished to have . . . this young girl, who stands so grave and quiet at the mouth of hell, looking collectedly at the gambols of a demon. I wanted her just as a change after that fierce ragout. . . . look at the difference! Compare these clear eyes with the red balls yonder – this face with that mask – this form with that bulk.' (*JE*, p. 308; emphases in original)

In so far as metaphor, the figure of speech which centrally enables *Jane Eyre* to articulate its domestic critique, is self-consciously re-enacted at the level of narrative, the status of Brontë's heroine as absolutely other to Bertha ('the antipodes of the Creole' [*JE*, p. 328]) might seem to create a contradiction. How can the projected marriage be viewed as a staging of metaphor when, on the one hand, the substitutions it involves are marked by radical difference while, on the other hand, those of the Aristotelian transference demand an analogical ground? Such an apparent difficulty is, however, exactly why the suspended union between Jane and Rochester can be seen in the way suggested. The 'impediment' (*JE*, p. 303) placed against the marriage functions as the sign of the text's own unspoken but nevertheless 'pronounced objection' (*JE*, p. 309) to the figurative policies which it seeks to implement – the representation of modes of domestic oppression in terms of slavery. The charade of marriage at the end of volume 2 is indeed a pantomime of metaphor but in a way which discloses *Jane Eyre*'s anxieties about the dubiety of its own tropological compulsions.

That the text's revelation of its narrative mysteries is also a metaphor for the exposure of rhetorical secrets is underscored by the language describing Jane's, and the reader's, first formal introduction to Bertha in the recesses of what is both Thornfield's and the novel's third story: 'In the deep shade, at the further end of the room, a figure ran backwards and forwards' (*JE*, p. 307). Narrative and rhetorical modes come together here as Bertha's movements suggest, by inversion, the oscillations of the slave trope itself. The figure of slavery moves forward from colonial to domestic worlds, in *Jane Eyre*, as a means of highlighting forms of oppression at home even as – once again – such a movement can only culminate in its own undoing, shifting the reader's attention back from the domestic to the colonial context from which the figure emanates. This pattern gives rise to a vantage from which a subsequent return to the realm of the domestic can occur, whose own effect is to bring the political dangers of the slave trope into focus: while it is integral to *Jane Eyre*'s ideological critique, the language of slavery purchases its effects at the expense of a veiling of the history of colonial oppression which is its literal ground.

Rebellions

For Gilbert and Gubar, Bertha's destructive impulses – directed as they are against men (Rochester and Richard Mason, her brother) as against marriage and Thornfield itself – enact Jane's own 'secret fantasies',[31] the 'fire and violence' (*JE*, p. 251) of her rage against patriarchal oppression. Yet the third of Bertha's actions (there are five in all)[32] suggests not only the limits of such a reading, but also provides a particularly spectacular illustration of the ways in which *Jane Eyre* sets its own linguistic operations in question.

This action involves the tearing of Jane's wedding-veil two nights before the scheduled marriage to Rochester and is recounted in detail in volume 2, chapter 10. While the veil is, as Adrienne Rich notes, a 'symbol of matrimony',[33] it is also the sign of Rochester's economic power. Purchased in London with 'princely extravagance' (*JE*, p. 294) for a reluctant bride, it consequently functions as an oblique token for slavery, the source from which Rochester's 'English gold' (*JE*, p. 146) – like Jane's own inheritance – derives. Thus to read its destruction in solely patriarchal terms is, in a metaphorical sense, critically to mend the veil, covering over the question of colonialism which *Jane Eyre* itself chooses to put aside.

By a strange cross-cultural and transhistorical coincidence, the action literally performed by Bertha is adopted by Toni Morrison as a metaphor for her own rewriting of the eighteenth- and nineteenth-century slave narrative tradition in *Beloved* (1987). Reflecting on the ideological and psychological constraints imposed upon the slave narratives (including Douglass's), Morrison remarks that her 'job becomes how to rip that veil drawn over "proceedings to terrible to relate"'.[34] However, in terms of the evasiveness of Brontë's novel towards the truth of British colonial slavery in the West Indies, the moment of Bertha's veil-tearing can be viewed as a model of what the text consistently fails to do, preferring to manipulate colonialism-as-figure rather than represent it directly, in its literality. Indeed, in those moments when the language of enslavement is made culturally specific (as in volume 2, chapter 9, for example), it is in a way that lures the reader beyond British frames of reference, safely transporting the material realities of slave-oppression and rebellion to Oriental contexts (*JE*, pp. 281–2).

However, it is not only that colonialism (literally absent at one level) is transformed by *Jane Eyre* into a consequential presence at another, that of figuration, but that it is also figured by Brontë's text. At one point, Jane deems herself to be 'purposely excluded' from the 'mystery at Thornfield' (*JE*, p. 174). Yet the irony is that in one sense Rochester's revelation of his secret only compounds it: as already noted, Bertha's status as a creole makes the question of her race significantly uncertain. Nevertheless, the suggestively indeterminate nature of Bertha's racial identity (as specified in volume 2, chapter 11 and volume 3, chapter 1) seems, at other junctures, equally suggestively, to be less vague. As Susan L. Meyer puts it:

> [Bertha] is clearly imagined as white – or as passing as white –
> in the novel's retrospective narrative. . . . But when she actually
> emerges in the course of the action, the narrative associates her
> with blacks, particularly with the black Jamaican antislavery rebels,
> the Maroons. In the form in which she becomes visible in the
> novel, Bertha has *become* black.[35]

In these terms it can be seen that the targets of Bertha's violence are not exclusively patriarchal: a 'crime' breaking out, 'now in fire and now in blood, at the deadest hours of night' (*JE*, p. 221) with a 'black and scarlet visage' (*JE*, p. 327), Bertha is also a figure for colonial rebellion, 'symbolically enacting precisely the sort of revolt feared by the British colonists in Jamaica'[36] in the years of their dominion prior to the writing of *Jane Eyre*.

The subtext of colonial rebellion not only supplements and disrupts feminist constructions of Bertha as patriarchal rebel, but in so doing also helps to reveal the continuing preoccupation of Brontë's novel with the propriety of its own figurative designs. As one confined to and subversive of what is literally a domestic space – Thornfield – Bertha metaphorizes Jane's own predicament as Englishwoman. Conversely, Bertha is a figure for the very literality (colonialism) that Jane exploits as a figurative system through which self-representation is facilitated: Bertha stands in, in other words, for the 'rebel' or 'revolted slave' to whom Jane systematically likens herself (and those like her) throughout the novel. However, the moment of their meeting in volume 2, chapter 10 is implicitly marked by Jane's failure to see the resemblances between Bertha's two roles – as her own patriarchally oppressed double, on the one hand, and as a surrogate for the victims of colonialism, on the other. Jane's statement of her nocturnal encounter with Bertha is given in a series of exchanges with Rochester on the next night. Asking whether Jane saw the face of her bedroom-intruder, Rochester prompts the following dialogue:

> 'Not at first. But presently she took my veil from its place; she held it up, gazed at it long, and then she threw it over her own head, and turned to the mirror. At that moment I saw the reflection of the visage and features quite distinctly in the dark oblong glass.'
> 'And how were they?'
> 'Fearful and ghastly to me – oh, sir, I never saw a face like it! It was a discoloured face – it was a savage face. I wish I could forget the roll of the red eyes and the fearful blackened inflation of the lineaments!'
> 'Ghosts are usually pale, Jane.'
> 'This, sir, was purple: the lips were swelled and dark; the brow furrowed; the black eye-brows wildly raised over the bloodshot eyes. Shall I tell you of what it reminded me?'
> 'You may.'
> 'Of the foul German spectre – the Vampyre.'
> 'Ah! – What did it do?'
> 'Sir, it removed my veil from its gaunt head, rent it in two parts, and flinging both on the floor, trampled on them.' (*JE*, p. 297)

As noted above, the division of the veil combines patriarchal with colonial aggressions. Despite both this, however, and the physiognomic stereotyping of Bertha as black, her 'savage face' is not revealed, in Jane's account, as what it is for Donaldson – the 'rem(a)inder of slavery'.[37] Instead it is reviled or masked through a Eurocentric association with 'the foul German spectre – the Vampyre': in what amounts to a moment of repressive bathos, Jane precisely fails to see the likeness between Bertha and the 'rebel slave' for which she is the hyperbolic or literally inflated figure. Yet since Bertha is also Jane's double, the failure of recognition is itself twofold – a failure to see the very correspondences between patriarchal and colonial oppression on which, ironically, Jane's text both insists and relies so fully.

Jane's non-apprehension of Bertha as a figure or counter-double for the colonial oppression and rebellion in terms of which she apprehends herself provides another instance of her text's scepticism towards its own rhetorical operations. One of the ironic consequences of this is to suggest the resemblances between Jane and Bertha. Being the signifier of 'matrimony' on the one hand, and slavery on the other, the veil concomitantly signifies precisely the kind of conjunctions which Brontë's text seeks to establish through metaphor. In rending the veil 'from top to bottom in two halves!' (*JE*, p. 298), Bertha thus aligns herself with the impulses of *Jane Eyre*'s rhetorical self-critique, grounded as it is in a subversive counter-emphasis on the discrepancies rather than similarities between the 'two parts' – domestic and colonial oppression – of the novel's central figure, the trope of slavery.

With its bafflements and loss of consciousness, the encounter with Bertha recalls the events in the red-room of volume 1, chapter 2, though this time it is a 'savage' rather than a 'white face' – a 'lurid visage' (*JE*, p. 298) – from which Jane is alienated. The encounter leads back briefly, equally, to the charade sequence, introduced in the following passage:

> Mrs. Fairfax was summoned to give information respecting the resources of the house in shawls, dresses, draperies of any kind; and certain wardrobes of the third story were ransacked, and their contents, in the shape of brocaded and hooped petticoats, satin sacques, black modes lace lappets, &c., were brought down in armfuls by the Abigails: then a selection was made, and such things as were chosen were carried to the boudoir within the drawing-room. (*JE*, p. 191)

Notwithstanding the improbable transvestism of Rochester's subsequent appearance as a gipsy-woman, 'almost as black as a crock' (*JE*, p. 202), these garments are Bertha's – their removal and appropriation to other uses itself a glancing reminder of the relocation of meaning from literal to figurative in *Jane Eyre* as a whole. In volume 2, chapter 10, however, Bertha begins her own charade with a counter-raid on the 'suit of wedding raiment' (*JE*, p. 288) in Jane's wardrobe, sorting out the veil (manifold symbol of marriage and slavery and marriage-as-slavery) from the rest.

In the act of Bertha's veil-tearing, as in the larger scene in which it occurs, Brontë's text dramatizes a rejection of the very rhetorical operations it brings into play, giving them what Jane calls 'the distinct lie' (*JE*, p. 298). It is in the context of this kind of textual self-critique that the opening events of volume 2, chapter 3 (*JE*, pp. 190–5) can be situated. What most obviously links the two scenes is their common concern with marriage. The first element of the word acted out by Rochester and his company is 'Bride!' (*JE*, p. 192), while the 'divining party' is asked to infer the second from a rendering of the biblical scene at the well in which Eliezer recognizes Rebekah as the future wife to Isaac, his master's son (Genesis 24. 14ff). Themselves married together in the '"tableau of the Whole"', the two verbal units spell out Rochester's private meaning, yet in a way which reveals his figurative mode, at this point at least, to be at odds with that of the text at large:

> Amidst this sordid scene, sat a man with his clenched hands resting on his knees, and his eyes bent on the ground. I knew Mr. Rochester; though the begrimed face, the disordered dress (his coat hanging loose from one arm, as if it had been almost torn from his back in a scuffle), the desperate and scowling countenance, the rough, bristling hair might well have disguised him. As he moved, a chain clanked: to his wrists were attached fetters.
>   'Bridewell!' exclaimed Colonel Dent, and the charade was solved.
> (*JE*, p. 193)

Through the metaphorical pun that turns marriage into a prison (for which 'Bridewell' in the nineteenth century is a synonym), Brontë's text appears indeed momentarily to have liberated itself from the confines of its own rhetorical system.

Such an impression is, however, self-undermining. At some level Rochester is no doubt the victim of the 'steps' (*JE*, p. 133) taken by his own and Bertha's father in order to procure his fortune. Yet the terms in which he figures this plight could hardly be more questionable: even as Rochester theatricalizes himself as marital prisoner, he stands as Bertha's literal warder, creating for her the material conditions in terms of which he sees himself. The fact subverts the figure.

Structurally, then, the metaphor with which Rochester entertains both himself and the reader (who, apart from the remembering Jane, is its sole audience) only extends the figurative closure which it seems, in terms of content, to transcend. His charade rehearses, in other words, the problems built into the emancipatory strategies of the novel as a whole. As if to confirm this point, the ostensible prisoner seems – from 'begrimed face' to clanking 'chain' and 'fetters' – much like a slave in poor disguise. In this way, he illustrates the wrong-headedness of Jane's assumption that the charade is 'solved' with 'Bridewell!' and hence the manner in which meaning escapes the (Rochesterean) attempt to fix it.[38]

Translations

The discovery of Bertha's place as prisoner at Thornfield causes Jane to lose her own. Leaving Rochester, she embarks upon the desperate moorland journey which leads to the eventual exhausted arrival at Moor House. In the course of her recuperation, Moor House becomes 'more' house, in two senses. Not only does Jane gain the Riverses – St. John, Diana and Mary – as her cousins but, through the mutual avuncular link of John Eyre, her fortune also (*JE*, pp. 396–409). This in turn – through John Eyre's Madeiran connection with Richard Mason, a Jamaican wine-maker – indicates, as Meyer notes, that Jane's wealth, like Rochester's, has colonial origins.[39] As throughout, the colonial realities at the 'ravished margin' (*JE*, p. 401) of the text have, in this part, a centrally figurative function, continuing to dictate Jane's constructions of female possibility. Nowhere is the clash of referential margin against figurative centre sharper than in Jane's struggle to persuade St. John that he and his sisters should share her windfall, rather than remain dispersed into hardship. As 'governesses in a large, fashionable, south-of-England city' (*JE*, p. 371), Diana and Mary are envisaged, for example, as 'slaving amongst strangers', while Jane is 'gorged with gold [she] never earned and [does] not merit!' (*JE*, p. 408). Similarly, imagining a life as Rochester's mistress in Marseilles turns Jane, at an earlier point, into a 'slave in a fool's paradise' (*JE*, p. 379), just as, later, she can only contemplate working as a missionary with St. John in India if her 'natural . . . feelings' remain 'unenslaved' by marriage (*JE*, p. 429).[40]

St. John's missionary ambitions in India indicate *Jane Eyre*'s expansion of its own frame of colonial reference.[41] This broadening of narrative range is accompanied by the incursion into the novel of what Suvendrini Perera calls a 'vocabulary of oriental misogyny'.[42] Such a vocabulary manifests itself in the form, particularly, of a series of references to the culturally specific practice of sati – the immolation of Hindu widows on the funeral pyres of their husbands.[43] Despite the obvious differences between *Jane Eyre*'s colonial contexts – or subtexts – the West Indies and India, they nevertheless become firmly interlocked by the ideological purposes to which Brontë's novel puts them.

Urged, in volume 3, chapter 8, by St. John to 'give up German and learn Hindostanee' (*JE*, p. 418), Jane soon enough finds herself 'poring over the crabbed characters and flourishing tropes of an Indian scribe' (*JE*, p. 421). Yet the figures she reads thrive equally well in the foreign soil of her own writing, as the trope of sati – like that of slavery – generates the inscription of the patriarchal and religious oppression of women. In the eyes of St. John, Jane's is 'a soul that revel[s] in the flame and excitement of sacrifice'. Such spiritual refinement prompts his proposal/ultimatum that she not only support his aims in the role of 'helper amongst Indian women' (*JE*, p. 425) but do so, moreover, by becoming his wife. Even before she comes to consider the hollow blisses of domestic relations with St. John, the prospect of giving assistance to 'Indian women' is figured as sati, precisely one of the practices which the nineteenth-century missionary sought to outlaw: 'if I *do* make the sacrifice he urges, I will make it absolutely: I will throw all on the altar – heart, vitals, the entire victim' (*JE*, p. 426; emphasis in original).[44] Marriage to St. John is represented, similarly, as a kind of sati from within:

> but as his wife – at his side always, and always restrained, and always checked – forced to keep the fire of my nature continually low, to compel it to burn inwardly and never utter a cry, though the imprisoned flame consumed vital after vital – *this* would be unendurable. (*JE*, p. 429; emphasis in original)[45]

At Moor House Brontë's novel mixes its metaphors – sati with slavery – in terms of marriage as in other respects.[46] The differences between the colonial spaces from which they are drawn – as also between the forms of oppression, the histories and cultures with which those spaces are associated – should not be overlooked. On the other hand, it is evident that in this section of the novel the language of 'oriental misogyny' effectively restates (like Rochester's figuring of marriage-as-prison) the problems inherent to the slave trope. *Jane Eyre*, that is, co-opts sati – like slavery – as metaphor and channels it into a process of ideological critique at home whose liberative aims are compromised by the discursive re-enactment of the very oppressions which form the ground of their enablement. It is almost as if the text were translating the dilemma at its tropological heart into another idiom whose limits, risks and delusions are already implied by the original.

Such an effect is not surprising because Moor House is itself a place where translation from and into other languages – German, Hindostanee – occurs continually. Translation is indeed the occupation of Diana and Mary during Jane's first uncanny sight of them:

> I had nowhere seen such faces as theirs: and yet, as I gazed on them, I seemed intimate with every lineament. I cannot call them handsome – they were too pale and grave for the word: as they each bent over a book, they looked thoughtful almost to severity. A stand between them supported a second candle and two great volumes, to which they frequently referred; comparing them seemingly with the smaller books they held in their hands, like people consulting a dictionary to aid them in the task of translation. (*JE*, p. 350)

Nor is the passage here from the strange to the familiar – 'I had nowhere seen such faces as theirs: and yet . . . I seemed intimate with every lineament' – entirely unexpected. Diana and Mary not only relate to Jane as her cousins but also because their 'task of translation' is one upon which she – as a metaphorist – has been engaged throughout the life of her writing. For Quintilian, metaphor is *translatio*, like translation a form of 'carrying over'. The translator strives to transport meaning intact from one language to another, while in metaphor it is transferred from one level to another, within the same language – the literal to the figurative. Such a metaphorical movement is also, as Cheyfitz points out, a translation from the 'familiar' to the 'foreign',[47] (even as the translation in this particular instance is from foreign to familiar, the German of Schiller's *Die Rauber*[48] to English). Translation, in this light, can be a figure for metaphor in the same way that metaphor can stand in for translation.

A significant example of the former possibility comes in volume 1, chapter 10, during the transition from Lowood to Thornfield. Having 'tired of the routine of eight years in one afternoon' (*JE*, p. 89), Jane resolves to 'get a new place' by advertising her services as a governess in the '——shire Herald' (*JE*, p. 90). Advertisement is concealment, however, the would-be governess styling herself as 'J. E.', rather than 'Jane Eyre', and citing Lowton post office, rather than Lowood, for an address. The act of acronymic substitution is a kind of translation at one remove: 'Jane Eyre' is an alias for the 'I' which names the self even as the letters which replace it – 'J. E.' – spell out that 'I''s foreign counterpart, the French 'Je'. In so far as Jane Eyre's 'I' – the self – literally emerges at this point in translation, it enacts a process which in turn provides a figure for *Jane Eyre*'s self-constitution through metaphor, and its translations of the language of slavery from literal to figurative, colonial to domestic settings. Appropriately, the kind of surveillance under which Brontë's novel places itself also marks the transactions carried out by the anxious post-seeker, 'J. E.': in the course of literally receiving the reply from Mrs. Fairfax which leads Jane on to Thornfield as a governess, she is also twice given an 'inquisitive and mistrustful glance' (*JE*, p. 92) by the 'old dame' who both runs the post office and hands over the 'document' (*JE*, p. 91) in question.

Jane Eyre's metaphorical translations are complemented by narrative structure, the series of crossings which take the heroine from place to place: Gateshead to Lowood, Lowood to Thornfield, Thornfield to Moor House, Moor House to Ferndean, as if Jane's life were itself a protracted play – or charade – of metaphor. The final removal, from Moor House to Ferndean, also sees her carried across another threshold through the marriage to Rochester which had been originally blocked at the end of the second volume. The earlier débâcle constitutes a narrative inscription of *Jane Eyre*'s misgivings with regard to its own textual strategies. In this light, as one of the 'incongruous unions' (*JE*, p. 328) to which he refers during the 'confession' to Jane at the beginning of volume 3, Rochester's marriage to Bertha suggests the interesting possibility that a bad match is itself an apposite figure for a suspect metaphor: both involve the joining together of two terms whose similarities cannot offset their differences. In this way, the text might be seen as advertising once again a certain discontent with its own characteristic rhetorical gestures. Conversely, Brontë's novel constructs Rochester's relation to Jane (at least in its ideal form) in terms of what Carolyn Williams calls a 'rhetoric of romantic congruence'.[49] As Williams notes, such rhetoric is 'most graphic' in the proposal scene of volume 2, chapter 8,[50] as, for example, in the fraught cries of the following:

> 'Do you think, because I am poor, obscure, plain, and little, I am soulless and heartless? – You think wrong! – I have as much soul as you, – and full as much heart! And if God had gifted me with some beauty, and much wealth, I should have made it as hard for you to leave me, as it is now for me to leave you. I am not talking to you now through the medium of custom, conventionalities, nor even of mortal flesh: – it is my spirit that addresses your spirit; just as if both had passed through the grave, and we stood at God's feet, equal, – as we are!' (*JE*, pp. 265–6)

As if to authenticate Jane's closing claim, Rochester mirrors its terms: ' "My bride is here," he said . . . "because my equal is here, and my likeness. Jane, will you marry me?" ' (*JE*, p. 267). Just as the 'rhetoric of romantic congruence' is here quite literally a question of the congruence of rhetoric, so the good match is by implication a kind of figuring – displaced into the register of marriage – of the adequation which the text suspects itself to lack at the level of metaphor. The eventual marriage of Jane and Rochester is similarly displaced into the form of a 'double retirement' (*JE*, p. 8) to Ferndean. On the one hand, such a conclusion can be seen as a realization of the 'feminist manifesto'[51] outlined in volume 1, chapter 12 where 'women feel just as men feel' (*JE*, p. 115). Yet, as several critics have observed, such egalitarianism is distinctly asocial.[52] *Jane Eyre* thus ends with the tacit admission that equality between men and women constitutes a sexual utopia which indeed has no place in the realms of the socially real. At the same time, *Jane Eyre* reaches a conclusion with regard to its own practices at which, from the outset, it seems already to have arrived, suggesting that the kind of rhetorical harmony metaphorized in the lovers' 'perfect concord' (*JE*, p. 475) is a textual utopia that has always lain beyond the novel's reach.

4
'Qui est là?': Race and the Politics of Fantasy in *Wide Sargasso Sea*

I was curious about black people. They stimulated me and I felt akin to them. It added to my sadness that I couldn't help but realise they didn't really like or trust white people – white cockroaches they called us. Sick with shame at some of the stories of the slave days.... Yet all the time knowing that there was another side to it. Sometimes seeing myself powerful... sometimes being proud of my great grandfather, the estate, and the good old days.... But the end of my thinking about them was always a sick revolt and I wanted to be identified with the other side which of course was impossible.

Jean Rhys[1]

Revision as repetition: negotiating *Jane Eyre*

As Jean Rhys suggests in a letter to Diana Athill, *Wide Sargasso Sea* (1966) emerges out of a certain scepticism with regard to the early Victorian text which it reinscribes, Charlotte Brontë's *Jane Eyre* (1847). The specific matrix of Rhys's disbelief – as of her novel indeed – is Brontë's representation of Rochester's 'mad' first wife, the Jamaican creole heiress, Bertha Mason:

I can see it all up to a point. I mean a man *might* come to England with a crazy wife. He *might* leave her in charge of a housekeeper and a nurse and dash away to Europe. She *might* be treated far more harshly than he knows and so get madder and madder. He *might* funk seeing her when he returns. But really, to give a house party in the same house – I can't believe that.

But then I've never believed in Charlotte's lunatic, that's why I wrote this book.[2]

From the perspective of the astonishment outlined in Rhys's letter, *Wide Sargasso Sea* can be seen to constitute a striking postcolonial expression of that 'incredulity toward metanarratives' which is a sure sign, according to Jean-François Lyotard, of the postmodern condition.[3] Failure to believe in the figure of 'Charlotte's lunatic' is, by the same token, a rejection of the *grands récits* of colonialism and empire by means of which, as several critics have noted, both Bertha and the problematic feminism of *Jane Eyre* as a whole are enabled and legitimated.[4]

Alluded to as 'Charlotte's lunatic' in the letter to Athill, Bertha is renamed in *Wide Sargasso Sea* as Antoinette. This renaming is itself a trope for the process by which (in its first and third parts at least), Rhys's text translates the marginalized and silent other of Brontë's 'reactionary 19th century romance'[5] into a central narrating 'I'. Yet Bertha is not only silenced but also crucially disfigured by *Jane Eyre* through the workings of a particular textual effect. As suggested in the previous chapter, Bertha's status within Brontë's novel as a creole renders her racial identity ambiguous, even as such a textual and racial aporia is something which *Jane Eyre* seems all too eager to resolve. To recall Susan L. Meyer's argument:

> [Bertha] is clearly imagined as white – or as passing as white – in the novel's retrospective narrative. . . . But when she actually emerges in the course of the action, the narrative associates her with blacks. . . . In the form in which she becomes visible in the novel, Bertha has *become* black.[6]

The mode of Bertha's blackness is twofold, changing as her status shifts between object and subject. As object – a figure in the accounts of other characters – Bertha is consistently represented in terms of three of the commonest stereotypes through which blackness, in the nineteenth century, is fetishistically constructed: sexual licence, madness and drunkenness.[7] Yet as a subject of action, punctuating 'the deadest hours of night' with 'fire and . . . blood'[8] by turns, she functions as a figure of colonial revolt, linked especially, to cite Meyer again, 'with the black Jamaican antislavery rebels, the Maroons'.[9]

The disfiguration of Bertha's identity in these ways is doubly significant for *Wide Sargasso Sea*. As well as seeking, that is, to re-cover a female history lost to the silences of Brontë's colonial fiction – to 'write . . . a life'[10] for Bertha – Rhys aims to reclaim the specificities of that history from the aberrant workings of Brontëan representa-tion. It turns out, however, that her own text participates in the very fantasmatics it seeks to undo because the story it tells is itself regulated by a desired self-identification on the part of its central female figure with a range of black others. While offering a postmodern and postcolonial critique of *Jane Eyre*'s carceral femi-nism, *Wide Sargasso Sea* at the same time elaborates its own complex version of the patterns of rhetorical and racial fantasy inscribed within Brontë's colonial pre-text.

Identification with blackness is not the only way in which *Wide Sargasso Sea* articulates what might be called its fantasies of racial crossing. There are several occasions when Antoinette identifies herself with images from the metropolis: her 'favourite picture', for example, is 'The Miller's Daughter', with its figure of 'a lovely English girl with brown curls and blue eyes'.[11] None the less, it is the principal mode in which such fantasies occur, what the text wishes most, as it were, to explore. This exploration commences at the very start of the novel as Antoinette's narrative obliquely positions Christophine (who is at once her nurse, an obeah woman and an ex-slave from Martinique) as an alternative mother-figure. It is developed throughout the text in Antoinette's involvement in a series of doublings: with Tia, Christophine herself and, most spectacularly, the crowd of ex-slaves who burn down Coulibri Estate, Antoinette's childhood home, in the novel's first part.

The problem with these forms of fantasmatic doubling is their politics. Having no basis in genetic science, the category of race might itself be described as a kind of fantasy. Yet the material force of its effects cannot be overstressed, manifesting itself – in the con-text of colonial slavery – in the production of forms of historical and psychic experience which are radically different from or in-commensurable with one another. The racial and gender-oppression to which Antoinette is subject throughout the text as white creole woman cannot, consequently, be equated with the black slave-history in terms of which it is persistently figured – so that her attempts to cross the colonial 'color-line'[12] through fantasy can themselves only seem exploitative. In resisting and critiquing its own procedures, as it does, *Wide Sargasso Sea* – like *Jane Eyre* before it – is a self-deconstructing text: it is not only an example of what Helen Tiffin

calls *'canonical counter-discourse'*[13] but also a text which runs counter
to itself. In so far as Rochester's narrative splits Antoinette's (taking
up almost all of the novel's second and longest part), it provides a
structural emblem for the self-divisions by which her own story is
marked.

'Doubts and hesitations': the perils of identification

In *Jane Eyre* domestic and textual locations mirror one another.
Secreted in the third story of Rochester's manor-house, Bertha is
introduced to the reader in the central third story of the novel,
Jane's account of her experiences at Thornfield Hall. These third
stories belong to one who might herself be described, in three senses,
as the novel's third person: Bertha is brought to England from the
'Third World', constitutes the scandalous 'impediment' which ensures
that the marriage between Jane and Rochester 'cannot proceed' (*JE*,
p. 303) as scheduled, and is constantly referred to as 'she' or 'it'.

   Yet in *Wide Sargasso Sea* the concern with the recuperation of
white creole narrative reinflects the notions of third story and third
person, causing them to become associated with the space between
the polarities of master and slave, white and black, European source
and African *re*source of colonial oppression. The point is under-
lined as Antoinette elucidates for Rochester the words sung by Amélie,
the 'little half-caste servant' (*WSS*, p. 39) in part two. 'It was a
song', she tells him:

> 'about a white cockroach. That's me. That's what they call all of
> us who were here before their own people in Africa sold them
> to the slave traders. And I've heard English women call us white
> niggers. So between you I often wonder who I am and where is
> my country and where do I belong and why was I ever born at
> all.' (*WSS*, p. 64)

This interstitial space is not a stable one, its borders remaining
permanently open to the traversals of fantasy. These take the shape,
most typically, of identifications with those whom Mr Mason –
Antoinette's stepfather or 'white pappy' (*WSS*, p. 16) – is correctively
advised by her mother, Annette, to call 'Black people' rather than
'nigger, [or] even Negro' (*WSS*, p. 15). Such identifications are integral, it might even be argued, to the intertextual or revisionary
project of *Wide Sargasso Sea per se*. On the one hand, Rhys's text

releases Antoinette from the silent Eurocentrism of *Jane Eyre*, in which she is fixed and framed as Bertha, even as the moment of Antoinette's inscription into language – her narrative origin – is coterminous with the emancipation of slaves in British colonies in 1833–4: the reclamation of the white creole female subject comes to coincide with and parallel black slave liberation.

Yet the parallelism between the two forms of liberation – the intertextual and the historical – is self-ironizing. *Wide Sargasso Sea* recovers the prehistory of the Bertha of *Jane Eyre* as the story of Antoinette, and in so doing provides a powerful counter-statement to Rochester's representation of his West Indian experiences in the earlier text. At the same time, however, the narrative liberated from *Jane Eyre* claims its space by means of a marginalization of the very slave-history with which it seeks alignment. The equation of canonically silenced woman with slave breaks down because the one is emancipated into a speech which itself excludes the utterance of the other.[14] It is not only Rochester's 'mind' but also Antoinette's narrative which contains 'blanks . . . that cannot be filled up' (*WSS*, p. 46): 'All Coulibri Estate had gone wild like the garden, gone to bush. No more slavery – why should *anybody* work? This never saddened me. I did not remember the place when it was prosperous' (*WSS*, p. 6; emphasis in original). Antoinette's failure to recall Coulibri when it was 'prosperous' forms an effacement of the 'Old time' (*WSS*, p. 10) of slavery which is all the more striking for the language in which it is articulated. In disremembering Coulibri's prosperity, Antoinette simultaneously recollects the very figure in whom notions of colonial mastery are perhaps most memorably embodied, the Prospero of William Shakespeare's *The Tempest*.

One feature of the previously cited passage on Africa and England concerns the way in which their difference is curiously slurred by the syntactic elision of the phrase 'So between you' (as opposed, for example, to 'So between the two of you'). Here for a moment the text suggests another doubling, between Antoinette and her 'younger brother Pierre who staggered when he walked and couldn't speak distinctly' (*WSS*, p. 6) and is classified by the 'smooth smiling people' at Annette's wedding to Mr Mason as an 'idiot' (*WSS*, p. 13). Antoinette's own sisterly failure of distinct speech similarly disturbs the novel's opening allusions to the 'trouble' of Emancipation:

They say when trouble comes close ranks, and so the white people did. But we were not of their ranks. The Jamaican ladies had

never approved of my mother, 'because she pretty like pretty
self' Christophine said.
    She was my father's second wife. (*WSS*, p. 5)

Antoinette's difference and exclusion from the martial 'ranks' of
the 'white people' (the English), is underscored by the patois formulation which she borrows from Christophine, originally given
to Annette as a 'wedding present' (*WSS*, p. 8) by Antoinette's father, old Cosway. Yet the complex of relations seems no sooner
fixed than it is unsettled in the equivocal movement between para-
graphs. 'She' refers, properly speaking, to Annette, even as the syntax
allows for a counter-reading in which it is Christophine who comes
to assume the place of the mother,[15] a position with which she is
strongly associated throughout the text. Nor is it surprising that
Antoinette's narrative should begin with a reimagining of maternal
origins, since the reality of the relation between mother and daughter
is characterized by the emotional absence of the one from the other
resulting from Annette's devotion to the disadvantaged Pierre. Yet
the daughter's replacement of the mother who rejects her not only
provides a way of negotiating the disappointment of psychic need.
It also constitutes an initial textual inscription of the desire to effect a kind of fabulous passage or crossing from one subject-position
(and history) to another, white creole to black.
    Antoinette's fleeting fantasy of being the daughter of an ex-slave,
herself deemed by Rochester to be 'blacker than most' (*WSS*, p. 44),
sets her in direct opposition to her mother, 'the daughter of a slave-
owner' (*WSS*, p. 15). The racialized family romance in which she
briefly indulges is given more sustained and explicit narrative em-
bodiment in her yearning to 'be like' (*WSS*, p. 24) Tia, her childhood
friend, daughter of Maillotte, Christophine's companion and another
ex-slave. Elaborated in terms of a tension between sameness and
difference, the relation between Antoinette and Tia is an important
medium through which Rhys's text articulates its ambivalence toward
the identificatory possibilities with which it engages.
    The place where the two girls meet is, accordingly, also where
they routinely take their leave of one another, as well as itself being
a point of convergence and/or separation: 'Soon Tia was my friend
and I met her nearly every morning at the turn of the road to the
river. . . . Late or early we parted at the turn of the road.' The 'turn
of the road' leads similarly to a place which is also a turning-point
in several respects, both literal and figurative – the 'pool' where

the two girls bathe. The 'pool' is literally a turning-point in the sense that it is where Tia goads Antoinette into performing a 'somersault under water "like [she] say [she] can"', the wager being the 'new pennies' (given to Antoinette by Christophine) that fall 'one morning' out of her dress-pocket (*WSS*, p. 9). Antoinette's claim to have fulfilled the terms of the wager is disputed by Tia who appropriates the gleaming coins, saying that she 'hadn't done it good and besides pennies didn't buy much'. The pool scene thus becomes the figurative turning-point in the girls' friendship. Antoinette calls Tia a 'cheating nigger', even as her own declaration – 'I can get more [money] if I want to' – is a self-deception which fails to convince her interlocutor:

> That's not what she hear, she said. She hear all we poor like beggar. We ate salt fish – no money for fresh fish. That old house so leaky, you run with calabash to catch water when it rain. Plenty white people in Jamaica. Real white people, they got gold money. They didn't look at us, nobody see them come near us. Old time white people nothing but white nigger now, and black nigger better than white nigger. (*WSS*, p. 10)

Antoinette's assertion that she has unlimited financial reserves is indeed a lie. At this juncture in the narrative she and her mother exist in a state of humiliating poverty which only the advent of the 'gold money' of Mr Mason, one of those 'Real white people', can alleviate. Deceptions are compounded, moreover, as Antoinette's narrative here creates the illusion of an authentic reproduction of her accuser's speech: the re-presentation of the contretemps with Tia precisely enacts a translation of self into other, 'white nigger' into 'black'. At the same time, however, the figuring of the fantasy of racial crossing through a linguistic identification with the other is disrupted, as the pronouns 'we' and 'us' maintain Antoinette in the position of the 'white nigger' from which she seeks to unfix herself.

Following Annette's remarriage to Mr Mason, the Coulibri estate house is restored, only to be set on fire and destroyed by the rioting ex-slaves. It is in the mayhem of the riot's closing scene that Antoinette re-encounters the figure of Tia, and once again their relation is defined in terms of a conflictual play of sameness and difference. If the scene ends by looking back to an earlier turning-point, it begins with the repetition of a backward look, as Antoinette's gaze follows the distressed line of her mother's:

she had turned and was looking back at the house and when
[Mr Mason] put his hand on her arm she screamed. . . . But now
I turned too. The house was burning, the yellow-red sky was
like sunset and I knew that I would never see Coulibri again.
Nothing would be left. . . . Then, not so far off, I saw Tia and
her mother and I ran to her, for she was all that was left of my
life as it had been. We had eaten the same food, slept side by
side, bathed in the same river. As I ran, I thought, I will live
with Tia and I will be like her. Not to leave Coulibri. Not to go.
Not. When I was close I saw the jagged stone in her hand but I
did not see her throw it. I did not feel it either, only something
wet, running down my face. I looked at her and I saw her face
crumple up as she began to cry. We stared at each other, blood
on my face, tears on hers. It was as if I saw myself. Like in a
looking-glass. (*WSS*, p. 24)

Like 'the turn of the road to the river', that which might seem to
bring the two young figures together also marks the gap between
them. The loss of home and resultant family destruction (Pierre
dies, Annette goes insane, Mr Mason vanishes) offer 'jagged' images of slave history, but are brought about in this instance by a
desire to avenge the wrongs of colonialism on the part of those
who have been its direct victims. The effects of this irony are regis-
tered, particularly lucidly, in the exchange of looks which concludes
the passage above, as identification, recognizing the self in the other,
is itself recognized to be both illusory and implausible: 'as if'. The
sense of the illusoriness of this moment is increased by its comparison to the experience of the 'looking-glass', with its traditional
connotations of treacherous likeness and seductive error.

Like the manoeuvrings that culminate in Rochester's marriage to
Antoinette, the orientation of Rhys's text towards its own fantasies
of identification is characterized by a play of 'advance and retreat . . .
doubts and hesitations' (*WSS*, p. 39). In the stone-throwing scene
with Tia, what might be called a racialized *méconnaissance* is subtly
thwarted by the intrusions of Antoinette's 'as if' and the mirror
simile. Yet if the crossing of identification is blocked at one level it
continues to be forged at another, for the scene in question is also
a mirroring revision of *Jane Eyre*, looking back to the domestic violence perpetrated upon the ten-year-old Jane by 'Master Reed' (*JE*,
p. 10):

I instinctively started aside with a cry of alarm: not soon enough, however; the volume was flung, it hit me, and I fell, striking my head against the door and cutting it. The cut bled, the pain was sharp: my terror had passed its climax; other feelings succeeded.

'Wicked and cruel boy!' I said, 'You are like a murderer – you are like a slave-driver – you are like the Roman emperors!' (*JE*, p. 11)

The interplay between texts turns Tia's stone into the book hurled by John Reed and in so doing comes to function as the surreptitious detour through which the desired crossing from one side of the colour-line to the other can be effected – albeit at one remove: Antoinette is identified with a figure (Jane) whose autobiographical project entails the hyperbolic construction of her own subjectivity in terms of a black other, a slave.

Antoinette's doubling in Tia is replicated in turn by the blurring of differences – similarly problematized by the text – between Antoinette and Christophine, one of whose roles, as already noted, is that of a kind of black counter-mother. One way in which Rhys's text links the two women concerns their mutual status as objects of exchange. As a slave, Christophine had first been a love-gift: 'She was your father's wedding present to me – one of his presents. He thought I would be pleased with a Martinique girl. I don't know how old she was when they brought her to Jamaica, quite young' (*WSS*, p. 8). In parallel to this Antoinette is exchanged between families by means of a patriarchal scheme combining economic with sexual exploitation: a narrative of slave-oppression is drawn into relation with the history of a white creole subject. These links are developed in the second of Antoinette's prefigurative dreams which, like the first (*WSS*, p. 11), is induced by the presence, actual or expected, of 'English friends' (*WSS*, p. 33). The dream looks forward both to the marriage to Rochester and the final incarceration in Thornfield and thus entails a double-crossing – from virginal bride to wife and the West Indies to England. While Antoinette's geographical displacement parallels and augments Christophine's own (from Martinique to Jamaica), the crossing into marriage and sexuality is adumbrated in the dream in such a way as to produce a merging of the two female figures. In this respect it symbolically conflates forms of oppressed experience which are quite distinct from one another. The sign of this conflation is a dress:

Again I have left the house at Coulibri. It is still night and I am walking towards the forest. I am wearing a long dress and thin slippers, so I walk with difficulty, following the man who is with me and holding up the skirt of my dress. It is white and beautiful and I don't wish to get it soiled. . . . Now we have reached the forest. . . . Now I do not try to hold up my dress, it trails in the dirt, my beautiful dress. We are no longer in the forest but in an enclosed garden surrounded by a stone wall and the trees are different trees. I do not know them. There are steps leading upwards. (*WSS*, p. 34)

As it 'trails in the dirt' and becomes 'soiled', Antoinette's 'white and beautiful' dress not only offers a premonitory metaphor for the rite of an undesired sexual loss but also anticipates a later textual scene situated towards the beginning of Rochester's narrative. Christophine has withdrawn from the bedroom where she has been serving the newly-weds their breakfast, prompting Rochester to initiate the following exchange:

'Her coffee is delicious but her language is horrible and she might hold her dress up. It must get very dirty, yards of it trailing on the floor.'
    'When they don't hold their dress up it's for respect,' said Antoinette. 'Or for feast days or going to Mass.' . . .
    'Whatever the reason it is not a clean habit.'
    'It is. You don't understand at all. They don't care about getting a dress dirty because it shows it isn't the only dress they have. Don't you like Christophine?' (*WSS*, pp. 52–3)

From this retrospect, the dream's prefiguring of sexual crossing becomes racialized. In the manner in which she reveals herself to have more than one dress, Christophine at the same time shows the dress code of Antoinette's dream to have more than one meaning, turning the dream itself into a site where identities intersect and blur.

At another point, also located in the early stages of Antoinette's honeymoon with Rochester, Rhys's text supplies a kind of gloss on the moment in the dream in which identities become doubled – white creole with black – through the interplay of scenes and dresses: 'She seemed pleased when I complimented her on her dress and told me she had it made in St Pierre, Martinique. "They call the fashion *à la Joséphine"'* (*WSS*, p. 49; emphasis in original). Just as Rochester fails to grasp the dress-sense in the passage above, so the meaning of 'fashion *à la Joséphine*' remains hidden and deferred, for Rochester and reader alike – 'Not here, not yet' (*WSS*, p. 34) – until both much later learn from Fraser, the magistrate, that 'Josephine' is Christophine's other name ('Josephine or Christophine Dubois' [*WSS*, p. 91]). Fashion *'à la Joséphine'* is thus *à la* Christophine as well, reality a deciphering of dream.

Yet the dress code which seems to bind together the stories and histories of Antoinette and Christophine also works to reinscribe their differences: 'But look me trouble', Christophine urges, 'a rich white girl like you and more foolish than the rest. A man don't treat you good, pick up your skirt and walk out. Do it and he come after you.' The practical reason for Antoinette's reluctance to take up this suggestion is that it would be ineffectual: Christophine is mistaken in thinking Antoinette still to be rich since, under 'English law' (*WSS*, p. 69), her money has become Rochester's, thus dissolving the incentive for him to 'come after' her. Yet at the level of fantasy, the counsel must equally be refused because the terms in which the prospect of leaving Rochester is figured themselves symbolically – if ingenuously – announce an immediate divorce between the two women.

Larger signs of *Wide Sargasso Sea*'s undoing of the links it establishes between 'rich white girl' and black ex-slave become visible by recalling Christophine's position, in fantasy, as alternative mother to Antoinette. For it is not so much Christophine's story which Antoinette's own comes to duplicate but that belonging to her real mother. Annette and Antoinette enter alike into disastrous marriages with Englishmen – Mr Mason and Rochester, respectively – which lead to 'madness' and imprisonment, and both come to be associated with sexual excess and drunkenness. It is as if this process of doubling, a narrativizing of the similarity between the names of mother and daughter – Annette/Antoinette[16] – were operating as a kind of strategic counter-plot to the designs of fantasy. Its literal sign takes the form of the frown shared by Antoinette and her mother, set so deep as to seem 'cut with a knife' (*WSS*, pp. 7, 88).

The shift in perspective between the novel's first and second parts entails not only a crossing from one narrative voice to another – Antoinette's to Rochester's – but also a revision or reinscription of the fantasmatics of blackness. In Rochester's narrative, the desire of the white creole subject to be 'like Tia', 'Like Christophine' (*WSS*,

p. 53) is not simply suspended until the point (in part three) when it can be resumed. Rather, it is uncannily translated into an idiom of paranoia, fear and disgust, seen from what Annette and Antoinette both allude to as 'the other side' (*WSS*, pp. 15, 82). This means, in turn, that while Rochester's 'racial imagination'[17] brings about the very identification Antoinette seems to seek, the manner in which it does so involves a profound inversion or grotesque parody of the terms in which she sees herself. The blackness fashioned by the overloaded colonial gaze of the 'fine English gentleman' (*WSS*, p. 80) is negative, stereotypical and racist, rather than being a positive, if problematic, means of self-definition.

Rochester's misgiving with regard to the racial identity of his wife – the repeatedly echoed question, precisely, of 'Qui est là?' (*WSS*, pp. 22, 25, 123) – is evident from the first:

> Long, sad, dark alien eyes. Creole of pure English descent she may be, but they are not English or European either. And when did I begin to notice all this about my wife Antoinette? After we left Spanish Town I suppose. Or did I notice it before and refuse to admit what I saw? (*WSS*, p. 40)

Far from suggesting recognition of and respect for the alterity of the other, this description serves only as the prelude to Antoinette's subsumption into blackness – an effect resulting from a set of 'fixed' ideas analogous to those which she herself is said by Rochester to hold in relation to 'England and . . . Europe' (*WSS*, p. 58).

The catalyst for this is the figure of Daniel Cosway/Boyd. Daniel first enters the text – claiming to be Antoinette's illegitimate mulatto half-brother – by means of a letter addressed to Rochester (*WSS*, pp. 59–62). Whatever the truth of this particular claim (denied alike by Antoinette and Christophine [*WSS*, pp. 82, 101]), it would appear that in denouncing Antoinette's family as 'Wicked and detestable slave-owners since generations' (*WSS*, p. 59), the letter constitutes a kind of revisionist historiography. It corrects the 'lies' of an official colonial narrative in which the slave-owner is monumentalized as 'Pious', 'Beloved by all', and 'Merciful to the weak' (*WSS*, p. 77). Daniel's letter also overturns an essentialist ideology of race by ascribing to the white creoles qualities which are supposed exclusively to define blackness: Daniel informs Rochester that there is 'madness' (*WSS*, p. 59) in Antoinette's family, as 'in all these white Creoles', challenges him to 'ask older people . . .

about [old Cosway's] disgusting goings-on' and documents the latter's marriage to Annette as being 'too much for him', so that he becomes 'Dead drunk from morning till night' (*WSS*, p. 60).

The effect on Rochester of this inauspicious family portrait is the confirmation of fears and anxieties he had previously 'refuse[d] to admit': 'I folded the letter carefully and put it into my pocket. I felt no surprise. It was as if I'd expected it, been waiting for it' (*WSS*, p. 62). Rochester's prejudice *avant la lettre* is that Antoinette, like 'all these white Creoles', is not only contaminated by a stereotypically defined blackness but also threatens him with her own pollution.[18] This is made clear in the narrative transformation of Antoinette that succeeds Daniel's first letter and the interview with Rochester prompted by his second (*WSS*, pp. 77–80). At the beginning of the night on which she attempts both to put forward 'the other side' to Daniel's story and win back her estranged husband through the agencies of obeah, Antoinette is identified with Amélie:

> She raised her eyebrows and the corners of her mouth turned down in a questioning mocking way. For a moment she looked very much like Amélie. Perhaps they are related, I thought. It's possible, it's even probable in this damned place. (*WSS*, p. 81)

A similar effect marks the point at which she urges Rochester to listen to her account of the past: '"I might never be able to tell you in any other place or at any other time. No other time, now. You frightened?" she said, imitating a Negro's voice, singing and insolent' (*WSS*, p. 82).

The likeness Rochester imagines between his wife and the mulatto girl is itself consolidated in the wake of his sexual intercourse with Amélie – which in turn follows on from the débâcle of the obeah plot. Amélie also becomes subjected to the transformative powers of the Rochesterian gaze: 'Another complication. Impossible. And her skin was darker, her lips thicker than I had thought' (*WSS*, p. 89). Antoinette and the newly darkened Amélie become further blurred during a brief lapse in Antoinette's arraignment of Rochester's sexual betrayal:

> Then to my astonishment she stopped crying and said, 'Is she so much prettier than I am? Don't you love me at all?'
>
> 'No, I do not,' I said (at the same time remembering Amélie

saying, 'Do you like my hair? Isn't it prettier than hers?'). 'Not at this moment,' I said. (*WSS*, p. 95)

Coming to see things in these ways, Rochester parodically performs for Antoinette just what she wishes to do for herself, carrying her over the colour-line between white creole and black other.

Wide Sargasso Sea's inscription of its own awareness of these processes takes the form of Rochester's renaming of Antoinette – as a result of Daniel's interventions – as Bertha, since in *Jane Eyre* the latter, to recall Meyer, is herself disfigured as black. Yet Rochester's vision of blackness is violently at odds with Antoinette's, the difference defining itself, precisely, in terms of the doubled figuration of the Bertha of *Jane Eyre* – as stereotype on the one hand, and figure of colonial defiance on the other. This suggests that Antoinette's rejection of the name Rochester foists upon her not only entails a questioning of the ideology of colonial representation, but also forms part of an ongoing struggle against the identificatory lures which structure and determine her relations with Tia and Christophine, both of whom have strongly anti-colonial roles in the text. The negotiation and refusal of the identities – the forms of blackness – collocated in Bertha is dramatized in the third and final part of Rhys's text, set in the Thornfield of Brontë's *Jane Eyre* and narrated by Antoinette.

This part begins with an overheard conversation in which Mrs Eff (the Mrs. Fairfax of Brontë's text) instructs Grace Poole in the conditions under which she is to serve as warder to Antoinette: '*But there must be no more gossip. If there is I will dismiss you at once. I do not think it will be impossible to fill your place. I'm sure you understand*' (*WSS*, p. 115; emphasis in original). Cautioning Grace against further gossip with the threat that her place can always be taken by someone else, Mrs Eff offers a metaphor for the processes of identification with which the text is concerned throughout, since the attempt to see oneself in the other can be viewed as a relocation of the self in the position which that other occupies. Yet it is precisely the impossibility of ever fully carrying out such processes – whether in the present of Thornfield or the past of the West Indies – which Rhys's novel is at pains to underscore:

There is no looking-glass here and I don't know what I am like now. I remember watching myself brush my hair and how my eyes looked back at me. The girl I saw was myself yet not quite myself. Long ago when I was a child and very lonely I tried to kiss her. But the glass was between us – hard, cold and misted over with my breath.

The literal absence of the 'looking-glass' is reversed in the specularities of language which image Antoinette as Bertha. In the 'sound of whispering' (*WSS*, p. 117) she is interpellated as Thornfield's 'ghost' (*WSS*, pp. 118, 122, 123) and accused by Rochester of being 'intemperate and unchaste', the 'Infamous daughter of an infamous mother' (*WSS*, p. 121).[19] Yet if the mirror-image remains subtly discrepant, 'not quite' the self, the figures of discourse themselves fail to elicit recognition.

This occurs, for example, at the start of Antoinette's third and final dream as she imagines escaping from the attic: 'Sometimes I looked to the right or to the left but I never looked behind me for I did not want to see that ghost of a woman whom they say haunts this place' (*WSS*, p. 122). Here the projected escape is both literal and by implication figurative, a liberation from the 'enclosure' (*WSS*, p. 59) of representation itself. In this latter sense it rehearses the revisionary intent of *Wide Sargasso Sea* as a whole, motivated as it is by Rhys's own desire to free Antoinette from incarceration in the Bertha – that 'poor ghost' as she calls her[20] – of *Jane Eyre*.

The 'someone else' (*WSS*, p. 94) from whom Antoinette seeks to distance herself is not only a discursive construct whose traits align her with a stereotypical blackness, but also, in Brontë's text, a figure of colonial rebellion: 'the Jamaican Bertha-become-black', as Meyer writes, 'is [*Jane Eyre*'s] incarnation of the desire for revenge on the part of the colonized races'.[21] From this perspective, it can be seen that the dream which separates Antoinette from Bertha brings them equally together, as the event in which the dream prophetically culminates – Antoinette's burning down of Thornfield (*WSS*, pp. 122–4) – itself looks back to and fuses with the firing of Coulibri carried out by the ex-slaves in the novel's first part.

By collapsing the difference between the 'desire for revenge' – against Rochester – of a white creole woman and that enacted – against slavery – by the 'colonized races' at Coulibri, Rhys's 'dream book'[22] would appear, as if despite itself, finally to have effected the crossing of identification with which it is preoccupied. It is crucial to recognize, however, that Thornfield's destruction is only dreamt, rather than realized, in *Wide Sargasso Sea*. Even as Antoinette leaves the attic, she moves towards a translation of dream into action, self into other, from which the text ultimately, and characteristically, steps back:

> I was outside holding my candle. Now at last I know why I was brought here and what I have to do. There must have been a draught for the flame flickered and I thought it was out. But I shielded it with my hand and it burned up again to light me along the dark passage. (*WSS*, p. 124)

Suspending Antoinette's narrative at a point before it reaches the 'terrible spectacle' (*JE*, p. 449) which completes Bertha's, *Wide Sargasso Sea* concludes by signalling once again a certain resistance with regard to its own fantasmatics. The translation of 'passage' into impasse bespeaks a recognition that the space between self and other cannot be crossed.

5
'I is an Other': Feminizing Fanon in *The Bluest Eye*

Of all the wishes people had brought him – money, love, revenge – this seemed to him the most poignant and the one most deserving of fulfillment. A little black girl who wanted to rise up out of the pit of her blackness and see the world with blue eyes.

Toni Morrison

We who come from the Antilles know one thing only too well: Blue eyes, the people say, frighten the Negro.

Frantz Fanon[1]

From Black Aesthetic to black Atlantic

For Madhu Dubey, the critical context most germane to a reading of Toni Morrison's *The Bluest Eye* (1970) is that of the Black Aesthetic movement which came to prominence in the America of the 1960s and early 1970s and was 'explicitly developed as the literary arm of black cultural nationalism'.[2] Yet, as Dubey points out, Morrison's fictional practice in *The Bluest Eye* – like that of other African American women writers of the time – is one that significantly exceeds the prescriptions of Black Aesthetic theory: the novel not only engages in an exploration of black female subjectivity which Black Aestheticians sought to discourage, but also emphasizes 'the sexual division between black men and women that can potentially disrupt the racial unity projected in black nationalist discourse'.[3]

While Dubey's analysis of Morrison's novel is as illuminating as it is sophisticated, it is symptomatic of what, for Paul Gilroy, is, ultimately, an over-particularized approach to the genealogy of black literary and cultural production. In *The Black Atlantic*, Gilroy challenges this approach by suggesting a somewhat broader and more flexible model for the examination of black cultures. They are not, he argues, to be treated as if hermetically sealed off from one another, but as elements in a constantly shifting network of relations, responses, crossings and hybridities:

> The fractal patterns of cultural and political exchange and transformation that we try and specify through manifestly inadequate theoretical terms like creolisation and syncretism indicate how both ethnicities and political cultures have been made anew in ways that are significant not simply for the peoples of the Caribbean but for Europe, for Africa . . . and of course, for black America.[4]

From the 'explicitly transnational and intercultural perspective'[5] opened up by Gilroy's black Atlantic, the critical possibilities for reading *The Bluest Eye* can themselves be 'made anew'. While Morrison's negotiation of the Black Aesthetic provides one framework in which to locate her novel, it does not exhaust the processes of 'exchange and transformation' in which the text is implicated. These processes draw *The Bluest Eye* into dialogue with the work of the Martinique-born anti-colonial theorist Frantz Fanon and, especially, Fanon's *Black Skin, White Masks* (1952), establishing an intertextual filiation which neither Morrison nor her novel's critics so far appear to have acknowledged.[6] At the same time, however, this dialogue is itself characterized by the kind of tension between race and gender operative in the context of the novel's relation to the Black Aesthetic programme: unlike Fanon, who routinely marginalizes 'the woman of color' (*BS*, p. 179), to the point, indeed, of claiming to 'know nothing about her' (*BS*, p. 180), Morrison makes black female subjectivity her novel's central question.

Black Skin, White Masks: uses and limits

The principal theoretical concern of *Black Skin, White Masks* is with what Michael Rossington calls 'the psychology of racial division'[7] as it operates in the postwar colonial context of French Martinique. '[D]ivision' here should be understood in two senses. It refers, most obviously, to the material tensions and conflicts between colonizer and colonized. These, as Fanon puts it, lead to 'a genuinely Manichean concept of the world' (*BS*, pp. 44–5) and set whiteness against black-ness as good opposes evil: 'Sin is Negro as virtue is white. All those white men in a group, guns in their hands, cannot be wrong. I am guilty. I do not know of what, but I know that I am no good' (*BS*, p. 139). Yet at the same time, the division between colonizer and colonized produces a self-division which pathologizes both parties and radically distorts their interaction. The precise nature of this self-division can be clarified by considering the use Fanon makes of the psychoanalytic tradition on which he draws and, in particu-lar, Jacques Lacan's influential notion of the 'mirror-stage'.

Lacan first developed this notion in 1936, subsequently expand-ing and revising it in 1949. For Lacan, the child's identification with its mirror-image, approximately between the ages of 6 and 18 months, constitutes a pivotal moment in the formation of the Western subject. Lacking any bodily co-ordination at this point in its growth, the child, Lacan argues, becomes fixated by his or her own marmo-real reflection in the mirror, precisely because that reflection appears to be imbued with the kind of coherence and unity that the child does not possess. Succumbing to 'the lure of spatial identification', the child becomes embroiled in a 'succession of phantasies' that culminates in 'the assumption of the armour of an alienating iden-tity, which will mark with its rigid structure the subject's entire mental development'.[8] The 'mirror-stage' is thus not only a mile-stone in the subject's psychic evolution but also a kind of metaphor for an abiding aspect of the structure of subjectivity itself.

Fanon engages in some detail with the 'mirror-stage' in a long technical footnote which appears in 'The Negro and Psychopathol-ogy', the sixth chapter of his text. For Fanon, as for Lacan, the subject is constituted or produced by means of an identification with the other that is at the same time alienating. The difference, however, between the kind of formative subjective misrecognition elaborated by Lacan and that which interests Fanon is that Fanon's other is racialized in a way that Lacan's is not. None the less, Lacan proves useful to Fanon. 'When one has grasped the mechanism described by Lacan', he announces:

> one can have no ... doubt that the real Other for the white man is and will continue to be the black man. And conversely. Only for the white man The Other is perceived on the level of the body image.... For the black man ... historical and econ-omic realities come into the picture. (*BS*, p. 161)

The 'black man's' identification with his white other – the donning of the white mask – is, as Fanon insists, inevitable: 'For the black man there is only one destiny. And it is white' (*BS*, pp. 12, 228). The reason for this inevitability relates to what might be called the semiotics of colonialism, the ways in which it organizes the signs of racial difference in terms of 'characteristic pairings' (*BS*, p. 183). Whiteness connotes 'beauty and virtue' (*BS*, p. 45) and is associated with all things civilized and human, while blackness, conversely, 'is the symbol of Evil and Ugliness' (*BS*, p. 180) and is linked with all things primitive and bestial. It is this hierarchical metaphorization of race, also at work in *The Bluest Eye*, which makes the identification of black with white so ironic, since it is the white other – supposedly fully human – that is the source of the black subject's dehumanization in the first place. As Jean-Paul Sartre remarks in his Preface to Fanon's *The Wretched of the Earth* (1961): 'the European has only been able to become a man through creating slaves and monsters'.[9]

The consequence of the Fanonian 'black man''s identification with whiteness is splitting and self-estrangement, since his blackness is derogated and disparaged and comes to assume, in Fanon's baleful phrase, the aspect of a 'corporeal malediction' (*BS*, p. 111). These processes of identification and alienation work in the opposite direction as well, as the white man both desires and fears 'the sexual potency' (*BS*, p. 164) with which he imagines his black counterpart to be invested. The colonial encounter in Fanon's text is thus one in which black man and white are adorned with a 'shameful livery put together by centuries of incomprehension' (*BS*, p. 14).

As Fanon's invocation of Lacan makes clear, *Black Skin, White Masks* is a text in which psychoanalytic theory plays an important, if somewhat contradictory, role. On the one hand, Fanon exploits a Western intellectual tradition for anti-Western and anti-colonial purposes. In Gwen Bergner's formulation, he 'transposes psychoanalysis – a theory of subject formation based on sexual difference – to a register where it accounts for race as one of the fundamental differences that constitute subjectivity'. Yet, on the other hand, as Bergner goes on to note, Fanon simultaneously perpetuates the masculinist bias of the tradition he inherits, taking 'the male as the norm' and figuring 'the exemplary colonized subject' as '*le noir*', 'the black man'.[10]

The *locus classicus* for the formation, or deformation, of black male subjectivity in Fanon's text occurs in chapter 5, 'The Fact of Blackness':

> 'Look, a Negro!' It was an external stimulus that flicked over me
> as I passed by. I made a tight smile.
> 'Look, a Negro!' It was true. It amused me.
> 'Look, a Negro!' The circle was drawing a bit tighter. I made
> no secret of my amusement.
> 'Mama, see the Negro! I'm frightened!' Frightened! Frightened!
> Now they were beginning to be afraid of me. I made up my
> mind to laugh myself to tears, but laughter had become impossible.
> I could no longer laugh, because I already knew that there
> were legends, stories, history, and above all *historicity* . . . . Then,
> assailed at various points, the corporeal schema crumbled, its
> place taken by a racial epidermal schema. In the train it was no
> longer a question of being aware of my body in the third per-
> son but in a triple person. (*BS*, pp. 111–12; emphasis in original)

Not only is the black man the spectacular object of the white gaze
in this moment but comes also, crucially, to see himself from the
point from which the gaze is launched. It is this internalization of
the white gaze which produces the dramatic and ruinous shift from
the 'corporeal' to the 'racial epidermal schema'. The black subject
is no longer able to experience his body merely as something he
neutrally inhabits, but as something that is racialized – assailed
and layered with 'legends, stories, history, and above all *historicity*'.

This paradigmatic passage illustrates both the similarities and the
differences between Fanon's text and Morrison's, the ways in which
the theoretical model articulated in the former at once enables and
constrains the fictional project of the latter. As Morrison herself
puts it (using a strikingly Fanonian idiom), *The Bluest Eye* forms a
'reaction . . . against the damaging internalization of assumptions
of immutable inferiority originating in an outside gaze' (*BE*, p. 168).
Yet, equally, in a major revision of Fanon, the text's principal –
though not exclusive – concern, as befits its emergent black feminist context, is to trace the effects of that 'outside gaze' as it infracts
upon black female subjectivity. Morrison's fictional translation of
the colonial insights of *Black Skin, White Masks* into her own African American context at the same time reconfigures them.

'Horror at the heart': reading *The Bluest Eye*

For Fanon 'every neurosis . . . in an Antillean is the product of his
cultural situation'. As he goes on:

there is . . . a series of propositions that slowly and subtly – with the help of books, newspapers, schools and their texts, advertisements, films, radio – work their way into one's mind and shape one's view of the world of the group to which one belongs. (*BS*, p. 152)

Fanon's insight into the contributory role of 'schools and their texts' in the fashioning of a sense of self is developed by Morrison. The narrative proper of *The Bluest Eye* is preceded by the representation, drawn from a 'Dick and Jane' reading primer, of an idealized white middle-class household. This is the kind of image of the family that any child in the 1940s America before Pearl Harbor, when the novel is set, would encounter in the school-room (whether s/he is white or black). Appearing *ex nihilo*, the image does not so much work 'slowly and subtly', in a process of insinuation. Rather, it asserts itself, fixing the socio-cultural norm by means of textual fiat:

Here is the house. It is green and white. It has a red door. It is very pretty. Here is the family. Mother, Father, Dick, and Jane live in the green-and-white house. They are very happy. See Jane. She has a red dress. She wants to play. Who will play with Jane? See the cat. It goes meow-meow. Come and play. Come play with Jane. The kitten will not play. See Mother. Mother is very nice. Mother, will you play with Jane? Mother laughs. Laugh, Mother, laugh. See Father. He is big and strong. Father, will you play with Jane? Father is smiling. Smile, Father, smile. See the dog. Bowwow goes the dog. Do you want to play with Jane? See the dog run. Run, dog, run. Look, look. Here comes a friend. The friend will play with Jane. They will play a good game. Play, Jane, play. (*BE*, 1)

Like the arrangements within the family which it describes, the language of this passage is ordered and stable, as grammar, syntax and spelling alike conform to recognized conventions. Such familial and linguistic harmonies are no sooner established, however, than they are disrupted, as the original passage is twice repeated. In the first repetition, the passage is reproduced with neither capitalization nor punctuation, as the boundaries between sentences are eroded and typography is compressed. The second repetition accentuates these effects: line-divisions are further reduced and gaps between words are removed altogether, as white space is overrun by a chaos of black print.

This pre-textual 'play' of repetition works to 'prime', or prepare, the reader for what is to follow.[11] The disintegration of familial and linguistic order prefigures the gradual dislocation which befalls the working-class black family at the heart of Morrison's text. In stark contrast to the romanticized figures in the primer, the ironically named Breedloves are far from being 'very happy' in their domestic relations. Cholly and Pauline Breedlove '[fight] each other with a darkly brutal formalism . . . paralleled only by their lovemaking', while Sammy, their son, 'was known, by the time he was fourteen, to have run away from home no less than twenty-seven times' (*BE*, p. 32). The novel's most pressing concern, however, is with the plight of the daughter, the 11-year-old Pecola, who is constantly denied love from Pauline, whom she impersonally refers to as 'Mrs. Breedlove' (*BE*, pp. 32, 83), only to receive it in the incestuous form of a rape carried out by Cholly. Considered as a violation of familial boundaries, this event (also leading to Pecola's pregnancy and miscarriage) is itself anticipated by the linguistic and typographical confusion of the novel's opening – as is the madness which, in conjunction with other abusive encounters, the event precipitates.

Divided into four sections keyed to an inverted seasonal cycle ('Autumn', 'Winter', 'Spring', 'Summer'), *The Bluest Eye* is structured in such a way as to suggest the inevitability of Pecola's madness. While the first three sections are introduced from the retrospective vantage of Claudia MacTeer, originally one of Pecola's young black friends, they are given over, in the main, to an unnamed third-person voice whose narrative is itself divided into sections preceded by headings based on the third version of the 'Dick and Jane' primer. The novel's final section has a slightly different organization: beginning and ending with Claudia, its main part is again prefaced by a heading from the primer, but this time takes the form of the unspoken dialogue which Pecola – now deranged – conducts with herself, somewhere 'in the valleys of [her] mind' (*BE*, p. 162). Morrison herself describes the world of the 'white-family primer' as 'barren' (*BE*, p. 172): like the affluent 'lakefront houses' visited at one point in the novel by the Claudia and Frieda, her sister, it contains 'no sign of life' (*BE*, p. 81). Yet in narrative terms, there is a sense in which the primer is profoundly generative. It provides a sequence – house, family, cat, mother, father, dog and the friend to play with Jane – which is taken up and rewritten from a contrapuntal black perspective. If Pecola's madness is inevitable, the narrative design of *The Bluest Eye* works to suggest that it is largely the product of an order of things embodied in institutions ranging from the white family to the 'nation' itself, of which, as Fanon observes, 'the family is a miniature' (*BS*, p. 142).

As its title suggests, *The Bluest Eye* is a novel preoccupied, like *Black Skin, White Masks*, with the visual. This emphasis is introduced by the 'Dick and Jane' primer itself, with its repeated exhortation that the reader 'See' and 'Look, look.' Yet the white and black bodies which compose and circulate within the novel's scopic field are not innocently precultural, but come loaded or inscribed with ideological meaning. The keynote is struck directly, with the narrative focus on the figure of Rosemary Villanucci in the opening paragraph of the narrative proper. Even as Claudia and Frieda, respectively 'nine and ten years old' (*BE*, p. 10), long to imprint 'red marks' on the 'white skin' of their 'next-door friend' (*BE*, p. 5), Rosemary's body is already marked by a kind of writing. The whiteness of its surfaces is associated with beauty, purity, goodness, value and presence and is something which American culture both privileges as the norm and prizes as the object of desire. Blackness, conversely, connotes ugliness, filth, evil, worthlessness and absence and is to be stigmatized, loathed and cast out.[12] The crucial insight of Morrison's novel – as of *Black Skin, White Masks* – is that there is a shaping or determining relation between the ideological construction of racial difference and subjectivity. As the novel demonstrates so inexorably, Pecola's tragedy is due to the way in which both she and the black community identify themselves – albeit with some notable exceptions – with whiteness as the signifier of beauty and value and hence become self-alienated, renouncing blackness as the signifier of ugliness and lack. That which is external to the self – culture, ideology, representation – has far-reaching effects within and upon the self.[13]

One of the earliest signs of this process of identification occurs when Pecola, already categorized as a '"case"' as the result of Cholly having 'burned up his house' (*BE*, p. 11), is temporarily staying with the MacTeers:

> Frieda brought [Pecola] four graham crackers on a saucer and some milk in a blue-and-white Shirley Temple cup. She was a long time with the milk, and gazed fondly at the silhouette of Shirley Temple's dimpled face. Frieda and she had a loving conversation about how cu-ute Shirley Temple was. (*BE*, pp. 12–13)

Here Pecola receives two gifts, one contained within another, whose symbolic meanings intersect. The milk over which Pecola lingers – later prodigiously imbibing '*three* quarts' *(BE, p. 16; emphasis in original)* in a single day – is a figurative substitute for the love her mother fails to provide. At the same time, the act of consuming it seems to literalize the 'kind of lactification' *(BS, p. 47)* desired by the black female subject in Fanon. Yet what interests Pecola even more than the milk contained in the 'blue-and-white Shirley Temple cup' is the cup itself. The image of the white child-star which it bears, widely disseminated by Hollywood cinema during the 1930s and here encountered in commodified form, holds her captive.

The presence of the grail-like Shirley Temple cup is perhaps to be expected in a household in which the MacTeer sisters are humorously greeted by Mr. Henry, the family lodger, as 'Greta Garbo' and 'Ginger Rogers'. Yet even as Claudia 'giggle[s]' *(BE, p. 10)* at such an interpellation, her response to Shirley Temple is very different from Pecola's, and indeed Frieda's. This is because she has 'not yet arrived at the turning point in the development of [her] psyche which would allow [her] to love' this particular icon of white culture. Claudia's 'unsullied hatred' 'for all the Shirley Temples of the world' derives, in its turn, from the experience of a 'more frightening thing', first prompted, as she recalls, by the Christmas gift of a 'big, blue-eyed Baby Doll' *(BE, p. 13)*. Instead of appreciating this present as she is supposed to, Claudia's impulse is to anatomize it:

> I had only one desire: to dismember it. To see of what it was made, to discover the dearness, to find the beauty, the desirability that had escaped me, but apparently only me. Adults, older girls, shops, magazines, newspapers, window signs – all the world had agreed that a blue-eyed, yellow-haired, pink-skinned doll was what every girl child treasured. *(BE, p. 14)*

Claudia is not one who unquestioningly assents to the cultural production of whiteness as beautiful. Like the novel itself, she strives, rather, to uncover the 'secret' that leads to this equation and 'destroy[s] white baby dolls' accordingly. As well as dissecting 'baby dolls', Claudia wishes, moreover, to destroy the 'little white girls' of which the dolls are the replicas in order, once again, to 'discover . . . the secret of the magic they weaved on others' *(BE, p. 15)*. Yet her resistance and questioning do not last. Like Pecola, though with less personally disastrous consequences, she also learns 'much later to worship' (*BE*, p. 16) Shirley Temple and the values she embodies – thus following the 'course of mutation' 'From black to white' (*BS*, p. 51) outlined by Fanon. At the same time, she self-consciously recognizes 'that the change was adjustment without improvement' (*BE*, p. 16).

Claudia's dissection of white female beauty is paralleled in the minute physiognomic examination carried out by the third-person narrator in order to locate the origins of the Breedloves' apparent ugliness:

> The Breedloves did not live in a storefront because they were having temporary difficulty adjusting to the cutbacks at the plant. They lived there because they were poor and black, and they stayed there because they believed they were ugly.... Except for ... Cholly ... the rest of the family ... wore their ugliness, put it on, so to speak, although it did not belong to them. The eyes, the small eyes set closely together under narrow foreheads. The low, irregular hairlines, which seemed even more irregular in contrast to the straight, heavy eyebrows which nearly met. Keen but crooked noses, with insolent nostrils. They had high cheekbones, and their ears turned forward. Shapely lips which called attention not to themselves but to the rest of the face. You looked at them and wondered why they were so ugly; you looked closely and could not find the source. Then you realized that it came from conviction, their conviction. It was as though some mysterious all-knowing master had given each one a cloak of ugliness to wear, and they had each accepted it without question.

Concluding the inventory of the Breedloves' family features with the opinion that what makes them 'so ugly' is 'their conviction', the narrator uses a term whose dual meaning precisely captures the processes of internalization with which *The Bluest Eye* is concerned as a whole. While the term seems primarily, in this context, to imply an inward persuasion on the Breedloves' part, it also carries the sense of a judgement passed against them from outside which condemns and criminalizes: even as the negative connotations of blackness are ideologically constructed and conspicuously endorsed in 'every billboard, every movie, every glance' (*BE*, p. 28), they come to be felt, the text suggests, with all the unmediated vigour of a subjective truth.

That the Breedloves' sense of themselves as 'ugly' is an ideological effect rather than ontological given is underscored by the metaphor of blackness as a 'cloak', something externally fabricated and 'woven', to use Fanon's phrase, 'out of a thousand details, anecdotes, stories' (*BS*, p. 111). This 'cloak' – additionally figured as 'mantle' (*BE*, p. 28) and 'shroud' (*BE*, p. 29) – is also textured by Fanon's '*historicity*'. The allusion to 'the all-knowing master' is a reminder that the racist ideology the black subject must negotiate in the present is part of an ongoing legacy derived from the institution of slavery, only formally abolished in America, following the Civil War, in 1865, less than a century before the time in which the novel's action takes place.

If the 'cloak' of blackness renders Pecola unsightly, it can, on other occasions, conceal her humanity altogether. This is exemplified in the scene of her visit to the 'grocery store' (*BE*, p. 35) owned by Mr. Yacobowski. Here the gaze of 'the fifty-two-year-old white immigrant storekeeper' offers Pecola no acknowledgement as she holds out the money with which to buy her three Mary Jane sweets. Even as Pecola's appearance 'urges [him] out of his thoughts', Mr. Yacobowski seems still to be largely lost within them, entranced, in particular, by reflections on 'the doe-eyed Virgin Mary' (*BE*, p. 36):

> She looks up at him and sees the vacuum where curiosity ought to lodge. And something more. The total absence of human recognition – the glazed separateness. She does not know what keeps his glance suspended. Perhaps because he is grown, or a man, and she a little girl. But she has seen interest, disgust, even anger in grown male eyes. Yet this vacuum is not new to her. It has an edge; somewhere in the bottom lid is the distaste. She has seen it lurking in the eyes of all white people. So. The distaste must be for her, her blackness. All things in her are flux and anticipation. But her blackness is static and dread. And it is the blackness that accounts for, that creates, the vacuum edged with distaste in white eyes. (*BE*, pp. 36–7)

Crushed by her non-encounter with the abysmal white male gaze, Pecola first feels shame as she leaves the store and then anger as she 'trips' (*BE*, p. 37) on 'the sidewalk crack shaped like a Y' (*BE*, p. 35) – the initial letter, of course, of the storekeeper's name. 'Anger is better' (*BE*, p. 37) than shame, she thinks, for it offers 'a sense of being .... A reality and presence. An awareness of worth.... a lovely surging' (*BE*, pp. 37–8). Its uplift is short-lived though, dissipated by shame's return. In order to block the tears that shame threatens, Pecola 'remembers the Mary Janes' she has managed to purchase:

> Each pale yellow wrapper has a picture on it. A picture of little Mary Jane, for whom the candy is named. Smiling white face. Blond hair in gentle disarray, blue eyes looking at her out of a world of clean comfort. The eyes are petulant, mischievous. To Pecola they are simply pretty. She eats the candy, and its sweetness is good. To eat the candy is somehow to eat the eyes, eat Mary Jane. Love Mary Jane. Be Mary Jane.

Here Pecola enacts a cannibalistic communion, which both parallels and reverses the rituals of the Catholicism associated with Mr. Yacobowski and the Virgin. In the Catholic version of the Eucharist, to eat the wafer and drink the wine is literally to eat and be one with the body and blood of Christ. By eating the precious candies Pecola imagines herself, similarly, becoming one with the girl whose image adorns their wrappers, as black is transubstantiated into its opposite. Yet whereas the Eucharist is a spiritual experience, Pecola's communion is emphatically sexual. The 'lovely surging' is no longer that of anger but *jouissance*: 'Three pennies had bought her nine lovely orgasms with Mary Jane. Lovely Mary Jane, for whom a candy is named' (*BE*, p. 38). It also merits comparison with that 'form of salvation that consists of magically turning white', about which, according to Fanon, 'It is in fact customary in Martinique to dream' (*BS*, p. 44).

Between the white and black communities within *The Bluest Eye* are a number of other figures whose identity is racially mixed. These range from Maureen Peal, the 'high-yellow dream child' (*BE*, p. 47) who arrives as a new pupil at Pecola's school and immediately 'enchant[s]' it (*BE*, p. 48), to Soaphead Church, a 'cinnamon-eyed West Indian with lightly browned skin' (*BE*, p. 132). Also prominent within this category are Geraldine (given no second name in the text) and Junior, her son, who becomes Pecola's tormentor in the scene which closes the novel's second section. Because of their lightness of skin, these hybrid figures have the advantage over their black rivals and can more easily approximate to the white ideal.

Maureen and Geraldine are closely linked to one another, to such an extent that the latter appears to be the adult fulfilment of the former. Both enjoy the class privileges associated with whiteness and revel, like Rosemary, in 'the pride of ownership' (*BE*, p. 5).

Maureen is 'as rich as the richest of the white girls' in Pecola's
school and 'swaddled in comfort and care' (*BE*, p. 47), while Geraldine
'build[s] her nest stick by stick' (*BE*, p. 65) around husband and
son and lives out the fantasy of a white middle-class femininity
within it. The two figures are further linked by the distinctions
which they seek to maintain between themselves and the 'malediction' of blackness. Following an altercation with Pecola and the
MacTeer sisters, Maureen declares herself – like Shirley Temple indeed – to be 'cute', dismissing her former friends, by contrast, as
'Black and ugly' (*BE*, p. 56). Similarly, Geraldine vigilantly patrols
the line between 'colored people and niggers' (*BE*, p. 67) and ensures that Junior's 'hair [is] cut as close to his scalp as possible to
avoid any suggestion of wool' (*BE*, pp. 67–8). Such strategies are
not without their ironies, however. In rejecting blackness, Maureen
and Geraldine at the same time disavow historical, cultural and
racial affiliations which are integral to their own identities. In this
way, they simply perform another version of the self-alienation by
which black subjectivities are themselves marked in the novel. As a
concise and disconcerting emblem for these processes of repudia-
tion, Maureen's 'long brown hair' is represented as 'braided into
two lynch ropes that [hang] down her back' (*BE*, p. 47).[14]

Geraldine's race and class identifications cause her to eradicate
from herself 'the dreadful funkiness of passion' (*BE*, p. 64), subli-
mating sexual energies into the methods and rituals of domestic
economy. The 'beautiful house' she fashions is not dissimilar, accordingly, to that sketched out by the 'Dick and Jane' primer,
complete with its 'red-and-gold Bible', 'Little lace doilies' (*BE*,
p. 69) and 'Potted plants'. Yet for Pecola, this place of beauty and
refinement, into which she is reluctantly enticed by Junior, turns
rapidly into a site of terror. Junior intimidates Pecola, whom he
calls his 'prisoner' and hurls the family cat 'right in her face'. He
subsequently whirls the creature – with its 'blue eyes' set in a 'black
face' (*BE*, p. 70) – in circles above his head and, when Pecola tries
to intervene, releases it in 'mid-motion'. The cat smashes against
the window and slithers onto the radiator where, after a 'few shud-
ders', it lies dead (*BE*, p. 71). Inevitably, Pecola, rather than Junior,
is blamed for the demise of the luckless feline by the returning
Geraldine, who has 'seen this little girl all of her life. . . . Hair un-
combed, dresses falling apart, shoes untied and caked with dirt'
(*BE*, pp. 71–2). Insulted by Geraldine as a 'nasty little black bitch',
Pecola can only retreat from the scene, dumbly agog 'at the pretty

milk-brown lady in the pretty gold-and-green house' (*BE*, p. 72). The implications of this incident have an almost typological clarity: the maltreatment and eventual death of the cat – blue-eyed, black-faced – precisely symbolize the self-destructiveness of Pecola's desire for the whiteness of which blue eyes are the token.

As Pecola's fascination with the image of Shirley Temple suggests, Hollywood cinema plays an important part in the mediation of black female subjectivities in Morrison's novel. Its effects are explored with particular detail in relation to Pauline, who – like her daughter – avidly consumes the 'black-and-white' (*BE*, p. 95) images projected by film. These images offer Pauline contrast and relief from the impoverishments, both economic and emotional, of her turbulent marriage to Cholly. They also provide a route back to the adolescent fantasies about 'men and love' and 'strangers who appear out of nowhere simply to hold one's hand' (*BE*, p. 88) which married life has not fulfilled:

> Then [Pauline] stopped staring at the green chairs, at the delivery truck; she went to the movies instead. There in the dark her memory was refreshed, and she succumbed to her earlier dreams. Along with the idea of romantic love, she was introduced to another – physical beauty. Probably the most destructive ideas in the history of human thought.

The destructiveness of the idea of 'physical beauty' arises, in the first instance, from the fact that it is invariably constructed by Western culture in terms of whiteness. Because Pauline is black, she is necessarily defined as unbeautiful. She is thus disenfranchised from the 'romantic love' that the white women who glide across the Hollywood movie screen appear to elicit so effortlessly and whose names drop like amulets into the text – Greta Garbo, Ginger Rogers, Claudette Colbert, Betty Grable, Hedy Lamarr, Jean Harlow. What is yet more destructive about the glamour of white beauty, however, is the way in which it is internalized and becomes, for Pauline, a ruthless standard of judgement: 'She was never able, after her education in the movies, to look at a face and not assign it some category in the scale of absolute beauty, and the scale was one she absorbed in full from the silver screen.'

While the use of the word 'education' implies a degree of overlap between Hollywood cinema and the school system betokened by the 'Dick and Jane' primer – they perform similar ideological

work – the term is at the same time ironic, because what is hap-
pening to the constantly movie-going Pauline is less an education
than its opposite, a kind of indoctrination. Pauline herself provides
an account of her collusion in these processes:

> *'The onliest time I be happy seem like was when I was in the picture*
> *show. Every time I got, I went. I'd go early, before the show started.*
> *They'd cut off the lights, and everything be black. Then the screen*
> *would light up, and I'd move right on in them pictures. White men*
> *taking such good care of they women, and they all dressed up in big*
> *clean houses with the bathtubs right in the same room with the toilet.'*
> (*BE*, p. 95; emphasis in original)[15]

From the perspective of the initial version of the 'Dick and Jane'
primer, Pauline's Southern vernacular defines her as linguistically
deviant or other. Yet the 'ungrammatical' nature of her language
has another significance, gesturing, as it does, toward a certain slippage
or confusion of identities. The distance between the black female
spectator and the '*White men*' and '*women*' whom she beholds is
undercut by the ambiguity of Pauline's opening confession: '*The*
onliest time I be happy seem like was when I was in the picture show.'
The overt meaning of this statement is that Pauline is only content when attending the cinema – perhaps the 'Dreamland Theater'
to which the text refers earlier and from whose billboards the al-
luring and beneficent face of 'Betty Grable smile[s] down' (*BE*,
p. 53). However, the sentence is phrased in such a way as to suggest
the idea of Pauline actually featuring in the movies which she watches.
Such ambiguous possibilities are evident elsewhere: '*Then the screen*
would light up, and I'd move right on in them pictures.' These ambiguities are the signs of Pauline's fantasmatic identification with the
white other and, in particular, with the figure of Jean Harlow, the
1930s' 'platinum blonde': '*I 'member one time I went to see Clark*
Gable and Jean Harlow. I fixed my hair up like I'd seen hers on a
magazine. A part on the side, with one little curl on my forehead. It
looked just like her. Well, almost just like.'
'*[S]itting back in [her] seat . . . tak[ing] a big bite of [her] candy*' and
imagining herself as her idol, Pauline is at the same time textually
doubled with Pecola, who is similarly capable of transforming herself into the image she craves: 'To eat the candy is somehow to eat
the eyes, eat Mary Jane. Love Mary Jane. Be Mary Jane.' In the
end, though, Pauline is less skilled than her daughter at sustaining

the delicious/orgasmic illusion of embodying all the things that are culturally associated with whiteness – beauty, desirability, value. The candy the mother consumes amid the chiaroscuro of the picture-house pulls out a front tooth (Harlow, ironically, was the daughter of a dentist), leaving in its place only the bathetic recognition of the unbridgable gap between black and white: '*it pulled a tooth right out of my mouth. I could of cried. I had good teeth, not a rotten one in my head. I don't believe I ever did get over that. There I was, five months pregnant, trying to look like Jean Harlow, and a front tooth gone. Everything went then. Look like I just didn't care no more after that*' (*BE*, p. 96; emphasis in original).

In the figure of Cholly, Pecola's delinquent father, *The Bluest Eye* complicates its critique of white oppression by demonstrating the effects which it produces upon black gender-relations. These are clearly delineated in the narrative sequence describing Cholly's first sexual encounter, when he is 14, with Darlene, 'a little country girl' (*BE*, p. 31):

> There stood two white men. One with a spirit lamp, the other with a flashlight. There was no mistake about their being white; he could smell it. Cholly jumped, trying to kneel, stand, and get his pants up all in one motion. The men had long guns. . . . The flashlight made a moon on his behind.
> 'Hee hee hee hee heeeeee.'
> 'Come on, coon. Faster. You ain't doing nothing for her.'
> 'Hee hee hee hee heeee.'
> Cholly, moving faster, looked at Darlene. He hated her. He almost wished he could do it – hard, long, and painfully, he hated her so much. The flashlight wormed its way into his guts and turned the sweet taste of muscadine into rotten fetid bile. (*BE*, p. 116)

What is important here is the movement of repression and displacement by which Cholly seeks to contain the humiliation he suffers at the hands of the two white hunters, with their 'long guns'. With 'The flashlight' trained 'on his behind' and 'worm[ing] its way into his guts', Cholly loses his position as heterosexual agent and becomes the object of what is – symbolically at least – a cross-racial homosexual rape. Yet rather than directing his hatred toward the perpetrators of this metaphorical rape, Cholly inexplicably transfers it onto Darlene, whom he 'almost wishe[s]' to wound sexually.

As the narrator puts it, in the abbreviated version of this moment which appears earlier in the text: 'For some reason, Cholly had not hated the white men; he hated, despised, the girl.' This defensive displacement of affect is in turn re-enacted in Cholly's relation to Pauline, his wife: 'He poured out on her the sum of all his inarticulate fury and aborted desires. Hating her, he could leave himself intact' (*BE*, p. 31).

Cholly's experience with Darlene and 'the white men' assumes its place amid the 'myriad . . . humiliations, defeats, and emasculations' (*BE*, p. 32) which have contributed to the making and marring of his subjectivity. These are catalogued in the section of the novel which takes him as its protagonist. As Cholly's narrative begins, his chances seem slim: 'When Cholly was four days old, his mother wrapped him in two blankets and one newspaper and placed him on a junk heap by the railroad.' Although this incident – identifying Cholly with waste or trash – is attributed to the fact 'that his mother wasn't right in the head' (*BE*, p. 103), it is also a powerful emblem of the disposability of the black subject within a white society driven by what Fanon calls the 'imbecility' of '"color prejudice"' (*BS*, p. 29). Cholly is rescued from his abjected state by his Great Aunt Jimmy – one of the few people to invest him with any worth. Jimmy dies, however, while Cholly is still an adolescent, causing him, together with the *coitus interruptus* with Darlene, to set out in search of Samson Fuller, the father who had abandoned him before he was born. This quest also ends in failure. Cholly eventually tracks his father down but is violently rejected by him in favour of a 'crap game' (*BE*, p. 126). The cumulative result of these events, 'The pieces of Cholly's life', as they are called, is to make 'Cholly . . . free. Dangerously free' (*BE*, p. 125). As the narrator elaborates:

> He was free to live his fantasies, and free even to die, the how and the when of which held no interest for him. In those days, Cholly was truly free. Abandoned in a junk heap by his mother, rejected for a crap game by his father, there was nothing more to lose. He was alone with his perceptions and appetites, and they alone interested him. (*BE*, p. 126)

Cholly's freedom takes the form of a radical self-negation, traceable either directly or indirectly to the terms in which his blackness is constructed ideologically. It reduces him to the status of 'a burned-out black man' (*BE*, p. 127): 'A feeling of inferiority', to cite Fanon, becomes 'a feeling of nonexistence' (*BS*, p. 139).

Like the 'group of boys' who earlier taunt Pecola in the school playground ('Black e mo Black e mo Ya daddy sleeps nekked'), Cholly is governed by 'an exquisitely learned self-hatred' (*BE*, p. 50) which is the middle link in the chain connecting racial to sexual oppression. Instead of directing his aggression towards his white oppressors, Cholly first internalizes it and then, crucially, aims it back out towards Pecola. Despite his 'love' for her, Cholly also feels a 'revulsion' grounded in the belief that he is unworthy of the affection which his daughter – despite his failings – feels for him. This complex ambivalence manifests itself most dramatically on the 'Saturday afternoon' when Cholly 'stagger[s] home reeling drunk and [sees] his daughter in the kitchen', 'washing dishes':

> If he looked into her face, he would see those haunted, loving eyes. The hauntedness would irritate him – the love would move him to fury. How dare she love him? Hadn't she any sense at all? . . . What could his heavy arms and befuddled brain accomplish that would earn him his own respect, that would in turn allow him to accept her love? His hatred of her slimed in his stomach and threatened to become vomit.

As Cholly is about to be sick, however, the whole scene suddenly shifts. Pecola performs an action – she 'scratch[es] the back of her calf with her toe' (*BE*, p. 127) – which reminds Cholly of his initial encounter with Pauline, for she was doing the same thing the 'first time he saw her in Kentucky'. Past and present blur into one another and lead to Cholly's arousal as he takes on the role of the sexualized father in the extemporized 'Black e mo' chant. They create a 'confused mixture', involving 'memories of Pauline and the doing of a wild and forbidden thing'. The confusion is not only of past and present, but also of 'lust' and 'politeness' (*BE*, p. 128), 'hatred' and 'tenderness' (*BE*, p. 129). It is under these disturbed conditions – in another dissolution of boundaries – that Cholly rapes Pecola:

> He wanted to fuck her – tenderly. But the tenderness would not hold. The tightness of her vagina was more than he could bear. His soul seemed to slip down to his guts and fly out into her,

and the gigantic thrust he made into her then provoked the only sound she made – a hollow suck of air in the back of her throat. Like the rapid loss of air from a circus balloon. (*BE*, p. 128)

The determining role of racial oppression in the production of the sexual violence meted out by black male against black female is underscored textually. The 'soul' that seems to 'fly out into' Pecola is projected from the very place – Cholly's 'guts' – previously penetrated by 'The flashlight' of his white tormentors.

With its harrowing blend of lyricism and brutality, this scene, rightly defined by Dubey as the novel's 'central incident',[16] has generated a variety of critical responses which see Cholly either as racial victim or sexual oppressor or – more subtly and accurately – as both (the reading Dubey herself favours).[17] Together with the interpretative controversy it has prompted, the rape scene is notable, as Jill Matus points out, for the fact that it is narrated from Cholly's perspective.[18] In this respect, it might be read as compounding Pecola's status as victim, silencing her textually as she is originally silenced by her father's incestuous assault, as well as inducing varying degrees of voyeurism, discomfort and complicity in the novel's readers – whether white or black, male or female. Yet as Matus also argues, the fact that 'Morrison does not, it seems, write Pecola's feelings into the scene' is very much to the point. As the sign of a 'collapse of witnessing',[19] Pecola's absence from the event of her own violation works powerfully to suggest the way in which, in the precise psychoanalytic sense outlined by Cathy Caruth, she is traumatized by her ordeal. With her 'shocked body', 'stunned throat' (*BE*, p. 128) and final loss of 'consciousness' (*BE*, p. 129), Pecola is represented as one caught in the paradox of traumatic experience. Such experience, as Caruth argues, is not properly experience at all, initially occurring 'too soon, too unexpectedly, to be fully known and . . . therefore not available to consciousness until it imposes itself again, repeatedly, in the nightmares and repetitive actions'[20] of the subject who is both its victim and survivor.

Even as the rape scene understands black male sexual violence to be the effect of larger structures of institutionalized racism, it none the less acknowledges the existence of such violence as it is played out upon the black female subject. Read in these terms, one of its most consequential effects is to demystify the Black Aesthetic construction of 'the black community as a cohesive monolith that [does] not admit differences and divisions'.[21] Yet if the scene has implications for Black Aesthetic ideology, the question of rape which it raises is also an important element in *The Bluest Eye*'s unstated dialogue with *Black Skin, White Masks*. Fanon poses his version of this question in 'The Negro and Psychopathology', as he undertakes 'an explanation of the [white female] fantasy: *A Negro is raping me*' (*BS*, p. 178; emphasis in original). For Morrison, Cholly's rape of Pecola is explicable, though not excusable, in terms of his own racial oppression. For Fanon, conversely, the rape-fantasy of the white woman is a racist phobia which needs, in fact, to be decoded, as the expression, in Diana Fuss's phrase, of 'a violent lesbian desire':[22] 'when a woman lives the fantasy of rape by a Negro', Fanon writes, 'it is in some way the fulfillment of a private dream, of an inner wish. . . . it is the woman who rapes herself' (*BS*, p. 179).

Fuss considers Fanon's reading of 'white women's rape fantasies' to be extremely 'questionable', going on to argue that:

> Ultimately, what may be most worrisome about the treatment of interracial rape in *Black Skin, White Masks* is not what Fanon says about white women and black men but what he does *not* say about black women and white men.[23]

For Fuss – as for Mary Ann Doane – the most serious problem with Fanon's analysis of 'interracial rape' lies in the displacement it entails. Fanon shifts the emphasis on rape, as Doane puts it, as 'the white man's prerogative as master/colonizer to the white woman's fears/desires in relation to the black male' and thus 'effectively eras[es] the black woman's historical role'.[24] To these critical rereadings of Fanon, *The Bluest Eye* adds its own doleful and provocative supplement, highlighting the ways in which a concern with the interracial can obscure sexual conflicts taking place in an intraracial (and intrafamilial) context.

The rape by her father causes Pecola to turn in 'dread' (*BE*, p. 136), to use the novel's own word, to Elihue Micah Whitcomb, *alias* Soaphead, whose migrant presence in the text overtly links the black American and West Indian contexts in which Morrison and Fanon are respectively located. Soaphead is, in every sense, a mixture: he is a 'fastidious' misanthrope with a 'fine education' (*BE*, p. 130) based on a reading of the classics of Western civilization – Shakespeare, the Bible, Gibbon, Dante. He is also a paedophile and self-styled '"Reader, Adviser, and Interpreter of Dreams"' (*BE*, pp. 130–1). Perhaps most significantly, he is the racially hybrid product of a complex colonial history. The chief agent in this history is one 'Sir Whitcomb', a 'decaying British nobleman' who euphemistically 'introduce[s] the white strain into [Soaphead's] family in the early 1800's' (*BE*, p. 132).[25] The white blood of this ancestral 'master/colonizer' brings with it a 'conviction of [the] superiority' of white over black, crystallized in the claims of Gobineau, the so-called 'father of racism', whom Morrison cites: '"all civilizations derive from the white race . . . none can exist without its help, and . . . a society is great and brilliant only so far as it preserves the blood of the noble group that created it"' (*BE*, p. 133). Though Soaphead is careful to stress that he is a native of 'the Greater of the two Antilles' (*BE*, p. 140), it is clear that he is descended from a family informed by just that sense of white supremacism which characterizes the Lesser Antillean context of Fanon's Martinique. As one critic puts it, 'Soaphead's story reveals the subliminal processes of a colonized mind that internalizes the belief that whiteness is superior'.[26]

What Pecola wants from Soaphead is what she has always wanted, the blue eyes which, she thinks, will make her beautiful and desirable. Although the local community invests Soaphead with supernatural powers, his abilities are fake. He does not fulfil Pecola's wish by means of 'miracles' (*BE*, p. 138) but instead plays a trick upon her which deludes her into thinking that her request has been granted, literally making her mad:

> 'Take this food and give it to the creature sleeping on the porch. Make sure he eats it. And mark well how he behaves. If nothing happens, you will know that God has refused you. If the animal behaves strangely, your wish will be granted on the day following this one.' (*BE*, p. 139)

The 'creature' in question is a 'mangy' (*BE*, p. 136) dog with running eyes called Bob. Unlike Pecola, Soaphead knows that the dog is sure to behave 'strangely' on receiving the 'food' because he has 'sprinkled' (*BE*, p. 139) it with poison, bought for the express purpose of killing this animal, by whom he is 'revolted' (*BE*, p. 136). Lacking the courage to administer the poison himself, Soaphead has Pecola do it instead. It is she who is thus subjected to the disgusting spectacle of the old dog's death-throes, its 'gagg[ing]', 'Choking [and] stumbling'. When Pecola next appears in the text, she has indeed got her blue eyes, having 'stepped over the threshold' (*BE*, p. 139) into a traumatized world of hallucination and repetition.

The final image of Pecola is as a divided being, as the novel concludes with a grotesque parody of its beginning. In the 'Dick and Jane' primer, Jane is given a friend who is imagined as playing a 'good game' with her. Yet Pecola, isolated and insane, resembles less the happily socialized Jane than the textually obscure and marginal figure of 'Auntie Julia', fleetingly reported, in the novel's opening pages, to be 'still trotting up and down Sixteenth Street talking to herself' (*BE*, p. 8). The subject of Pecola's own interminable interior dialogue is, predictably enough, the blue eyes of which she is now both owner and admirer:

> What? What will we talk about?
> *Why, your eyes.*
> Oh, yes. My eyes. My blue eyes. Let me look again.
> *See how pretty they are.*
> Yes. They get prettier each time I look at them.
> *They are the prettiest I've ever seen.*
> Really?
> *Oh, yes.*
> Prettier than the sky?
> *Oh, yes. Much prettier than the sky.*
> Prettier than Alice-and-Jerry Storybook eyes?
> *Oh, yes. Much prettier than Alice-and-Jerry Storybook eyes.* (BE, p. 159; emphases in original)

Although the silent conversation in which Pecola encircles herself is the symptom of madness, her delusional state is not without its own perfectly transparent logic. The blue eyes which she covets are the charismatic sign of a whiteness which her society deems beautiful and which endows the self with value and calls forth love from others. Identification with whiteness is thus the means by which the black female subject can gain access to such possibilities. The irony, however, is that Pecola's alienation from herself as ugly, worthless and undesirable is itself a delusion, albeit one sanctioned culturally.

The deranged and haunting exchange between the two voices within Pecola's psyche reinforces the novel's central contention. While the exchange takes place in the recesses of Pecola's mind, it is the effect of wider structures of power and ideology which circumscribe and regulate the self. The reader is left in no doubt as to the violence which such structures are capable of producing within and upon the black subject, body and mind. As Claudia puts it in the novel's final pages: 'So it was. A little black girl yearns for the eyes of a little white girl, and the horror at the heart of her yearning is exceeded only by the evil of fulfillment' (*BE*, p. 162).

6
'The Geography of Hunger': Intertextual Bodies in *Nervous Conditions*

Now that the mouth is shut, the heart is proud.

Tsitsi Dangarembga

The relations of man with matter . . . and with history are in the colonial period simply relations with food. . . . The fact is that the only perspective is that belly which is more and more sunken, which is certainly less and less demanding, but which must be contented all the same.

Frantz Fanon

Take the matter as you find it: ask no questions; utter no remonstrances: it is your best wisdom. You expected bread, and you have got a stone; break your teeth on it, and don't shriek because the nerves are martyrized: do not doubt that your mental stomach – if you have such a thing – is strong as an ostrich's – the stone will digest.

Charlotte Brontë[1]

Establishing relations: Dangarembga, Fanon, Brontë

On its appearance in 1988, Tsitsi Dangarembga's *Nervous Conditions* became the first novel by a black Zimbabwean woman to be published in English, meeting with immediate critical acclaim by winning the Africa section of the Commonwealth Writers Prize in the following year. The novel is preceded by an epigraph (also the source of its title) derived from Jean-Paul Sartre's Preface to Frantz Fanon's

The Wretched of the Earth (1961) – 'The condition of native is a nervous condition.' As might be expected, Dangarembga's allusion (via Sartre) to *The Wretched of the Earth* has led numerous critics to locate her text within a Fanonian frame of reference. At the same time, however, these critics are rightly at pains to stress how Dangarembga's fiction not only deploys Fanon's theoretical insights into the pathological workings of colonial domination but also extends and revises them from a black feminist perspective. As M. Keith Booker writes, in the most recent instance of this approach: '*Nervous Conditions* goes beyond Fanon, whose male-oriented analysis of the colonial condition does not explore gender issues in any substantive way'.[2]

While it is both necessary and productive to read *Nervous Conditions* in the light of *The Wretched of the Earth*, it is also possible to read Fanon's text in the light of Dangarembga's. This reversal of priorities generates some curious effects, not the least of which is to bring into focus rhetorical or figurative dimensions of Fanon's writing which critics have largely overlooked. As a critique of the complicitous orders of colonialism and patriarchy, *Nervous Conditions* is pervaded, as Charles Sugnet points out, by images of 'eating, digestion, nutrition, vomiting, and excretion'. These provide 'crucial metaphors for domination and resistance',[3] most spectacularly in the anorexia nervosa of Nyasha, anglicized and slightly older cousin to Tambudzai, the novel's first-person narrator. Yet what is much less frequently noted is the degree to which such a language also informs the representation of colonial relations in Fanon's text, organizing the 'Manichaean world' (*WE*, p. 31) of colonizer and colonized in terms of an opposition between bodily satiety and excess, on the one hand and starvation and lack, on the other: in an early example of this pattern, 'The settler's town' is 'well-fed' and has a 'belly . . . always full of good things', while 'The native town', by contrast, 'is a hungry town, starved of bread, of meat, of shoes, of coal, of light' (*WE*, p. 30).

The gastrological tendencies of *The Wretched of the Earth* are important not only in themselves, but also because they draw attention to the ways in which colonial struggle in Fanon's Algeria intersects with the 'question of gender difference'[4] which Fanon otherwise seems not to address. While there is little space in *The Wretched of the Earth* for women as literal agents of colonial resistance or even as colonized subjects, the metaphorics of the text provide a vehicle for the return of the feminine, contriving to suggest that colonial conflict in Fanon's text is in many respects a battle of the sexes. In this gender-clash, 'the starving native' (*WE*, p. 38) – invariably male – archetypally confronts a Europe recurrently figured as a devouring and ultimately vampiristic or monstrous woman.

For most readers, *The Wretched of the Earth* sets the limit to the intertextual operations of Dangarembga's novel. Yet there is another allusive gesture in *Nervous Conditions* which is just as likely as the invocation of Fanon to attract the attentions of the postcolonial critic. This occurs in chapter 5, as Tambudzai recalls how her 'fourteen-year-old fantasies' find gratification in an initial encounter with the low and high classics of English literature, as she 'Plung[es] into [the] books' contained in Nyasha's 'various and extensive library', reading 'everything from Enid Blyton to the Brontë sisters' (*NC*, p. 93). The allusion here to 'the Brontë sisters' – if not Blyton[5] – opens the possibility for a reading of *Nervous Conditions* in terms of a different but conplementary intertextual relation to that advertised by its epigraph. If Tambudzai reads the Brontës, the novel in which she is located rewrites them for its own postcolonial purposes, and Charlotte Brontë's *Shirley* (1849) in particular.[6] The central figure around which such a rewriting is performed is that of the female anorexic, textually embodied in the Nyasha of Dangarembga's novel, on the one hand, and the Caroline Helstone and Shirley Keeldar of Brontë's, on the other.

Bodies in trouble: gendering colonialism in *The Wretched of the Earth*

'The colonial world' (*WE*, p. 31) evoked in *The Wretched of the Earth* is overwhelmingly an androcentric one, rarely disrupted by the incursions of women, whether Algerian or French. On those occasions when women do appear in the text, they are principally figured as bodies to be possessed or appropriated by settler and native alike, paradoxically uniting men in a mutual conflict from which they themselves are excluded. This is clearly illustrated in the first of the case-histories included in 'Colonial War and Mental Disorders', the penultimate chapter of Fanon's text. Even as this case features a woman who is twice raped by colonial soldiers, Fanon is more concerned with the effects of these experiences on her husband. The husband suffers a 'loss of appetite' which is at once physical and political ('a marked lack of interest in everything to do with the national struggle' [*WE*, p. 206]) and, above all, entails a '"sexual failing"' (*WE*, p. 207) which renders him impotent. The violated female body – which, in the husband's phrase, has 'tasted the French' (*WE*, p. 206) – functions as the self-cancelling middle term in a narrative of colonial struggle in which it seems to have no place. In Michelle Vizzard's formulation, 'Fanon cannot conceive of women as political actors, even when theirs are stories of direct involvement in the violence of war.'[7]

In contrast to its female counterpart, the body of the colonized male subject features prominently in Fanon's text, even as its representation is marked by contradiction, as it fluctuates between emancipatory and defeatist postures. On the one hand, Fanon claims that 'The native's muscles are always tensed' (*WE*, p. 41), permanently geared to 'the moment when, deciding to embody history in his own person, he surges into the forbidden quarters' (*WE*, p. 31). Yet, on the other hand, the potentially insurgent native is a figure burdened by what Supriya Nair calls 'colonial melancholy',[8] 'starving and enfeebled' (*WE*, p. 57), with 'atrophied muscles' (*WE*, p. 77). His famishment is both literal – a matter of the 'shrunken bellies [which] outline what has been called the geography of hunger' (*WE*, p. 76) – and metaphorical. Colonial exploitation produces not only 'a veritable emaciation of the stock of national culture' (*WE*, p. 191) but also makes the native ravenous for even a soupçon of his own humanity:

> The native is so starved for anything, anything at all that will turn him into a human being, any bone of humanity flung to him, that his hunger is incoercible, and ... poor scraps of charity may, here and there, overwhelm him. (*WE*, p. 112)

It is in relation to the variously starving native and his nation that the feminine re-enters Fanon's text. While the agents of colonialism are typically male for Fanon, the colonizing powers in whose name they act – whether France or Europe in general – are repeatedly figured as despoliating females:

> The settler makes history and is conscious of making it. And because he constantly refers to the history of his mother country, he clearly indicates that he himself is the extension of that mother country. Thus the history which he writes is not the history of the country which he plunders but the history of his own nation in regard to all that she skims off, all that she violates and starves. (*WE*, p. 40)

Among those things which this 'mother country' 'violates' is the very conventional coding of motherhood in terms of nourishment and growth, qualities perhaps hinted at in the glancingly lactic allusion 'to all that she skims off'. By figuring the 'colonial mother' (*WE*, p. 170) as one who is neither 'gentle [nor] loving' (*WE*, p. 169), Fanon suggests that the practices in which she engages not only pathologize the colonized but are themselves pathological or 'fundamentally perverse' (*WE*, p. 170). As Sartre puts it: 'In other days France was the name of a country. We should take care that in 1961 it does not become the name of a nervous disease' (*WE*, p. 25).

The direct textual corollary to the emaciation of the colonized male native/nation is a feminized colonial power whose body is grotesquely surfeited and swollen. If France is a bad or neurotic mother-figure in Fanon's text, Europe, for Sartre, is a 'fat, pale continent [which] ends by falling into . . . narcissism' (*WE*, p. 22), while, for Fanon, it is 'suspicious and bloated' (*WE*, p. 77). In the most striking instance of these rhetorical transformations, Europe emerges as a giantess battening on her spoils:

> For in a very concrete way Europe has stuffed herself inordinately with the gold and raw materials of the colonial countries: Latin America, China and Africa. From all these continents, under whose eyes Europe today raises up her tower of opulence, there has flowed out for centuries towards that same Europe diamonds and oil, silk and cotton, wood and exotic products. Europe is literally the creation of the Third World. The wealth which smothers her is that which was stolen from the under-developed peoples. The ports of Holland, the docks of Bordeaux and Liverpool were specialized in the Negro slave-trade, and owe their renown to millions of deported slaves. (*WE*, p. 81)

As she 'stuff[s] herself inordinately with gold and raw materials', Europe is turned into a prodigious eating compulsion. She is not so much 'continent' as incontinent, foully overdeveloped and 'smother[ed]' in the 'wealth' she takes into herself through her capacious 'ports'. Fanon typically figures colonialism as a 'violence' that 'will only yield when confronted with greater violence' (*WE*, p. 48). Yet the language of his text suggests that colonialism's defeat is equally a question of one appetite being outstripped by another. Shortly after the passage cited above, Fanon reminds the reader that – in an even more gargantuan effort of consumption – the

'Third World . . . is rising like the tide to swallow up all Europe' (*WE*, p. 84).

Towards the end of *The Wretched of the Earth*, the figures of France and Europe are not only feminized but also strangely Gothicized. In 'Colonial War and Mental Disorders', Fanon records the case of a young Algerian resistance fighter who has killed the wife of 'an active colonist' in revenge for the murder of his mother, shot 'point-blank by a French soldier' (*WE*, p. 211). As a result of this action, he suffers from hallucinations, striking 'attitudes' which give 'the impression to observers that the patient [is] witnessing a play' (*WE*, p. 210). This play – in which the patient's body is ceaselessly drained by a violent orality – casts him in a very different role from that scripted in the revolutionary theatres of decolonization, where 'spectators crushed with their inessentiality' are transformed 'into privileged actors with the grandiose glare of history's floodlights upon them' (*WE*, p. 28):

> the patient talked of his blood being spilt, of his arteries which were being emptied and of his heart which kept missing a beat. He implored us to stop the haemorrhage and not to let him be 'sucked by a vampire' within the very precincts of the hospital. (*WE*, p. 210)

The hallucinations are accompanied by nightmares in which the native loses the 'muscular prowess' (*WE*, p. 40) he so cherishes and the persecutory 'vampire' reappears:

> At nightfall . . . as soon as the patient went to bed, the room was 'invaded by women'. . . . It was a manifold repetition of the same woman. Every one of them had an open wound in her stomach. They were bloodless, pale and terribly thin. They tormented the young patient and insisted that he should give them back their spilt blood. At this moment the sound of running water filled the room and grew so loud that it seemed like a thundering waterfall, and the young patient saw the parquet of his room drenched with blood – his blood – while the women slowly got their colour back, and their wounds began to close up. The patient awoke. (*WE*, p. 212)

Faced with these symptoms, Fanon speculates that he might be dealing with 'an unconscious guilt complex following on the death

of the mother, as Freud has described in *Mourning and Melancholia'*
and 'direct[s] the investigation towards the maternal image' (*WE*,
p. 211). At the same time, however, the text sends the reader in
another direction, which leads beyond the private symptomatology
of the patient's 'disrupted personality' (*WE*, p. 212) and back out
towards the larger gendered paradigm of colonial strife. The halluci-
natory 'vampire' who torments Fanon's patient and multiplies herself
indefinitely as the invader of his dreams is another incarnation of
colonial France as the predatory and negating mother who so dev-
astates her 'offspring' (*WE*, p. 170). What this proliferating vampire
figure wants, however, is not to starve the native but to drink his
blood, decanting it into her body in order to 'close up' the gaping
'wound'/mouth slashed into her 'stomach'.

In the final chapter of *The Wretched of the Earth*, the focus switches
back from France to Europe. Here the gendering of colonialism as
a conflict in which a destructive female exclusively starves and
consumes the 'colonized man' (*WE*, p. 249) is made explicit. In an
extraordinary claim, Fanon writes that Europe 'has only shown herself
parsimonious and niggardly where men are concerned; it is only
men that she has killed and devoured' (*WE*, p. 251). Yet Europe,
like France, is also a bad mother, though in a different sense. Her
attempts at giving birth have been a spectacular failure and must
not be repeated by Fanon and his labouring 'brothers' (*WE*, p. 251):

> Let us decide not to imitate Europe; let us combine our muscles
> and our brains in a new direction. Let us try to create the whole
> man, whom Europe has been incapable of bringing to triumphant
> birth.
>
> Two centuries ago, a former European colony decided to catch
> up with Europe. It succeeded so well that the United States of
> America became a monster, in which the taints, the sickness and
> the inhumanity of Europe have grown to appalling dimensions.
> (*WE*, p. 252)

In giving birth to America, European colonialism produces a nation
which, in subsequently giving birth to itself, only reproduces and
exceeds its mother's monstrosities.

To reproduce the errors of Euro-American history would, in Fanon's
estimation, be a 'nauseating mimicry' (*WE*, p. 251). Yet the history
whose pathology Fanon wants to avoid – 'We today can do everything, as long as we do not imitate Europe' (*WE*, pp. 251–2) – is

itself a familiar tale, imitating, as it does, the Gothic ironies of Mary Shelley's *Frankenstein* (1818). Aspiring, in 'a torrent of light', to usher forth 'A new species' consisting of 'many happy and excellent natures',[9] Frankenstein engenders only 'catastrophe'[10] in the literally monstrous shape of the creature he fashions. Driven alike by mother-figures who create monstrous doubles of themselves, Fanon's history and Shelley's fiction, appropriately, double one another.

Figures of starvation in *Nervous Conditions* and *Shirley*

Nervous Conditions is set in the Rhodesia of the 1960s and early 1970s, during a period which saw the beginnings of 'the *chimurenga* struggle for national liberation' from white rule. As Sugnet points out, however, Dangarembga's novel 'barely mentions'[11] this struggle, decentring the colonized male subject who – as in *The Wretched of the Earth* – might carry it forward. This decentring is effected in the novel's seemingly brutal first sentence, 'I was not sorry when my brother died' (*NC*, p. 1), which clears the space for Tambudzai's narrative. Yet even as *Nervous Conditions* is Tambudzai's story, a good deal of its attention is directed towards Nyasha, Tambudzai's 'companion, double and sometime guide'[12] on the journey which takes her from impoverished African homestead to mission-school to the Young Ladies College of the Sacred Heart and culminates in the production of the narrative itself. Despite Tambudzai's hopes to the contrary, Nyasha suffers, throughout the novel, from a 'wasting disease which progresse[s] imperceptibly in the early stages only to ravage quickly and finally at the end' (*NC*, p. 131).

As an anorexic, Nyasha is afflicted by a condition whose aetiology and meanings notoriously tend to baffle the interpreter's grasp, stimulating what Abigail Bray calls an 'epidemic of signification'.[13] In an ironic digest of the ways in which anorexia has been constructed in Western feminist discourse, Bray lists some twenty possible interpretations. These variously define the disease as anything from a 'mourning for a pre-Oedipal . . . body', to a 'psychosomatic phenomenon which articulates the pathologies of the patriarchal capitalist nuclear family' to a 'reading disorder',[14] in which culturally dominant representations of the perfectly slenderized female form are consumed by the girls and young women about whom they circulate.

The glutting of potential and sometimes contradictory meanings which anorexia tends to provoke is certainly evident in Dangarembga's text. From one perspective, Nyasha's condition can be seen to parallel – and feminize – the kind of alienating identification with the white other outlined by Fanon in *Black Skin, White Masks* (1952). This is suggested, for example, in the exchange which takes place in the bedroom shared by Nyasha and Tambudzai at the mission-school where they both study and where Babamukuru, Nyasha's father and Tambudzai's uncle, is headmaster. Newly arrived at the school and having dressed herself in her uniform, Tambudzai 'admire[s her]self in the mirror':

> 'Not bad,' she agreed, standing beside me to observe my reflection. 'Not bad at all. You've got a waist. One of these days you'll have a bust. Pity about the backside,' she continued, slapping it playfully as she turned away. 'It's rather large. Still, if you can look good in that old gym-dress, you'll look good in anything.' (*NC*, p. 91)

In this mirror-scene, with its delicate pun on 'waist'/waste, it is Nyasha's bodily self-image as much as Tambudzai's reflection that is made visible: 'turn[ing] away' from Tambudzai, whose 'backside' she considers 'rather large', 'believ[ing] that angles [are] more attractive than curves' (*NC*, p. 135) and preferring 'bones to bounce' (*NC*, p. 197), Nyasha is clearly figured, as Sugnet notes, as one who has incorporated 'Western notions about the ideal female form'[15] into her own sense of self. As Nyasha's black classmates sneeringly remark, 'She thinks she is white' (*NC*, p. 94).

Yet as well as entailing an identification with the aesthetics of white femininity, Nyasha's anorexia is at the same time the sign of a complex 'rebellion' (*NC*, p. 1), bespeaking 'alternatives and possibilities' (*NC*, p. 76). In one respect, it follows the classical white feminist model of 'anorexia as an unconscious protest against patriarchal oppression',[16] whether Western or African. Yet, ultimately, Nyasha's weight loss is not reducible to the 'question of femaleness. . . . as opposed and inferior to maleness' (*NC*, p. 116): it also figures as a mode of resistance to the processes of colonialism which have subjugated her 'country' and 'people' (*NC*, p. 147) alike. If 'Decolonization', as Fanon puts it, 'is . . . a programme of complete disorder' (*WE*, p. 27), it takes the form, in Nyasha's case, of an eating disorder.

There is a sense in which Nyasha's patriarchal and colonial defiance is also a transgression of Western feminism on Dangarembga's part. For in making the anorexic body an African body, Dangarembga challenges the Western feminist consensus that anorexia is a disease typically afflicting the white middle-class female subject.[17] Such an assumption is reinforced by the first of the two white psychiatrists to whom Nyasha is rushed as her condition deteriorates in the final chapter of Dangarembga's novel. Nyasha 'could not be ill', he tells her family, because 'Africans did not suffer in the way [they] had described. She was making a scene' (*NC*, p. 201). While this opinion is not explicitly contradicted, it is at least moderated by the second white psychiatrist to whom Nyasha is referred and who recommends that she be 'put into a clinic' (*NC*, p. 202). Perhaps this psychiatrist has read Fanon, who himself underwent psychiatric training and whose work with both colonized and colonizing subjects during the Algerian War of Independence is documented in 'Colonial War and Mental Disorders'? As Sugnet notes, several of the (male) Algerian patients who appear in this chapter suffer from 'eating disturbances'[18] which, in Fanon's estimation, are 'the direct product of oppression' (*WE*, p. 201).

As 'the body's symptomatic resistance to . . . different but related forms of domination',[19] Nyasha's illness is the principal means through which the dialogue between *Nervous Conditions* and its Brontëan intertext is articulated. While anorexia does not enter Victorian medical discourses until the early 1870s,[20] critics have none the less been inclined to read Brontë's *Shirley* as powerfully prefiguring those discourses. According to Rod Edmond, *Shirley* 'is probably the longest, most detailed study of wasting illness in nineteenth-century writing',[21] the 'conspicuous symptom' of such illness being, he goes on to note, 'a refusal or inability to eat'[22] which 'seems to be a form of anorexic suicide'.[23] Similarly, in a much more sustained discussion of Brontë's text, the illness that first grips Caroline and then Shirley herself is viewed by Deirdre Lashgari as distinctly anorexic in its cast. 'Individual eating disorders . . . in *Shirley*', she writes:

> are portrayed as part of a much larger picture, in which a dysfunctional society starves women . . . and women internalize that dis/order as self-starvation. Contrary to some readings of the novel, Brontë is not selling the two heroines out to conventional female passivity, either when she has them stop eating or when she marries them off at the end of the story. Caroline and Shirley have both struggled against gender roles and relationships that

are 'killing them.' When each in turn finds herself blocked from any effective overt protest and barred from speaking her pain, she asserts control over her life in the only arena available, inscribing her hunger on her own body in a desperate plea to be 'read aright.'[24]

The literal complaints that assail the bodies of *Shirley*'s two main female figures work as symptoms of a broader and otherwise unspeakable dissatisfaction with what *Nervous Conditions* ironically calls 'the real tasks of feminine living' (*NC*, p. 34). In Brontë's novel, these are urged on Caroline by Mr. Helstone, her uncle: 'stick to the needle – learn shirt-making and gown-making, and pie-crust-making, and you'll be a clever woman some day' (*S*, pp. 98–9). Evidently, Helstone is to be numbered with those guardians of the patriarchal nation openly addressed by the narrator shortly before the onset of Caroline's illness:

> Can you give [your daughters] a field in which their faculties may be exercised and grow? Men of England! look at your poor girls, many of them fading around you, dropping off in consumption or decline; or, what is worse, degenerating to sour old maids, – envious, backbiting, wretched, because life is a desert to them; or, what is worst of all, reduced to strive, by scarce modest coquetry and debasing artifice, to gain that position and consideration by marriage, which to celibacy is denied. Fathers! cannot you alter these things? (*S*, p. 392)

Read as anorexics potentially diminished to the activity of 'backbiting', the 'natives' of Brontë's nineteenth-century Yorkshire – Caroline and Shirley – would thus appear to share the dilemma which besets the Nyasha of Dangarembga's twentieth-century Rhodesia. By the same token, the somatic strategies deployed by their postcolonial counterpart function as a rejection of the patriarchal norm, figured pre-eminently, in Dangarembga's text, in the shape of Babamukuru. Babamukuru poses several problems for Nyasha which arise, in the first instance, from his ambiguously hybrid location between cultures – African and English, black and white – that are themselves in direct colonial tension with one another. Even as he is 'revered patriarch' (*NC*, p. 197), in Nyasha's scathing phrase, to his extended Shona family, Babamukuru is also what she astutely calls 'a historical artefact' (*NC*, p. 160): taken in by 'holy wizards'

(*NC*, p. 19), he is the product of a colonial/missionary education, followed by third-level study in South Africa and then England. Nyasha's father thus takes his place among the kind of black colonial élite satirized so heavily by Sartre – echoing Fanon – in the Preface to *The Wretched of the Earth*:

> The European *élite* undertook to manufacture a native *élite*. They picked out promising adolescents; they branded them, as with a red-hot iron, with the principles of western culture; they stuffed their mouths full with high-sounding phrases, grand glutinous words that stuck to the teeth. After a short stay in the mother country they were sent home, whitewashed. These walking lies had nothing left to say to their brothers; they only echoed. (*WE*, p. 7)

The contradictions and conflicts generated by Babamukuru's role as 'good African' (*NC*, p. 107) – 'not even the replica of Europe, but its caricature' (*WE*, p. 141) – themselves find bodily or even hysterical expression: his 'nerves' are said to be 'bad' (*NC*, p. 102) as a result of the hectic daily routines he carries out as family breadwinner and mission-school head.

In terms of gender and sexuality, however, the native/Shona and colonial/missionary discourses regulating Babamukuru's subjectivity are not at odds, coalescing, as they do, around ideals of 'feminine decency, submissiveness and respect'.[25] These ideals are challenged and violated by Nyasha throughout the novel. She reads *Lady Chatterley's Lover*, 'forgetting to eat' (*NC*, p. 83) when her father slyly confiscates the book and she thinks she has mislaid it, dresses in a Western style which Babamukuru deems 'ungodly' (*NC*, p. 109) and returns late and unchaperoned from the mission-school Christmas dance because she has been dallying with a white boy. This last transgression precipitates what is quite literally the novel's most striking scene. Babamukuru is scandalized and repeatedly accuses Nyasha of behaving 'like a whore' (*NC*, p. 114). The violent verbal exchange between father and daughter rapidly escalates into bodily conflict as they flail and wrestle on Nyasha's bedroom floor, threatening, as they always do, according to Maiguru, Nyasha's mother, to 'tear[ ] each other to pieces' (*NC*, p. 118). While she is both silenced and physically worsted at the end of this scene, Nyasha is ultimately – as Tambudzai recognizes – the 'victim of her femaleness' (*NC*, p. 115) or, more properly, the patriarchal codes by which that femaleness is circumscribed. Like Caroline and Shirley, however, Nyasha has developed alternative ways of continuing her struggle against Babamukuru and the patriarchal authority invested in him. Throughout the week after the fight, Nyasha grows increasingly vague and detached from those around her: she neither sees the hand that Tambudzai passes before her eyes nor hears her voice and, above all, 'stop[s] eating again' (*NC*, p. 118).

Shirley's disorderly female eaters cannot, however, be placed in straightforward or unproblematic alliance with the Nyasha of *Nervous Conditions*. This is evident from the following passage in which the narrator undertakes to explain to the reader who is not '"au fait"' with them, the 'mysteries of the "Jew-basket" and "Missionary-basket"':

> these . . . are willow-repositories, of the capacity of a good-sized family clothes-basket, dedicated to the purpose of conveying from house to house a monster collection of pincushions, needle-books, card-racks, work-bags, articles of infant-wear, &c., &c., &c., made by the willing or reluctant hands of the Christian ladies of a parish, and sold perforce to the heathenish gentlemen thereof, at prices unblushingly exorbitant. The proceeds of such compulsory sales are applied to the conversion of the Jews, the seeking up of the ten missing tribes, or to the regeneration of the interesting coloured population of the globe. (*S*, p. 112)

Brontë's 'willow-repositories' serve a double purpose. On the one hand, they subjugate women – including Caroline, most notably – to the drudgery of preparing the trivial domestic items that go into them. Yet on the other hand, the profits from the sale of such stereotypically 'feminine' items are channelled into a range of colonial/missionary projects designed for the apparent benefit of another 'monster collection', whose members include 'Jews', 'missing tribes' and 'the interesting coloured population of the globe': the form taken by one of the restrictions placed upon the female subject in *Shirley* thus implicates her, albeit obliquely, in the oppression of the colonized other.

Nor does *Nervous Conditions* simply repeat or mirror *Shirley*'s representation of disorderly female eating as patriarchal rebellion. Rather, Dangarembga's novel also figures it as a form of colonial resistance. For example, Tambudzai's mother, Mainini, believes that the colonial education received by Nhamo has caused his death. When

Tambudzai is chosen by Babamukuru to take Nhamo's place at the mission-school, Mainini's protests are first verbal ('You and your education have killed my son' [*NC*, p. 54]) and then somatic:

> In the week before I left she ate hardly anything, not for lack of trying, and when she was able to swallow something it lay heavy in her stomach. By the time I left she was so haggard and gaunt she could hardly walk to the fields, let alone work in them. (*NC*, pp. 56-7)

This pattern recurs when Tambudzai is about to depart for the predominantly white Sacred Heart: Mainini 'ate less and less and did less and less, until within days she could neither eat nor do anything' (*NC*, p. 184).

Like Mainini's, Nyasha's corporeal guerrilla tactics are mobilized against the system of colonial education to which both she and Tambudzai are subject and, in particular, against the corpus of texts by which colonialism represents itself – to itself and to others. While the black colonial élite of which Babamukuru is a part relies on and 'remembers what it has read in European textbooks' (*WE*, p. 141) and thus also necessarily internalizes a sense of its own inferiority, Nyasha critiques such a process as a form of forgetting. Sacred Heart represents for her 'a marvellous opportunity ... to forget' (*NC*, p. 178):

> The process, she said, was called assimilation, and that was what was intended for the precocious few who might prove a nuisance if left to themselves, whereas the others – well really, who cared about the others? So they made a little space into which you were assimilated. ... But, she insisted, one ought not to occupy that space. (*NC*, p. 179)

The digestive and spatial metaphors Nyasha uses here are highly appropriate, not least because they are ones which her body appears to literalize. Refusing colonial 'assimilation' by a refusal to eat, Nyasha seems to want her body to be without volume altogether, not to 'occupy ... space' – however 'little' – at all: at one point, accordingly, 'her nightdress' is described as falling 'through the space where her thighs had been' (*NC*, p. 200).

The link between the anorexic body and colonial representation, the one dramatizing a rejection of the other, first emerges in the

course of a sequence of references to books and eating which begins in the novel's second chapter. Lamenting the fact that her
family does not have sufficient funds to send both Nhamo and
herself to school, Tambudzai is comforted by Jeremiah, her father:
'Is that anything to worry about? . . . Can you cook books and feed
them to your husband? Stay at home with your mother. Learn to
cook and clean. Grow vegetables' (*NC*, p. 15). Yet Tambudzai is
not persuaded by the mutually exclusive opposition between education and subsistence, reading and eating which Jeremiah sets up.
Her father's logic is refuted, as Tambudzai notes, by the counter-
example of Babamukuru's wife: 'Maiguru was educated, and did she
serve Babamukuru books for dinner? I discovered to my unhappy
relief that my father was not sensible' (*NC*, p. 16). Tambudzai's
father is not only 'not sensible' but also manages to contradict
himself, implicitly revoking his earlier culinary metaphor. Having
asserted that it is not possible to 'cook books', he none the less
suggests, in chapter 3, that the colonizer's texts are quite edible.
Exhibiting 'his usual ability to jump whichever way was easiest'
(*NC*, p. 15), Jeremiah greets Babamukuru, on his return from com-
pleting his education in England, with the following eulogy:

> '[Babamukuru] has returned appeased, having devoured English
> letters with a ferocious appetite! Did you think degrees were in-
> digestible? If so, look at my brother. He has digested them! If
> you want to see an educated man, look at my brother, big brother
> to us all!' (*NC*, p, 36)

This figure of the colonizer's texts as food to be 'devoured' is taken
up and incorporated into her own narrative of educational nourishment by Tambudzai in her second reference to Nyasha's library,
which she describes as a 'various and exotic' collection for its reader
to 'digest' (*NC*, p. 178).

Babamukuru's own digestion of 'English letters' renders him 'Full
of knowledge' (*NC*, p. 36), in the words of one of Tambudzai's
aunts. Yet while such epistemological repletion is the ground of
Babamukuru's characteristically 'grave and weighty' (*NC*, p. 46)
presence, the assimilation of colonial ideology produces the opposite effect upon Nyasha. As she crams for her Form Two
examinations at Babamukuru's school, 'reading and memorising all
the time. To make sure [she gets] it all in', she suffers from 'nerves'
(*NC*, p. 108) which manifest themselves in familiar ways:

Everybody agreed that she was overdoing it. She was looking drawn and had lost so much of her appetite that it showed all over her body in the way the bones crept to the surface, but she did not seem to notice. (*NC*, p. 107)

These disrupted temporal and bodily rhythms are not just the prosaic index of a desire to excel academically, though Babamukuru certainly construes them in that way and is suitably 'impressed by his daughter's industry' (*NC*, p. 108). They constitute, rather, the complex symptomatic expression of a struggle – as 'ferocious' as Babamukuru's reputed 'appetite' – against the educational processes that are integral to Nyasha's anglicization and which she herself abets. As these expressions appear 'all over her body' and creep to its 'surface', it becomes evident that it is far more difficult for Nyasha than for her father to 'stomach' the 'Englishness' (*NC*, p. 203) to which they are both exposed. As if to underscore the destructiveness of the colonial texts which she reads – the ways in which the assimilator is herself assimilated – Nyasha's emaciated frame takes on a striking resemblance to the textualized white bodies, 'their skin hanging in papery folds from their bones' (*NC*, p. 27), by whom Tambudzai is so repulsed in chapter 2.

By the final chapter of Dangarembga's novel the staging of anorexia as a contestation of the 'truths' incarnated in the texts of colonialism is at its most flamboyant. Having graduated from the mission-school to Sacred Heart, Tambudzai returns on vacation to find that in the three months since their last meeting her cousin is not just 'svelte' (*NC*, p. 197) but has 'grown skeletal' (*NC*, p. 198) and is studying 'fourteen hours a day to make sure that she passe[s] her "O" levels' (*NC*, p. 200). Nyasha is now also the protagonist in a 'horribly weird and sinister drama' largely enacted – like so many of the critical scenes in the novel – around the family dining-table, in which the relations between reading and eating are grotesquely inverted. Having been 'absorbed in a history text' and 'worked until suppertime', Nyasha sits down 'very quietly' to the evening meal to which she has been summoned:

> Babamukuru dished out a large helping of food for his daughter and set it before her, watching her surreptitiously as he picked casually at his own meal to persuade us that he was calm. Nyasha regarded her plate malevolently, darting anguished glances at her father, drained two glasses of water, then picked up her fork

and shovelled the food into her mouth, swallowing without chewing and without pause except to sip between mouthfuls from a third glass of water. Maiguru ate steadily and fussed over me, placing another chunk of meat, another spoonful of vegetables on my plate and making cheerful conversation about my lessons, my friends and the food at Sacred Heart. When Nyasha's plate was empty they both relaxed and the atmosphere returned almost to normal. Nyasha excused herself immediately. I thought she had gone to the bedroom to read but when I followed her there the room was empty. I could hear retching and gagging from the bathroom. (*NC*, p. 198)

The metaphorical interplay between food and text is distinctly Fanonian. As Booker points out, Nyasha is literally sickened by 'the ways in which colonialist historiographies have distorted the African past'.[26] She clearly reacts *à la* Fanon, who writes: 'In the period of decolonization, the colonized masses mock at [Western] values, insult them and vomit them up' (*WE*, p. 34). In a subsequent scene, the mouth which figuratively expels the colonizer's history strives to dismember it. Condemning her father, in a 'Rhodesian accent' as 'a good boy, a good munt. A bloody good kaffir' (*NC*, p. 200), Nyasha is finally 'beside herself with fury':

She rampaged, shredding her history book between her teeth ('Their history. Fucking liars. Their bloody lies.'), breaking mirrors, her clay pots, anything she could lay her hands on and jabbing the fragments viciously into her flesh, stripping the bedclothes, tearing her clothes from the wardrobe and trampling them underfoot. (*NC*, p. 201)

In figuring texts as food, *Nervous Conditions* provides one sign of its rhetorical continuity with *Shirley*, since it is precisely in such terms that Brontë's novel proffers itself to the reader. This is evident from as early on as the second paragraph:

If you think, from this prelude, that anything like a romance is preparing for you, reader, you never were more mistaken. Do you anticipate sentiment, and poetry, and reverie? Do you expect passion, and stimulus, and melodrama? Calm your expectations; reduce them to a lowly standard. Something real, cool, and solid, lies before you; something unromantic as Monday morning, when all who have work wake with the consciousness that they must rise and betake themselves thereto. It is not positively affirmed that you shall not have a taste of the exciting, perhaps towards the middle and close of the meal, but it is resolved that the first dish set upon the table shall be one that a Catholic – ay, even an Anglo-Catholic – might eat on Good Friday in Passion Week: it shall be cold lentiles and vinegar without oil; it shall be unleavened bread with bitter herbs and no roast lamb. (*S*, p. 5)

This would appear to be a fairly accurate description of what is on the fictional menu for the romance-hungry reader of Brontë's 'English book' (*S*, p. 63). Recently dieted on *Jane Eyre*, published two years earlier, such a reader might well demand that Brontë supply more of the 'passion, and stimulus, and melodrama' by which the earlier text, for contemporary reviewers, was strongly characterized. These elements are indeed part of *Shirley*'s narrative recipe, in the overlapping contexts of its central love-stories – between Caroline and the Anglo-Belgian mill-owner Robert Moore, on the one hand, and Shirley and Louis Moore, Robert's brother and Shirley's ex-tutor, on the other. Before s/he can indulge the 'taste' for romance, however, the reader must force down 'the first dish set upon the table', whose main ingredients include class struggle and industrialization, political economy and military conflict. These ingredients are already being obliquely served up in the reference to 'all who have work', with its concomitant suggestion that some do not. For the reader fed on the romantic melodrama of *Jane Eyre*, such a 'meal' is no doubt as unpalatable as it sounds: 'it shall be cold lentiles and vinegar without oil ... unleavened bread with bitter herbs and no roast lamb'.

As one of the texts contained in Nyasha's library, Brontë's novel, figured as a 'meal', itself contains a text which is represented in comparable terms, Shakespeare's *Coriolanus*. This text first enters Brontë's novel as 'an old English book' (*S*, p. 89) which Caroline gives to Robert to read during one of their romantic *soirées* at Hollow's Cottage, Robert's home:

The very first scene in 'Coriolanus' came with smart relish to his intellectual palate, and still as he read he warmed. He delivered the haughty speech of Caius Marcius to the starving citizens with unction; he did not say he thought his irrational pride right, but he seemed to feel it so. Caroline looked up at him with a singular smile.

The 'very first scene' of Shakespeare's play that Robert so relishes – while enjoying the 'warlike portions' of the text much less (*S*, p. 91) – is one in which, as this passage hints, questions of food and hunger are paramount. The scene in question dramatizes a conflict between the 'starving citizens' of Rome and the state which, they believe, in the person of Coriolanus in particular – 'very dog to the commonality'[27] – is responsible for the dearth of food from which they suffer. As befits *Shirley*'s own corporeal concerns, it is marked, also, by Menenius's extended allegorical reflection on the Roman body politic, whose 'senators' are figured as a 'good belly' while the citizens play the role of 'mutinous members'.[28]

What is uncanny about this Shakespearean scene is that it is one that Robert finds himself acting out shortly afterward. In chapter 8 of *Shirley*'s first volume, Robert is not only explicitly described by Caroline as a Coriolanus figure (*S*, p. 131), but also, like his Roman counterpart, confronted by beings 'haggard with want' (*S*, p. 138). This is the plea of William Farren, one of the workers who have been made redundant as a result of Robert's desire to modernize cloth-production at Hollow's Mill:

> 'Ye see we're ill off, – varry ill off: wer families is poor and pined. We're thrawn out o' work wi' these frames: we can get nought to do: we can earn nought. What is to be done? Mun we say, wisht! and lig us down and dee? Nay: I've no grand words at my tongue's end, Mr. Moore, but I feel that it wad be a low principle for a reasonable man to starve to death like a dumb cratur': – I will n't do't. I'm not for shedding blood: I'd neither kill a man nor hurt a man; and I'm not for pulling down mills and breaking machines: for, as ye say, that way o'going on 'll niver stop invention; but I'll talk, – I'll mak' as big a din as ever I can. Invention may be all right, but I know it isn't right for poor folks to starve.' (*S*, p. 137)

Like Coriolanus, Robert is perceived to be 'chief enemy to the people',[29] though, to be more precise, this description really applies to the technologizing impulse with which he identifies himself. He is 'the Divil of Hollow's-miln' (*S*, p. 33), whose indifference to the workers' plight precipitates the set-piece attack on his property that takes place at the novel's mid-point. This attack, as the spectating Shirley recognizes, is 'a struggle about money, and food, and life' (*S*, p. 342). It is also one in which language – the 'talk' of a 'reasonable man' – disintegrates into a 'Yorkshire rioters' yell' (*S*, p. 343) that becomes, in its turn, a physical violence carried out by the 'famished and furious mass of the Operative Class' against the 'Middle Rank' (*S*, p. 344).

Shirley's obsession with the starving bodies of middle-class women and working-class men is neither accidental nor gratuitous. Rather, like the novel's troping of itself and *Coriolanus* in terms of food, it is the reflex of the historical moment in which the novel is produced. Even as *Shirley* is set 'in eighteen-hundred-eleven-twelve' (*S*, pp. 5–6), against the background of the Napoleonic Wars, it is written in a context marked, precisely, by the crisis of food's absence, the Irish Famine of 1845–51. The result, in the first instance, of a fungus (*phytophthora infestans*) that attacked and destroyed the Irish potato crop, the Famine was 'the most important episode of modern Irish history and the greatest social disaster of nineteenth-century Europe',[30] killing approximately one million Irish and leading to the emigration – to England, Australia and especially America – of over a million more.

While the 'Irish cataclysm', as Elsie Michie calls it, constitutes a 'crucial historical event' in which 'the Brontës were particularly interested' (not least because of the Reverend Patrick Brontë's own working-class Irish origins), Michie's concern is with the curious status which the Famine occupies within their fiction. In an essay on *Wuthering Heights* and *Jane Eyre*, Michie begins by taking issue with the assumption that the Famine is simply 'absent' from the novels of the 1840s. She argues, instead, that it is something that is 'present but invisible'.[31] In *Wuthering Heights* and *Jane Eyre*, she writes:

> direct references to the Irish are difficult to identify because they are screened by references to China, India, Turkey and the West Indies. By moving from a troubling instance of local colonialism to more distant imperialist scenarios, the ... novels offer their Victorian readers a chance to project ... the sense of uneasiness elicited by a situation at work closer to home. At the same time, the novels' shift in focus from the Irish to peoples conceived of as more 'exotic' or more explicitly racially differentiated also allows those readers ... to accede to their own wildest fantasies as colonizers.[32]

These remarks provide a useful point of departure for a reading of the inscription of the Famine in *Shirley*. In this text, as in *Wuthering Heights* and *Jane Eyre*, 'direct references to the Irish' are indeed 'difficult to identify'. They not only appear sparingly but also are generally dispersed into the novel's margins where they retain, none the less, a casually dehumanizing force. One illustration of this comes in Shirley's cursory conjectures as to the 'soothsayers' she would choose to 'consult' in order to divine her romantic fortunes:

> 'Neither man nor woman, elderly nor young: – the little Irish beggar that comes barefoot to my door; the mouse that steals out of the cranny in the wainscot; the bird that in frost and snow pecks at my window for a crumb; the dog that licks my hand and sits beside my knee.' (*S*, p. 218)

To this could be added the narratorial reflection on the different ways in which 'poverty' is experienced and negotiated by the 'Irish girl' and her more fastidious and resourceful colonial counterpart: 'That British love of decency will work miracles: the poverty which reduces an Irish girl to rags is impotent to rob the English girl of the neat wardrobe she knows necessary to her self-respect' (*S*, p. 296).

In the one instance when the Irish allusion is more overt and sustained it is 'screened' in the ways that Michie suggests. Peter Augustus Malone, the curate who first appears in *Shirley*'s opening chapter and whose principal occupations, it is worth noting, would seem to be eating and drinking, certainly qualifies as one of Brontë's 'few identifiably Irish characters'[33] and is variously stereotyped as 'a native of the land of shamrocks and potatoes' (*S*, p. 8) or 'priestly Paddy' (*S*, p. 10). Yet no sooner does Malone appear in the text than he seems, also, to be transfigured:

> he is a tall, strongly-built personage, with real Irish legs and arms, and a face as genuinely national; not the Milesian face – not Daniel O'Connell's style, but the high-featured, North-American-Indian sort of visage, which belongs to a certain class of the Irish gentry, and has a petrified and proud look, better suited to the owner of an estate of slaves, than to the landlord of a free peasantry. (*S*, p. 8)

Even as Malone's 'face' marks him as 'genuinely national', it is swiftly masked by the narrative imposition of a 'North-American-Indian sort of visage'. This in turn is the cue for the fantasmatic reversal of the colonized other – 'vent[ing] bitter hatred against English rule' (*S*, p. 10) – into an oppressor-figure, 'the owner of an estate of slaves'.

The movement from 'a troubling instance of local colonialism to more distant imperialist scenarios' which this passage traces out in cameo is further expanded towards the end of the text, in the series of bizarre exchanges which take place between Shirley and Louis Moore. In these exchanges, it is not only the novel's readers but Shirley and Louis themselves who are given the opportunity to 'accede to their own wildest fantasies as colonizers'. At one point in the third volume of the novel, Shirley collaborates with Louis in the project of reinventing herself beyond English horizons:

> 'Oh, for rest under my own vine and my own fig-tree! Happy is the slave-wife of the Indian chief, in that she has no drawing-room duty to perform, but can sit at ease weaving mats, and stringing beads, and peacefully flattening her picaninny's head in an unmolested corner of her wigwam. I'll emigrate to the western woods.'
> Louis Moore laughed.
> 'To marry a White Cloud or a Big Buffalo; and after wedlock to devote yourself to the tender task of digging your lord's maize-field, while he smokes his pipe or drinks fire-water.'
> (*S*, p. 468)

Shirley's fantasy of emigration to 'the western woods' of course parallels the pattern of the Irish diaspora. It is also ironic. Even as she is reimagined, here, as 'the slave-wife of [an] Indian chief', it would appear that her envisaged escape only reproduces conditions of confinement that prevail at home and circumscribe the possibilities for middle-class women. The occupation of the 'slave-wife' in this passage is not very far removed, as she weaves her mats and strings her beads, from that of the 'Christian ladies' who expend their labours and lives in contributing to the 'monster collection' of clothes and other sundries to be included in the '"Jew-basket" and "Missionary-basket"'.

This strange cross-racial fantasy recurs, in a different form, in the novel's penultimate chapter, in the context of Louis Moore's diary. This 'little blank book' (*S*, p. 610) records the sequence of conversational manoeuvrings between Louis and Shirley that lead eventually to Shirley's agreement to marry her suitor. One of their discussions includes Shirley's vision of the Moore brothers as pioneers:

> '"You two might go forth homeless hunters to the loneliest western wilds; all would be well with you. The hewn tree would make you a hut, the cleared forest yield you fields from its stripped bosom, the buffalo would feel your rifle-shot, and with lowered horns and hump pay homage at you feet."
>
> '"And any Indian tribe of Black-feet, or Flat-heads, would afford us a bride, perhaps?"
>
> '"No (hesitating): I think not. The savage is sordid: I think, – that is, I *hope*, – you would neither of you share your hearth with that to which you could not give your heart."
>
> '"What suggested the wild West to your mind, Miss Keeldar?"'
> (*S*, p. 613; emphasis in original)

This passage to some degree effects a reversal of the previous one where Shirley had entertained the possibility of being the 'slave-wife of [an] Indian chief'. Now it seems that the 'savage' is not noble but 'sordid' and reduced to an impersonal 'that'. The prospect of interracial desire, between Anglo-European adventurer and Native American 'bride', is not idealized as it is in some narratives of colonial encounter (between John Smith and Pocahontas, for example), but regarded as transgressive and unthinkable. This is somewhat ironic since both Shirley herself and Caroline are attracted to men whose Anglo-Belgian lineage makes them 'hybrid' (*S*, p. 27), 'outcast and alien' (*S*, p. 38). The further irony of this passage emerges around the term 'savage'. Shirley applies this to the native, and yet the passage shows that savagery belongs more properly to the Anglo-European 'frontiersmen'. These 'homeless hunters' violently turn a natural environment to their own 'civilizing' purposes as they chop down trees, clear forests, shoot buffalo and have the power to appropriate the native woman for sexual pleasure and domestic oppression.

If these two passages are indicative of the textual screening to which Michie refers, they at the same time suggest the doubleness of the process. To screen something is to hide or conceal it and it is in this sense that Michie uses the term. Yet it is also to do the exact opposite – to project or reveal, as when a film is screened, for example. Just as the Irishness of Malone's 'face' is screened/concealed by a 'North-American-Indian sort of visage', so *Shirley*'s narrative excursions into 'the wild West' only gesture back towards its more immediate geopolitical location. This simultaneous play of concealment and revelation is all the more perceptible in terms of corporeal representation: like the starving frames of the working-class men in the novel, the anorexic bodies of its middle-class women disguise and disclose at once the traces of the historical trauma which the novel negotiates.

To read *Shirley* in this way is to suggest that the Famine possesses the status of a kind of colonial unconscious, analogous to that of slavery in Jane Austen's *Mansfield Park*: it is something unspeakable whose role is nonetheless determinate. To recall Pierre Macherey:

> it is not a question of introducing a historical explanation which is stuck on to the work from the outside. On the contrary, [there is] a sort of splitting within the work: this division is *its* unconscious, in so far as it possesses one – the unconscious which is history, the play of history beyond its edges, encroaching on those edges: this is why it is possible to trace the path which leads from the haunted work to that which haunts it. Once again it is not a question of redoubling the work with its unconscious, but a question of revealing in the very gestures of expression that which it is not. Then, the reverse side of what is written will be history itself.[34]

Viewed from the perspective of this Macherean model, for which 'The speech of the book comes from a certain silence',[35] Brontë's text could be said to be organized and behave in ways that are not dissimilar to those of the anorexic/hysterical bodies displayed within it. As Elizabeth Grosz writes, hysteria is 'the *symptomatic acting out* of a proposition the hysteric cannot articulate',[36] taking the form, in *Shirley*'s case, of protest against the meagre nourishment provided by patriarchy for what Brontë calls women's 'mental stomach'. Grosz's definition of hysteria can be applied, equally, to *Shirley*, in which representation is itself pathologized and rendered '*symptomatic*', obliquely rehearsing, as it does, an event – in the haunting shape of the Famine – which cannot otherwise be named.

The nature of the 'nervous condition' with which representation might thus be said to be marked in *Shirley* accordingly necessitates a reconsideration or refocusing of the processes involved in Dangarembga's postcolonial rewriting of Brontë. *Nervous Conditions* reconfigures anorexia in Brontë's text in such a way as to extend its signifying range, as Nyasha's 'rebellion' assumes a colonial as well as patriarchal dimension. At the same time, however, the gender and class conflicts which Brontë's text addresses cannot be disentangled from the specificities of the historical moment in which the text is produced. Appropriated and reinscribed by Dangarembga, *Shirley*'s anorexic bodies – like those of its hungry and insurgent male workers – are freighted already with their own colonial burdens.

Notes

Introduction

1 The epigraph to the Introduction is taken from Walter Benjamin, *Illuminations: Essays and Reflections*, trans. Harry Zohn, ed. and intro. Hannah Arendt (New York: Schocken, 1969), p. 255.

2 See, for example, the following: *Oxford Literary Review*, 13. 1–2 (1991); *Social Text*, 31/2 (1993); *Yale French Studies*, 82/3 (1993); *PMLA*, 110. 1 (1995) and *Yearbook of English Studies*, 27 (1997).

3 Amongst the most prominent collections of postcolonial criticism and theory are: *Colonial Discourse and Post-Colonial Theory: A Reader*, ed. and intro. Patrick Williams and Laura Chrisman (Hemel Hempstead: Harvester, 1993); *The Post-Colonial Studies Reader*, ed. Bill Ashcroft *et al.* (London and New York: Routledge, 1995), and *Postcolonial Criticism*, ed. and intro. Bart Moore-Gilbert *et al.* (London and New York: Longman, 1997). Notable introductions to the field include: Peter Childs and Patrick Williams, *An Introduction to Post-Colonial Theory* (Hemel Hempstead: Prentice Hall, 1997); Bill Ashcroft *et al.*, *Key Concepts in Post-Colonial Studies* (London and New York: Routledge, 1998); Leela Gandhi, *Postcolonial Theory: A Critical Introduction* (Edinburgh: Edinburgh University Press, 1998), and Ania Loomba, *Colonialism/Postcolonialism* (London and New York: Routledge, 1998). For book-length reflections on postcolonialism see, in particular, Robert Young, *White Mythologies: Writing History and the West* (London and New York: Routledge, 1990) and *Colonial Desire: Hybridity in Theory, Culture and Race* (London and New York: Routledge, 1995), and Bart Moore-Gilbert, *Postcolonial Theory: Contexts, Practices, Politics* (London and New York: Verso, 1998).

4 For a fuller discussion of these developments in the contemporary postcolonial scene, see Bart Moore-Gilbert, 'Crises of Identity? Current Problems and Possibilities in Postcolonial Criticism', *European English Messenger*, 6. 2 (1997), pp. 35–42.

5 Benjamin, p. 257.

6 For representative analyses of the implications of postcolonialism's 'post', see Anne McClintock, 'The Angel of Progress: Pitfalls of the Term "Postcolonialism"', in Williams and Chrisman, pp. 291–304; Ella Shohat, 'Notes on the "Post-colonial"', *Social Text*, 31/2 (1993), pp. 99–113, and Aijaz Ahmad, 'Postcolonialism: What's in a Name?', in *Late Imperial Culture*, ed. Román de la Campa *et al.* (London and New York: Verso, 1995), pp. 11–32.

7 Isobel Armstrong, 'Foreword', in *The Discourse of Slavery: Aphra Behn to Toni Morrison*, ed. and intro. Carl Plasa and Betty J. Ring, Foreword by Isobel Armstrong (London and New York: Routledge, 1994), p. xi.

8 Paul Gilroy, *The Black Atlantic: Modernity and Double Consciousness* (London and New York: Verso, 1993), p. x.

9 This is Françoise Vergès's description of Fanon, in 'Creole Skin, Black Mask: Fanon and Disavowal', *Critical Inquiry*, 23 (1997), p. 578.

10 John Newton, *Thoughts upon the African Slave Trade* (1788). Cited in David Dabydeen and Nana Wilson-Tagoe, *A Reader's Guide to West Indian and Black British Literature* (Kingston-upon-Thames: Rutherford Press, 1987), p. 117.

11 The metaphorical/textual potential of the notion of the Middle Passage is more explicitly recognized in Derek Walcott's 'The Sea is History', as, for example, at lines 24–5: 'but the ocean kept turning blank pages / looking for History'. See Derek Walcott, *Collected Poems 1948–1984* (London and Boston: Faber and Faber, 1992), p. 365.

12 Olaudah Equiano, *The Interesting Narrative of the Life of Olaudah Equiano, or Gustavus Vassa, the African. Written by Himself.*, in *The Interesting Narrative and Other Writings*, ed. and intro. Vincent Carretta (Harmondsworth: Penguin, 1995), p. 92.

13 Homi K. Bhabha, *The Location of Culture* (London and New York: Routledge, 1994), p. 89 (emphasis in original).

14 Frantz Fanon, *Black Skin, White Masks*, trans. Charles Lam Markmann, Foreword by Homi K. Bhabha (London: Pluto Press, 1993), p. 179.

15 Toni Morrison, *The Bluest Eye*, with a new Afterword (London: Picador, 1994), p. 162.

16 Arthur Rimbaud's phrase, cited as third epigraph to Jan Nederveen Pieterse, *White on Black: Images of Africa and Blacks in Western Popular Culture* (New Haven and London: Yale University Press, 1992), p. 7.

Chapter 1

1 The epigraph to this chapter is taken from David Murray, 'Racial Identity and Self-Invention in North America: The Red and the Black', in *Writing and Race*, ed. Tim Youngs (London and New York: Longman), p. 90.

2 William Shakespeare, *The Tempest*, ed. Frank Kermode (London and New York: Routledge, 1992), pp. 81–2.

3 Olaudah Equiano, *The Interesting Narrative of the Life of Olaudah Equiano, or Gustavus Vassa, the African. Written by Himself.*, in *The Interesting Narrative and Other Writings*, ed. and intro. Vincent Carretta (Harmondsworth: Penguin, 1995), p. 138. All subsequent references are to this edition – abbreviated as *IN* – and included in parenthesis after quotations in the text.

4 Henry Louis Gates, Jr., *The Signifying Monkey: A Theory of African-American Literary Criticism* (New York and Oxford: Oxford University Press, 1989), p. 156.

5 For detailed discussion of this trope as it is used by these writers (together with Equiano's relation to them) see Gates, pp. 132–58.

6 Ibid., p. 158.

7 Ibid., p. 127.

8 *Race and the Enlightenment: A Reader*, ed. Emmanuel Chukwudi Eze (Cambridge, MA and Oxford: Blackwell, 1997), p. 6.

9   Ibid., p. 33.
10 Ibid., p. 55.
11 Ibid., pp. 97, 99.
12 Ibid., p. 7.
13 For the etymological association of candour with whiteness, still current in Equiano's day, see *OED*.
14 Susan M. Marren, 'Between Slavery and Freedom: The Transgressive Self in Olaudah Equiano's Autobiography', *PMLA*, 108 (1993), p. 95.
15 Homi K. Bhabha, *The Location of Culture* (London and New York: Routledge, 1994), p. 86.
16 Ibid., p. 89 (emphases in original).
17 Marren, p. 94.
18 Ibid., p. 100.
19 The notion of the 'color-line' was, of course, originally developed by W. E. B. Du Bois in the context of the racial problematic of early twentieth-century America. See W. E. B. Du Bois, *The Souls of Black Folk*, ed. Candace Ward (New York: Dover Publications, 1994), p. 9.
20 Gates, pp. 129–30.
21 Robert Young, *White Mythologies: Writing History and the West* (London and New York: Routledge, 1990), p. 123.
22 Joseph Fichtelberg, 'Word between Worlds: The Economy of Equiano's *Narrative*', *American Literary History*, 5 (1993), p. 463.
23 Marren, p. 97.
24 Peter Childs and Patrick Williams, *An Introduction to Post-Colonial Theory* (Hemel Hempstead: Prentice Hall, 1997), p. 132.
25 Bryan Edwards, *The History, Civil and Commercial, of the British Colonies in the West Indies*, 2 vols (London: Stockdale, 1793), II, pp. 74–5.
26 Paul Gilroy, *The Black Atlantic: Modernity and Double Consciousness* (London and New York: Verso, 1993), p. 4.
27 Ibid., pp. 16–17.
28 For a brief but suggestive reading of *The Interesting Narrative* along these lines, see Gilroy's own 'Diaspora and the Detours of Identity', in *Identity and Difference*, ed. Kathryn Woodward (London: Sage, 1997), pp. 321–9.
29 Frantz Fanon, *Black Skin, White Masks*, trans. Charles Lam Markmann, Foreword by Homi K. Bhabha (London: Pluto Press, 1993), p. 11.
30 Fichtelberg, p. 463.
31 Fanon, pp. 17–18.
32 Paul Gilroy, *Small Acts: Thoughts on the Politics of Black Cultures* (London: Serpent's Tail, 1993), pp. 27–8 (emphasis in original).
33 Chinosole, 'Tryin' to Get Over: Narrative Posture in Equiano's Autobiography', in *The Art of Slave Narrative: Original Essays in Criticism and Theory*, ed. John Sekora and Darwin T. Turner (Macomb, IL: Western Illinois University Press, 1982), p. 45.
34 Bhabha, p. 87 (emphasis in original).
35 Graham Huggan, 'A Tale of Two Parrots: Walcott, Rhys, and the Uses of Colonial Mimicry', *Contemporary Literature*, 35 (1994), p. 645.
36 Richard Dyer, *White* (London and New York: Routledge, 1997), pp. 14–15 (emphasis in original).

37 Winthrop D. Jordan, *White Over Black: American Attitudes Toward the Negro, 1550–1812* (Chapel Hill: University of North Carolina Press, 1968), p. 94.

38 Dyer, p. 68.

39 For a discussion of the Mansfield Judgement, arising out of the case of the slave James Somerset, see Edward Heward, *Lord Mansfield* (Chichester and London: Barry Rose, 1979), pp. 139–49. See also Gretchen Gerzina, *Black England: Life before Emancipation* (London: John Murray, 1995), pp. 116–20, 124–32.

40 Marren, p. 103.

41 Dyer, p. 15 (emphasis in original).

42 Ibid., p. 31.

43 Houston A. Baker, Jr., *Blues, Ideology, and Afro-American Literature: A Vernacular Theory* (Chicago and London: University of Chicago Press, 1984), p. 34.

44 Ibid., p. 35.

45 Ibid., p. 36.

46 Ibid., p. 35.

47 Marion Rust, 'The Subaltern as Imperialist: Speaking of Olaudah Equiano', in *Passing and the Fictions of Identity*, ed. Elaine K. Ginsberg (Durham, NC and London: Duke University Press, 1996), p. 25.

Chapter 2

1 The epigraphs to this chapter are taken from Pierre Macherey, *A Theory of Literary Production*, trans. Geoffrey Wall (London: Routledge & Kegan Paul, 1978), pp. 94 and 85 respectively (emphasis in original).

2 Jane Austen, *Mansfield Park*, ed. James Kinsley, intro. Marilyn Butler (Oxford and New York: Oxford University Press, 1998), p. 337. All subsequent references are to this edition – abbreviated as *MP* – and included in parenthesis after quotations in the text.

3 The most comprehensive critical readings of Austen's text in terms of its oblique relation to questions of colonialism and slavery are: Moira Ferguson, *Colonialism and Gender Relations from Mary Wollstonecraft to Jamaica Kincaid: East Caribbean Connections* (New York: Columbia University Press, 1993), pp. 65–89; Maggie Malone, 'Patriarchy and Slavery and the Problem of Fanny', *Essays in Poetics: Journal of the Neo-Formalist Circle*, 18. 2 (1993), pp. 28–41; Maaja A. Stewart, *Domestic Realities and Imperial Fictions: Jane Austen's Novels in Eighteenth-Century Contexts* (Athens, GA and London: University of Georgia Press, 1993), pp. 105–36, and Edward W. Said, *Culture and Imperialism* (London: Vintage, 1994), pp. 95–116. See also Susan Fraiman's important metacritical feminist response to Said in 'Jane Austen and Edward Said: Gender, Culture and Imperialism', *Critical Inquiry*, 21 (1995), pp. 805–21. Questions of colonialism, slavery and related issues are addressed in less detail but with equal insight (in *Mansfield Park* and other Austen texts) in Isobel Armstrong, *Mansfield Park* (London: Penguin, 1988); Meenakshi Mukherjee, *Jane Austen* (Basingstoke and London: Macmillan, 1991), pp. 49–69, and

Suvendrini Perera, *Reaches of Empire: The English Novel from Edgeworth to Dickens* (New York: Columbia University Press, 1991), pp. 35–57. The links between Austen's own family and slavery (established through the Reverend George Austen's trusteeship of an estate owned by James Langford Nibbs) are documented in Frank Gibbon, 'The Antiguan Connection: New Light on *Mansfield Park*', *Cambridge Quarterly*, 11 (1982), pp. 298–305.

4   *Jane Austen's Letters to her Sister Cassandra and Others*, ed. R. W. Chapman, 2 vols (Oxford: Clarendon Press, 1932), II, p. 298.

5   See chapter 1, note 39 above.

6   Ferguson, p. 82.

7   James Walvin, *Black Ivory: A History of British Slavery* (London: HarperCollins, 1992), p. 11.

8   Ibid., p. 12.

9   Ibid.

10   Ferguson, p. 71.

11   In assuming such a role, Fanny's narrative would seem to enact the logic of the very naval office of lieutenant which is William's own professional goal. Defined by the *OED*, a lieutenant is 'One who takes the place of another; usually an officer, civil or military, who acts for a superior; a representative, substitute, vice-gerent'.

12   Ronald Hyam, *Empire and Sexuality: The British Experience* (Manchester and New York: Manchester University Press, 1991), p. 92.

13   For a useful reading of the intersections between colonial and patriarchal oppression in Blake's text, see Steven Vine, '"That Mild Beam": Enlightenment and Enslavement in William Blake's *Visions of the Daughters of Albion*', in *The Discourse of Slavery: Aphra Behn to Toni Morrison*, ed. and intro. Carl Plasa and Betty J. Ring, Foreword by Isobel Armstrong (London and New York: Routledge, 1994), pp. 40–63.

14   Armstrong, p. 46.

15   Claudia L. Johnson, 'Gender, Theory and Jane Austen Culture', in *Mansfield Park*, ed. and intro. Nigel Wood (Buckingham and Philadelphia: Open University Press, 1993), p. 110.

16   Armstrong, p. 64.

17   Edmund Spenser, *A View of the Present State of Ireland*, ed. W. L. Renwick (Oxford: Clarendon Press, 1970), pp. 15–16.

18   The foregoing remarks on colonial and theatrical fantasy in *As You Like It* are indebted to an unpublished essay by the late Victor Neo, who was a doctoral student in the Centre for Critical and Cultural Theory at the University of Wales, Cardiff.

19   Said, p. 104. Said's reference is to Warren Roberts, *Jane Austen and the French Revolution* (London and Basingstoke: Macmillan, 1979), pp. 138–41. See also Avrom Fleishman, *A Reading of Mansfield Park: An Essay in Critical Synthesis* (Baltimore and London: Johns Hopkins University Press, 1970), pp. 36–9.

20   As Joseph Litvak notes, Austen's figuration of acting as disease echoes the rhetorical strategies of Thomas Gisborne's *Enquiry into the Duties of the Female Sex* (1797). For Gisborne, predictably, it is women rather than men who are especially prone to the dangers of acting because

they evidently possess a greater disposition towards imitation and impersonation. See Joseph Litvak, *Caught in the Act: Theatricality in the Nineteenth-Century English Novel* (Berkeley: University of California Press, 1992), p. 7.

21 *The Quarterly Review* (August 1809), p. 1.

22 Ferguson, p. 67.

23 Marilyn Butler, *Jane Austen and the War of Ideas* (Oxford: Clarendon Press, 1975), p. 232 (emphasis in original). Trilling's reading of the role of *Lovers' Vows* in *Mansfield Park* appears in Lionel Trilling, *The Opposing Self: Nine Essays in Criticism* (London: Secker and Warburg, 1955), pp. 206–30.

24 August von Kotzebue, *Lovers' Vows*, adapt. by Elizabeth Inchbald, ed. and intro. Jonathan Wordsworth (Oxford and New York: Woodstock, 1990), p. 39.

25 Ibid., p. 4.

26 Ferguson, p. 85.

27 Von Sack, cited in an unsigned review in *The Quarterly Review* (May 1811), p. 490.

28 Ibid.

29 On this point, see L. F. Thompson, *Kotzebue: A Survey of his Progress in France, and England Preceded by a Consideration of the Critical Attitude to him in Germany* (Paris: Librairie Ancienne Honoré Champion, 1928), p. 60.

30 Unsigned review, *The Quarterly Review* (May 1811), p. 490.

31 See August von Kotzebue, *The Negro Slaves, A Dramatic-Historical Piece, in Three Acts, Translated from the German of the President de Kotzebue* (London: T. Cadell *et al.*, 1796), pp. 51–6.

32 Walvin, p. 167.

33 Lady Maria Nugent, *Lady Nugent's Journal: Jamaica One Hundred Years Ago, Reprinted from a Journal Kept by Maria, Lady Nugent, from 1801 to 1815, Issued for Private Circulation in 1839*, ed. Frank Cundall (London: Adam and Charles Black, 1907), pp. 65–6.

34 Walvin, p. 168.

35 It is no accident, in this context, that the 'nest of comforts' in Fanny's 'East room' should include, as well as William's 'small sketch' of 'H. M. S. Antwerp' (*MP*, p. 137), a transparency of Tintern Abbey. For in Wordsworth's poem of the same name, of course, the historical ruin prompts a poetic excavation of subjective memory which climaxes with an affirmation of just that love between brother and sister, William and Dorothy, whose 'precious remains' are celebrated in Austen. For detailed analyses of the incest motif in *Mansfield Park*, see Glenda A. Hudson, 'Incestuous Relationships: *Mansfield Park* Revisited', *Eighteenth-Century Fiction*, 4 (1991), pp. 53–68, and Johanna M. Smith '"My Only Sister Now": Incest in *Mansfield Park*', *Studies in the Novel*, 19 (1987), pp. 1–15.

36 In realizing such a fantasy, albeit at one remove, the text would thus appear to have overcome earlier resistances: the part which Fanny almost comes to play in *Lovers' Vows* ('Cottager's wife' [*MP*, p. 131]) is precisely the one she is accorded in William's projected pastoral.

37   For a fascinating account of the abolitionist emblem in both its male
     and female versions and British and American contexts see Jean Fagan
     Yellin, *Women and Sisters: The Antislavery Feminists in American Culture*
     (New Haven and London: Yale University Press, 1989), pp. 3–28.
38   Ferguson, p. 73.
39   Ibid., p. 74.
40   Kotzebue, *The Negro Slaves*, p. 105.
41   Ibid., p. 136.
42   Ibid., pp. 138, 140.
43   Ibid., p. 142.
44   Mary Prince, *The History of Mary Prince, A West Indian Slave, Related by
     Herself*, ed. and intro. Moira Ferguson (Ann Arbor: University of Michi-
     gan Press, 1993), p. 64.

Chapter 3

1   The epigraphs to this chapter are taken from Alain Robbe-Grillet, *Snap-
    shots and Towards a New Novel*, trans. Barbara Wright (London: Calder
    and Boyars, 1965), p. 78; George Eliot, *Felix Holt: The Radical*, ed. and
    intro. Peter Coveney (Harmondsworth: Penguin, 1987), p. 129 and *The
    Mill on the Floss*, ed. and intro. A. S. Byatt (Harmondsworth: Penguin,
    1985), p. 494, and Mary Prince, *The History of Mary Prince, A West In-
    dian Slave, Related by Herself*, ed. and intro. Moira Ferguson (Ann Arbor:
    University of Michigan Press, 1993), p. 64.
2   Sandra M. Gilbert and Susan Gubar, *The Madwoman in the Attic: The
    Woman Writer and the Nineteenth-Century Literary Imagination* (New Ha-
    ven and London: Yale University Press, 1979), p. 338. In this respect,
    Gilbert and Gubar at once repeat, while also transvaluing, the contem-
    porary Victorian response to Brontë's novel as a radical or subversive
    text. Such a response is most strongly formulated by Elizabeth Rigby in
    The Quarterly Review (December 1848): 'We do not hesitate to say that
    the tone of the mind and thought which has overthrown authority
    and violated every code human and divine abroad, and fostered Chartism
    and rebellion at home, is the same which has also written Jane Eyre.'
    Cited in *The Brontës: The Critical Heritage*, ed. Miriam Allott (London:
    Routledge & Kegan Paul, 1974), pp. 109–10. For readings which argue
    that *Jane Eyre* involves a containment rather than affirmation of female
    transgression see Bette London, 'The Pleasures of Submission: *Jane Eyre*
    and the Production of the Text', *English Literary History*, 58 (1991), pp.
    195–213, and Kathryn Sutherland, '*Jane Eyre*'s Literary History: The Case
    for *Mansfield Park*', *ELH*, 59 (1992), pp. 409–40.
3   Gilbert and Gubar, p. 338. As is evident from the very title of their
    project, *Jane Eyre* certainly provides the 'pattern' or paradigm for the
    feminist poetics which *The Madwoman in the Attic* itself seeks to formu-
    late: along with Brontë's other novels, it occupies a 'central position'
    in Gilbert and Gubar's analytic schema, generating 'new ways in which
    all nineteenth-century works by women can be interpreted' (p. xii). See
    also pp. 77–9.

4   Ibid., p. 339. The ascription of 'hunger, rebellion, and rage' to Brontë
    is Matthew Arnold's, made (in relation to the recently published *Villette*)
    in a letter to John Forster of 14 April 1853. See Matthew Arnold, *Letters
    of Matthew Arnold 1848–1888*, ed. George W. E. Russell, 2 vols (London
    and New York: Macmillan, 1895), I, p. 29.
5   The tendency of 'narrowly . . . race-blind interpretations' to construct
    Jane Eyre as a feminist epic of self-realization is discussed by Penny
    Boumelha in *Charlotte Brontë* (Hemel Hempstead: Harvester, 1990),
    p. 60. One of the most influential critical attempts to reinscribe the
    questions of race and colonialism elided by the kind of analysis pur-
    sued by Gilbert and Gubar is made by Gayatri Chakravorty Spivak in
    'Three Women's Texts and a Critique of Imperialism', *Critical Inquiry*,
    12 (1985), pp. 243–61. See also Laura E. Donaldson's critique of both
    Gilbert and Gubar and Spivak in 'The Miranda Complex: Colonialism
    and the Question of Feminist Reading', *Diacritics*, 18 (Autumn 1988),
    pp. 65–77; Susan L. Meyer, 'Colonialism and the Figurative Strategy of
    Jane Eyre', *Victorian Studies*, 33 (1990), pp. 247–68; Suvendrini Perera,
    Reaches of Empire: The English Novel from Edgeworth to Dickens (New York:
    Columbia University Press, 1991), pp. 79–102, and Firdous Azim, *The
    Colonial Rise of the Novel* (London and New York: Routledge, 1993),
    pp. 172–97.
6   On this point see Meyer, pp. 252–3.
7   Gilbert and Gubar, p. 360.
8   Yet at the same time such differences reappear in the linguistic ten-
    sions of the very critical formulation which seeks to deny them, Bertha
    being not only Jane's 'truest' but also 'darkest double'. See also Elaine
    Showalter's analogous comment that Bertha's death constitutes for Jane
    a symbolic destruction of 'the dark passion of her own psyche', *A Lit-
    erature of Their Own: British Women Novelists from Brontë to Lessing* (London:
    Virago, 1978), p. 122.
9   See note 5 above.
10 William Shakespeare, *The Tempest*, ed. Frank Kermode (London and New
    York: Routledge, 1992), p. 27.
11 Donaldson, p. 66.
12 Ibid., p. 68.
13 A term used by Elizabeth Baer in her analysis of Rhys's rewriting of
    Brontë. See 'The Sisterhood of Jane Eyre and Antoinette Cosway', in
    The Voyage In: Fictions of Female Development, ed. Elizabeth Abel *et al.*
    (Hanover and London: University Press of New England, 1983), p. 132.
14 The writing of Antoinette's narrative is, for Spivak, an ambiguous en-
    terprise. On the one hand, it can be viewed as itself a startling disruption
    of the canonical authority enshrined in *Jane Eyre*. Yet on the other
    hand, Rhys's recuperation of Antoinette/Bertha's story is inseparable,
    according to Spivak, from a repetition of the very sort of silence it
    seeks to oppose. Rhys's novel 'marks with uncanny clarity the limits of
    its own discourse in Christophine, Antoinette's black nurse. . . . She cannot
    be contained by a novel which rewrites a canonical English text . . . in
    the interest of the white Creole rather than the native' (pp. 252–3).
    Spivak could be said, however, to want to have it both ways, since in

her reading of *Jane Eyre*, Bertha precisely occupies the position of the 'native "subject"' (p. 248), which she is here described as having usurped. This double bind is succinctly formulated by Meyer, p. 251: 'Bertha is either native or not native in the interests of Spivak's critique. Thus it is by sleight of hand that Spivak shows feminism to be inevitably complicitous with imperialism.'

15   As Meyer points out, 'it may not be possible to pinpoint the closing moment of the novel further than within a range of twenty-seven years, between 1819 and 1846' (p. 254). This means that Jane's marriage to Rochester, ten years prior to the writing of her autobiography, occurs either in 1809 or 1836. Within the calendar of colonialism, it is thus located, at the earliest, either two years after the abolition of the slave trade by Britain and America in 1807 or, at the latest, two years after the formal abolition of slavery in British colonies (1834), but also two before the granting of full emancipation, in 1838. Despite the considerable discrepancies between these two chronologies, it is evident that both place the experiences of the heroine/narrator firmly in the context of British colonial oppression in the West Indies.

16   Frederick Douglass, *The Frederick Douglass Papers: Vol 1: Speeches, Debates and Interviews*, ed. John W. Blassingame (New Haven and London: Yale University Press, 1979), p. 317.

17   See note 15 above. For a meticulous account of these events (and the processes leading up to them) see Robin Blackburn, *The Overthrow of Colonial Slavery: 1776–1848* (London and New York: Verso, 1988), pp. 419–72.

18   Prince, p. 84.

19   Charlotte Brontë, *Jane Eyre*, ed. and intro. Margaret Smith (Oxford and New York: Oxford University Press, 1998), p. 115. All subsequent references are to this edition – abbreviated as *JE* – and included in parenthesis after quotations in the text.

20   See Brontë's letter of 28 January 1848 to W. S. Williams in *The Brontës: Their Lives, Friendships and Correspondence*, ed. T. J. Wise and J. A. Symington, 4 vols, (Oxford: Blackwell, 1932), II, p. 183. The circumstances of Thackeray's marriage are documented in Gordon N. Ray, *Thackeray: The Uses of Adversity 1811–1846* (London: Oxford University Press, 1955), pp. 250–77. See also Gilbert and Gubar's comments on Thackeray's marriage, pp. 680–1, note 23.

21   Thomas Babington Macaulay, *Miscellaneous Writings and Speeches* (London and New York: Longmans, Green and Co., 1889), p. 487. Cited in Blackburn, p. 448. The context of the phrase is Macaulay's speech on parliamentary reform (2 March 1831). As well as citing the American and French Revolutions as admonitory signs of the dangers involved in ignoring the popular desire for reform, he also invokes 'the struggle which the free people of colour in Jamaica are now maintaining' against colonial oppression.

22   Jane is figured in similar terms at Thornfield where she not only engages in what Rochester calls 'governessing slavery' (*JE*, p. 283) but is also looked upon, as governess, as part of an 'anathematized race' (*JE*, p. 186).

23 Eric Cheyfitz, *The Poetics of Imperialism: Translation and Colonization from The Tempest to Tarzan* (New York and Oxford: Oxford University Press, 1991), p. 35.

24 Aristotle, *Poetics*, 1457[b] 6–9 (Bywater's translation). Cited in Paul Ricœur *The Rule of Metaphor: Multi-Disciplinary Studies in the Creation of Meaning in Language*, trans. Robert Czerny *et al.* (Toronto and Buffalo: University of Toronto Press, 1977), p. 13.

25 See Quintilian, *The Institutio Oratoria of Quintilian*, trans. H. E. Butler, 4 vols (Cambridge, MA: Harvard University Press, 1976), III. viii, p. 303.

26 Ricœur, p. 19.

27 Patricia Parker, *Literary Fat Ladies: Rhetoric, Gender, Property* (London and New York: Methuen, 1987), p. 36.

28 As for example in his relation to Rosamond Oliver: 'His chest heaved once, as if his large heart, weary of despotic constriction, had expanded, despite the will, and made a vigorous bound for the attainment of liberty' (*JE*, p. 384). Against his 'large heart''s struggles for 'liberty', St. John is always 'preparing some iron blow of contradiction, or forging a fresh chain to fetter [it]' (*JE*, p. 393), labours of self-enslavement which find apotheosis in the form of his 'missionary's career' (*JE*, p. 414).

29 Jane herself is oddly to be discovered, at the end of volume 1, 'standing in a pool!' (*JE*, p. 158) made by the water she uses to extinguish the fire Bertha lights in an attempt to burn the sleeping Rochester in his bed.

30 Gilbert and Gubar, p. 360 (emphasis in original).

31 Ibid., p. 361.

32 This count includes Bertha's attempted strangulation of Rochester at the end of volume 2 (*JE*, pp. 307–8). Consistent with Bertha's marginalization throughout *Jane Eyre*, the ambiguous drama of her final moments – setting fire to Thornfield and finally leaping to death before the advancing Rochester – is presented from an obscure narrative perspective. It is a story told to Jane by one of the novel's more *recherché* figures, Rochester's father's butler (*JE*, pp. 448–52).

33 Adrienne Rich, *On Lies, Secrets and Silence: Selected Prose 1966–1978* (London: Virago, 1980), p. 99.

34 Toni Morrison, 'The Site of Memory', in *Inventing the Truth: The Art and Craft of Memoir*, ed. William Zinsser (Boston, MA: Houghton Mifflin, 1987), p. 110. The immediate source for Morrison's comment is in fact Lydia Maria Child's own veil-figure in the Introduction to Harriet A. Jacobs's *Incidents in the Life of a Slave Girl Written by Herself* (1861). Referring to the sexual ordeals inflicted upon female slaves, Child writes: 'This peculiar phase of Slavery has generally been kept veiled; but the public ought to be made acquainted with its monstrous features, and I willingly take the responsibility of presenting them with the veil withdrawn.' See Harriet A. Jacobs, *Incidents in the Life of A Slave Girl Written by Herself*, ed. and intro. Jean Fagan Yellin (Cambridge, MA and London: Harvard University Press, 1987), p. 4.

35 Meyer, p. 252 (emphasis in original).

36 Ibid., p. 255. As James Walvin notes, an example of just such anticipated violence, particularly disturbing to the colonizers in its scale, occurs

in the 'Baptist War' of 1831–2 as 'slaves in Jamaica erupted in the latest of that island's seemingly endless slave revolts'. See James Walvin, *Black Ivory: A History of British Slavery* (London: HarperCollins, 1992), p. 265. See also pp. 276–8, and Blackburn, pp. 432–3. For an interesting recuperative account of the role of black women in shaping the history of slave-resistance in the British colonies see Stella Dadzie, 'Searching for the Invisible Woman: Slavery and Resistance in Jamaica', *Race & Class: A Journal for Black and Third World Liberation*, 32 (Autumn 1990), pp. 21–38.

37 Donaldson, p. 66.

38 Rochester's inadvertent likening of himself to a slave is anticipated by his self-description, during an early conversation with Jane, as 'a man and a brother' (*JE*, p. 145), an oblique reference to the seal of the Slave Emancipation Society manufactured by Josiah Wedgwood in 1787. On this point see R. J. Dingley, 'Rochester as Slave: An Allusion in *Jane Eyre*', *Notes and Queries*, 31 (March 1984), p. 66. It should also be juxtaposed with a passage from Walsh's 'Notices of Brazil' cited by Thomas Pringle in his 'Supplement to the History of Mary Prince' in order to illustrate the corrupting effects of slavery upon its practitioners: 'I never walked through the streets of Rio', Walsh writes, 'that some house did not present to me the semblance of a Bridewell, where the moans and the cries of the sufferers, and the sounds of whips and scourges within, announced to me that corporal punishment was being inflicted. Whenever I remarked this to a friend, I was always answered that the refractory nature of the slave rendered it necessary, and no house could properly be conducted unless it was practised. But this is certainly not the case; and the chastisement is constantly applied in the very wantonness of barbarity, and would not, and dared not, be inflicted on the humblest wretch in society, if he was not a slave, and so put out of the pale of pity.' Cited in Prince, p. 112.

39 Meyer, p. 267.

40 See also, among further instances, Jane's description of the goodnight kiss ritually conferred upon her by St. John as 'a seal affixed to [her] fetters' (*JE*, p. 419) or, again, the rhetorical question concerning marriage that she directs towards Diana: 'Would it not be strange, Die, to be chained for life to a man who regarded one but as a useful tool?' (*JE*, p. 438).

41 Such an expansion lends support to the argument that Jane Eyre completes the writing of her narrative at the later date of 1846 (rather than 1819) since, as Blackburn notes, 'by the 1820s and 1830s a thorough-going reorientation of Britain's imperial interests was already well underway', towards the Orient and particularly India (p. 434).

42 Perera, p. 79.

43 The first direct reference to sati (anglicized by the text as 'suttee') comes while Jane is still at Thornfield. Despite the coercive lyricism of Rochester's serenade ('My love has sworn, with sealing kiss, / With me to live – to die'), Jane stubbornly asserts the 'right to die' when she pleases rather than 'be hurried away in a suttee': she will not be 'melted to marrow', as Rochester grudgingly concedes, by the 'stanzas crooned in her praise'

(*JE*, p. 286). For a fuller discussion of this particular exchange see Perera, pp. 87–8.

44 The motivation behind British colonial attempts to abolish the practice of sati (criminalized in 1829) was far from purely altruistic, a benign concern with Occidental female rights and liberation: as Perera puts it, 'Throughout the mid-nineteenth century, sati continued to provide justification both for empire and for increased missionary penetration' (p. 92).

45 On this point see ibid., p. 89.

46 As, for example, in terms of Jane's imagination of the silent conflict within St. John between desire for Rosamond and Christian vocation: 'He seemed to say, with his sad and resolute look, if he did not say it with his lips, "I love you. . . . If I offered my heart, I believe you would accept it. But that heart is already laid on a sacred altar: the fire is arranged round it. It will soon be no more than a sacrifice consumed"' (*JE*, p. 387).

47 Cheyfitz, pp. 35–6, 89–90.

48 An appropriate text, whose title – when translated into English, as *The Robbers* – is a reminder of the processes by which Rochester comes to acquire his wealth and hence, also, the past from which Jane had sought to escape. Hannah's remark, as she apologizes for having initially misconstrued the destitute Jane as a beggar, produces a similar effect: 'I was quite mista'en in my thoughts of you: but there is so many cheats goes about, you mun forgie me' (*JE*, p. 360).

49 Carolyn Williams, 'Closing the Book: The Intertextual End of *Jane Eyre*', in Jerome J. McGann, ed., *Victorian Connections* (Charlottesville: University Press of Virginia, 1989), p. 61.

50 Ibid., p. 85, note 2.

51 Rich, p. 97.

52 See Gilbert and Gubar, pp. 369–71; Pat Macpherson, *Reflecting on Jane Eyre* (London and New York: Routledge, 1989), p. 117 and Sutherland, pp. 434–5.

Chapter 4

1 The epigraph to this chapter is taken from the unpublished manuscript of Jean Rhys's *The Black Exercise Book*. Cited in Coral Ann Howells, *Jean Rhys* (Hemel Hempstead: Harvester, 1991), p. 21.

2 Jean Rhys, *Jean Rhys Letters, 1931–1966*, ed. Francis Wyndham and Diana Melly (London: André Deutsch, 1984), p. 296 (emphases in original).

3 See Jean-François Lyotard, *The Postmodern Condition: A Report on Knowledge*, trans. Geoff Bennington and Brian Massumi (Manchester: Manchester University Press, 1984), p. xxiv.

4 On criticism which examines the intersections between *Jane Eyre*'s feminism and its colonialist biases, see chapter 3, note 5 above.

5 Rhys, *Jean Rhys Letters*, p. 157.

6 Susan L. Meyer, 'Colonialism and the Figurative Strategy of *Jane Eyre*', *Victorian Studies*, 33 (1990), p. 252 (emphasis in original). The specificity

of Antoinette's status as white creole woman is discussed in Veronica Marie Gregg, *Jean Rhys's Historical Imagination: Reading and Writing the Creole* (Chapel Hill and London: University of North Carolina Press, 1995), pp. 82–115.

7 For detailed analysis of the hypersexualized black female, see Sander L. Gilman, 'Black Bodies, White Bodies: Toward an Iconography of Female Sexuality in Late Nineteenth-Century Art, Medicine, and Literature', *Critical Inquiry*, 12 (1985), pp. 204–42, and Barbara Bush, *Slave Women in Caribbean Society 1650–1838* (London: James Currey, 1990), pp. 11–22. The frequent association of blackness with drunkenness and madness is noted by Meyer, p. 253.

8 Charlotte Brontë, *Jane Eyre*, ed. and intro. Margaret Smith (Oxford and New York: Oxford University Press, 1998), p. 221. All subsequent references are to this edition – abbreviated as *JE* – and included in parenthesis after quotations in the text.

9 Meyer, p. 252.

10 Rhys's comment appears in an interview with Elizabeth Vreeland, 'Jean Rhys: The Art of Fiction LXIV', *Paris Review*, 21 (1979), p. 235.

11 Jean Rhys, *Wide Sargasso Sea*, ed. and intro. Angela Smith (Harmondsworth: Penguin, 1997), p. 18. All subsequent references are to this edition – abbreviated as *WSS* – and included in parenthesis after quotations in the text.

12 See chapter 1, note 19 above.

13 See Helen Tiffin, 'Post-Colonial Literatures and Counter-Discourse', *Kunapipi*, 9 (1987), p. 22: '*canonical counter-discourse*. . . . is [a strategy] in which a post-colonial writer takes up a character, or characters or the basic assumptions of a British canonical text, subverting the text for post-colonial purposes' (emphasis in original). Notable readings of *Wide Sargasso Sea* along these lines include Judie Newman, *The Ballistic Bard: Postcolonial Fictions* (London: Edward Arnold, 1995), pp. 13–28, and Romita Choudhury '"Is There a Ghost, a Zombie There?" Postcolonial Intertextuality and Jean Rhys's *Wide Sargasso Sea*', *Textual Practice*, 10 (1996), pp. 315–27.

14 For a brief gloss on this point see chapter 3, note 14 above.

15 See Maggie Humm, *Border Traffic: Strategies of Contemporary Women Writers* (Manchester: Manchester University Press, 1991), p. 69.

16 See Ronnie Scharfman, 'Mirroring and Mothering in Simone Schwarz-Bart's *Pluie et Vent sur Telumeé Miracle* and Jean Rhys' *Wide Sargasso Sea*', *Yale French Studies*, 62 (1981), p. 103: 'In the first part of the novel we learn that the mother's name is Annette. Antoinette is of course phonetically related to Annette, being a combination of Annette and "toi": a hidden, built-in bond between mother and daughter can be read into these names.'

17 Lee Erwin's phrase, '"Like in a Looking-Glass": History and Narrative in *Wide Sargasso Sea*', *Novel: A Forum on Fiction*, 22 (1989), p. 146.

18 For an excellent discussion of *Wide Sargasso Sea* as a text dramatizing anxieties about racial contamination, see Laura E. Ciolkowski, 'Navigating the *Wide Sargasso Sea*: Colonial History, English Fiction, and British Empire', *Twentieth Century Literature*, 43 (1997), pp. 339–59.

19 Rochester's phrases, reported by Antoinette, are citations from *Jane Eyre* (*JE*, p. 323), the second involving a minor alteration of its original counterpart, 'true daughter of an infamous mother'.
20 Rhys, cited in Vreeland, p. 235.
21 Meyer, p. 254.
22 Rhys, *Jean Rhys Letters*, p. 214.

Chapter 5

1 The epigraphs to this chapter are taken from Toni Morrison, *The Bluest Eye*, with a new Afterword (London: Picador, 1994), p. 138, and Frantz Fanon, *Black Skin, White Masks*, trans. Charles Lam Markmann, Foreword by Homi K. Bhabha (London: Pluto Press, 1993), p. 43. All subsequent references are to these editions – abbreviated as *BE* and *BS* respectively – and included in parenthesis after quotations in the text.
2 Madhu Dubey, *Black Women Novelists and the Nationalist Aesthetic* (Bloomington and Indianapolis: Indiana University Press, 1994), p. 15. See pp. 33–50 for Dubey's reading of *The Bluest Eye*.
3 Ibid., p. 20. In viewing *The Bluest Eye* as a critique of the gender politics of the Black Aesthetic, Dubey echoes Morrison's own reflections, in a talk originally delivered in 1985, on the motives informing the writing of the novel. Simultaneously casting herself in the roles of writer and reader, Morrison comments: 'I wrote [*The Bluest Eye*] because I had not read it before. There were no books about me. I didn't exist in all of the literature I had read.... When I reached this moment, the writing was important because I had to bear witness to what was not recorded. This person, this female, this black, did not exist "centre-self."' Cited in Sandi Russell, *Render Me My Song: African-American Women Writers from Slavery to the Present* (London: Pandora, 1990), p. 92. Morrison's critical distance from the Black Aesthetic and black nationalist movements (whose political projects are concentrated in the slogan 'Black is Beautiful') also forms the starting-point for Jill Matus's more recent analysis of *The Bluest Eye*: 'Morrison's first novel', she writes, 'implicitly takes on assertions of racial pride – black is beautiful – and scrutinises the historical backlog of self-devaluation that such assertions cannot magically erase'. Jill Matus, *Toni Morrison* (Manchester and New York: Manchester University Press, 1998), p. 37.
4 Paul Gilroy, *The Black Atlantic: Modernity and Double Consciousness* (London and New York: Verso, 1993), p. 15.
5 Ibid.
6 The critical absence of *Black Skin, White Masks* as an intertext for *The Bluest Eye* contrasts sharply with the wide recognition received by Fanon's more directly political *The Wretched of the Earth* as an influential text for the militant black nationalist thinkers of 1960s America. For a brief discussion of *The Wretched of the Earth* in this context see Matus, p. 11. In more general terms, the absence is consistent with the way in which African American writing tends, as Sally Keenan points out, to be largely under-theorized from the postcolonial perspective with which Fanon's

work is associated. To use Keenan's own word, this situation is, historically speaking, somewhat 'surprising'. Even as America finally came into being as a postcolonial nation by liberating itself from British rule in the American War of Independence of 1776–83, it was constituted out of and remained spectacularly implicated in forms of colonial oppression – from the attempted genocide of indigenous peoples to the enslavement of Africans – which continue to exert their effects in the present. See Sally Keenan, '"Four Hundred Years of Silence": Myth, History, and Motherhood in Toni Morrison's *Beloved*', in *Recasting the World: Writing after Colonialism*, ed. Jonathan White (Baltimore: Johns Hopkins University Press, 1993), p. 45. For a sustained and important recent consideration of the possible translations of postcolonial theory into an African American context, see also Christine Macleod, 'Black American Literature and the Postcolonial Debate', *Yearbook of English Studies*, 27 (1997), pp. 51–65.

 7 Michael Rossington, 'Frantz Fanon', in *The A-Z Guide to Modern Literary and Cultural Theorists*, ed. Stuart Sim (Hemel Hempstead: Prentice Hall/ Harvester Wheatsheaf, 1995), p. 124.

 8 Jacques Lacan, *Écrits: A Selection*, trans. Alan Sheridan (London: Tavistock, 1980), p. 4.

 9 Jean-Paul Sartre, Preface to *The Wretched of the Earth*, trans. Constance Farrington (Harmondsworth: Penguin, 1990), p. 22.

10 Gwen Bergner, 'Who is That Masked Woman? or, The Role of Gender in Fanon's *Black Skin, White Masks*', *PMLA*, 110 (1995), p. 76.

11 Some of the dictionary meanings of 'priming' are usefully noted by Gurleen Grewal: 'A primer is "a person or thing that primes," the verb *to prime* being defined as follows: "to prepare or make ready for a particular purpose or operation"; "to cover (a surface) with a preparatory coat or color, as in painting"'. Gurleen Grewal, '"Laundering the Head of Whitewash": Mimicry and Resistance in *The Bluest Eye*', in *Approaches to Teaching the Novels of Toni Morrison*, ed. Nellie Y. McKay and Kathryn Earle (New York: Modern Language Association of America, 1997), p. 125.

12 For a fuller discussion of Rosemary's whiteness, as it is inscribed with 'the intimate relation between sexual politics and racial and economic privilege', see Giavanna Munafo, '"No Sign of Life" – Marble-Blue Eyes and Lakefront Houses in *The Bluest Eye*', *LIT: Literature Interpretation Theory*, 6 (1995), pp. 2–3.

13 The most positive resistance to this dominant pattern comes in 'the form of the folk community embodied in the three prostitutes', as noted in Dubey, p. 45.

14 This point is amplified in Linden Peach, *Toni Morrison* (Basingstoke and London: Macmillan, 1995), p. 33: 'Ironically, the lynch rope into which Maureen's hair is said to have been braided reminds us of slavery and oppression, the past on which black solidarity ought to be constructed. . . . a symbol of torture and death has been transformed into an adornment and robbed of its power.'

15 While Pauline's cinematic encounters entail an identification with white women, the emphasis, in Fanon, falls, by contrast, on the black male

subject's disidentification with the celluloid images by which he is beset: 'I cannot go to a film without seeing myself. I wait for me. In the interval, just before the film starts, I wait for me. The people in the theater are watching me, examining me, waiting for me. A Negro groom is going to appear. My heart makes my head swim' (*BS*, p. 140).

16 Dubey, p. 36.
17 For an overview and negotiation of these conflicting critical positions on the rape-scene see Dubey, pp. 36–7.
18 See Matus, pp. 49–51.
19 Ibid., p. 50.
20 Cathy Caruth, *Unclaimed Experience: Trauma, Narrative, and History* (Baltimore and London: Johns Hopkins University Press, 1996), p. 4.
21 Dubey, p. 49.
22 Diana Fuss, *Identification Papers* (New York and London: Routledge, 1995), p. 155.
23 Ibid., p. 156 (emphasis in original).
24 Mary Ann Doane, *Femmes Fatales: Feminism, Film Theory, Psychoanalysis* (New York and Routledge, 1991), p. 222. Cited in Fuss, p. 156.
25 Like his personality, Soaphead's family history – which the novel provides in unusual detail – is 'an arabesque' (*BE*, p. 131) and seems to confirm Françoise Vergès's recent description of 'the Caribbean as a matrix of hybridization and creolization'. Its violent origins in miscegenation and colonial slavery (marked in the abolitionist allusion to 'the early 1800's') also provide another instance of the way in which Morrison's text supplements Fanon's. For, as Vergès argues, the path traced by Fanon's work – from *Black Skin, White Masks* to *The Wretched of the Earth*, colonial neurosis in Martinique to revolutionary struggle in Algeria – is a path of disavowal. In Martinique, Vergès writes, Fanon 'is confronted with the difficulty of working through a story that begins with deportation, violence, and the rape of the mother. . . . Fanon never evokes slavery as a symbolic, economic, and cultural system. The colonized Antillean's ancestor is ignored.' See Françoise Vergès, 'Creole Skin, Black Mask: Fanon and Disavowal', *Critical Inquiry*, 23 (1997), pp. 579, 581.
26 Joyce Irene Middleton, 'Confronting the "Master Narrative": The Privilege of Orality in Toni Morrison's *The Bluest Eye*', *Cultural Studies*, 9 (1995), p. 312.

Chapter 6

1 The epigraphs to this chapter are taken from Tsitsi Dangarembga, *Nervous Conditions* (London: The Women's Press, 1997), p. 33; Frantz Fanon, *The Wretched of the Earth*, Preface by Jean-Paul Sartre, trans. Constance Farrington (Harmondsworth: Penguin, 1990), p. 249, and Charlotte Brontë, *Shirley*, ed. and intro. Herbert Rosengarten and Margaret Smith (Oxford and New York: Oxford University Press, 1998), p. 105. All subsequent references are to these editions – abbreviated as *NC*, *WE* and *S* respectively – and included in parenthesis after quotations in the text.

2 M. Keith Booker, *The African Novel in English: An Introduction* (Portsmouth, NH: Heinemann, 1998), p. 191. Other critics who have explored *Nervous Conditions* as a black feminist response to *The Wretched of the Earth* include, most notably, Sue Thomas, 'Killing the Hysteric in the Colonized's House: Tsitsi Dangarembga's *Nervous Conditions'*, *Journal of Commonwealth Literature*, 27. 1 (1992), pp. 26–36; Michelle Vizzard, '"Of Mimicry and Woman": Hysteria and Anticolonial Feminism in Tsitsi Dangarembga's *Nervous Conditions'*, *SPAN: Journal of the South Pacific Association for Commonwealth Literature and Language Studies*, 36 (1993), pp. 202–10, and Charles Sugnet, '*Nervous Conditions*: Dangarembga's Feminist Reinvention of Fanon', in *The Politics of (M)Othering: Womanhood, Identity, and Resistance in African Literature*, ed. Obioma Nnaemeka (London and New York: Routledge, 1997), pp. 33–49.

3 Sugnet, p. 35.

4 Thomas, p. 35.

5 Dangarembga's reference to Blyton is considerably less peripheral to the ideological and thematic concerns of her text than it might seem: Blyton's work not only offers a version of Englishness that has been condemned by many as simultaneously racist, sexist and classist and is consequently unlikely to do much to nourish the self-image of the Tambudzai who reads her but also, like *Nervous Conditions* itself, is strikingly food-centred. As Michael Woods puts it, Blyton's evocations of food and eating are 'reminiscent of an orgy in an Edwardian emporium . . . tongues, ham, pies, lemonade and ginger beer. This is not just food, it is archetypal feasting'. Cited in Stephen Moss, 'The Eternal Child', *Guardian*, Friday Review, 11 April 1997, p. 3.

6 That the work of 'the Brontë sisters' should resonate with the anticolonial feminism of an African novelist such as Dangarembga is far from surprising. As numerous critics have demonstrated, the feminist fictions of Charlotte and Emily Brontë in particular need to be situated – and critiqued – from the perspective of the larger discourses of colonialism and empire in which they are implicated. The most influential illustration of such an approach is, of course, Gayatri Chakravorty Spivak's analysis of *Jane Eyre* in 'Three Women's Texts and a Critique of Imperialism', *Critical Inquiry*, 12 (1985), pp. 243–61. For examples of more recent critical decolonizations of Charlotte and Emily Brontë see, respectively, Firdous Azim, *The Colonial Rise of the Novel* (London and New York: Routledge, 1993), pp. 109–213, and Susan Meyer, *Imperialism at Home: Race and Victorian Women's Writing* (Ithaca, NY and London: Cornell University Press, 1996), pp. 96–125. It should also be recalled that Charlotte Brontë's early writings – produced in collaboration with her brother, Branwell – are themselves located in Angria, an imaginary colonial space 'carved', in the words of Juliet Barker, 'out of the interior of Africa'. See Juliet Barker, ed. *Charlotte Brontë: Juvenilia 1829–1835* (Harmondsworth: Penguin, 1996), p. 270.

7 Vizzard, p. 205.

8 Supriya Nair, 'Melancholic Women: The Intellectual Hysteric(s) in *Nervous Conditions'*, *Research in African Literature*, 26. 2 (1996), p. 132.

9 Mary Shelley, *Frankenstein*, ed. and intro. Marilyn Butler (London: Pickering, 1993), p. 35.
10 Ibid., p. 38.
11 Sugnet, p. 33.
12 Ibid., p. 34.
13 Abigail Bray, 'The Anorexic Body: Reading Disorders', *Cultural Studies*, 10 (1996), p. 413.
14 Ibid., p. 414.
15 Sugnet, p. 43.
16 Bray, p. 419.
17 Dangarembga underlines this point in an interview with Kirsten Holst Petersen in which she notes that cases of what might be called black anorexia 'have been reported in Zimbabwe'. At the same time she recognizes, like Bray, that 'The diagnosis of anorexia is something difficult. If a woman in Zimbabwe, rural or urban is depressed, loses weight etc. who is to say whether that is anorexia or not? . . . When does a depression become a disease?' See 'Between Gender, Race and History: Kirsten Holst Petersen Interviews Tsitsi Dangarembga', *Kunapipi: Journal of Post-Colonial Writing*, 16 (1994), p. 346. For discussion of the conflicting ways in which the incidence of eating disorders in Zimbabwean and other non-Western contexts has been handled, see Heidi Creamer, 'An Apple for the Teacher? Femininity, Coloniality, and Food in *Nervous Conditions*', ibid., pp. 359–60, note 8.
18 Sugnet, p. 35.
19 Ibid., p. 47.
20 For detailed discussion of the historical institution of anorexia as a diagnostic category – together with its affiliations to hysteria – see Helen Malson, *The Thin Woman: Feminism, Post-Structuralism and the Social Psychology of Anorexia Nervosa* (London and New York: Routledge, 1998), pp. 61–75.
21 Rod Edmond, *Affairs of the Hearth: Victorian Poetry and Domestic Narrative* (London and New York: Routledge, 1988), p. 193.
22 Ibid., p. 195.
23 Ibid., p. 196.
24 Deirdre Lashgari, 'What Some Women Can't Swallow: Hunger as Protest in Charlotte Brontë's *Shirley*', in *Disorderly Eaters: Texts in Self-Empowerment*, ed. Lilian R. Furst and Peter W. Graham (Pennsylvania: The Pennsylvania State University Press, 1992), p. 141.
25 Thomas, p. 30.
26 Booker, p. 194.
27 William Shakespeare, *Coriolanus*, ed. Philip Brockbank (London: Methuen, 1976), p. 96.
28 Ibid., pp. 102–6.
29 Ibid., p. 95.
30 Terry Eagleton, *Heathcliff and the Great Hunger: Studies in Irish Culture* (London and New York: Verso, 1995), p. 23.
31 Elsie Michie, 'From Simianized Irish to Oriental Despots: Heathcliff, Rochester and Racial Difference', *Novel: A Forum on Fiction*, 25 (1992), p. 125.

32 Ibid., pp. 125–6.
33 Ibid., p. 128.
34 See chapter 2, note 1 above.
35 See chapter 2, note 1 above.
36 Elizabeth Grosz, *Sexual Subversions: Three French Feminists* (Sydney: Allen & Unwin, 1989), p. 134 (emphasis in original). Cited in Thomas, p. 27.

Select Bibliography

Ahmad, Aijaz, 'Postcolonialism: What's in a Name?', in *Late Imperial Culture*, ed. Román de la Campa *et al.* (London and New York: Verso, 1995), pp. 11–32

Armstrong, Isobel, 'Foreword', in Plasa and Ring, pp. xi–xii

——, *Mansfield Park* (London: Penguin, 1988)

Ashcroft, Bill *et al.*, *Key Concepts in Post-Colonial Studies* (London and New York: Routledge, 1998)

—— *et al.*, ed., *The Post-Colonial Studies Reader* (London and New York: Routledge, 1995)

Austen, Jane, *Mansfield Park*, ed. James Kinsley, intro. Marilyn Butler (Oxford and New York: Oxford University Press, 1998)

Azim, Firdous, *The Colonial Rise of the Novel* (London and New York: Routledge, 1993)

Baker, Jr., Houston A., *Blues, Ideology, and Afro-American Literature: A Vernacular Theory* (Chicago and London: University of Chicago Press, 1984)

Benjamin, Walter, *Illuminations: Essays and Reflections*, trans. Harry Zohn, ed. and intro. Hannah Arendt (New York: Schocken, 1969)

Bergner, Gwen, 'Who is That Masked Woman?, or, The Role of Gender in Fanon's *Black Skin, White Masks*', *PMLA*, 110 (1995), pp. 75–88

Bhabha, Homi K., *The Location of Culture* (London and New York: Routledge, 1994)

Blackburn, Robin, *The Overthrow of Colonial Slavery: 1776–1848* (London and New York: Verso, 1988)

Booker, M. Keith, *The African Novel in English: An Introduction* (Portsmouth, NH: Heinemann, 1998)

Boumelha, Penny, *Charlotte Brontë* (Hemel Hempstead: Harvester, 1990)

Bray, Abigail, 'The Anorexic Body: Reading Disorders', *Cultural Studies*, 10 (1996), pp. 413–29

Brontë, Charlotte, *Jane Eyre*, ed. and intro. Margaret Smith (Oxford and New York: Oxford University Press, 1998)

——, *Shirley*, ed. Herbert Rosengarten and Margaret Smith (Oxford and New York: Oxford University Press, 1998)

Bush, Barbara, *Slave Women in Caribbean Society 1650–1838* (London: James Currey, 1990)

Butler, Marilyn, *Jane Austen and the War of Ideas* (Oxford: Clarendon Press, 1975)

Caruth, Cathy, *Unclaimed Experience: Trauma, Narrative, and History* (Baltimore and London: Johns Hopkins University Press, 1996)

Cheyfitz, Eric, *The Poetics of Imperialism: Translation and Colonization from The Tempest to Tarzan* (New York and Oxford: Oxford University Press, 1991)

Childs, Peter and Patrick Williams, *An Introduction to Post-Colonial Theory* (Hemel Hempstead: Prentice Hall, 1997)

Chinosole, 'Tryin' to Get Over: Narrative Posture in Equiano's Autobiography', in *The Art of Slave Narrative: Original Essays in Criticism and Theory*, ed. John Sekora and Darwin T. Turner (Macomb, IL: Western Illinois University Press, 1982), pp. 45–54

Choudhury, Romita, '"Is There a Ghost, a Zombie There?" Postcolonial Intertextuality and Jean Rhys's *Wide Sargasso Sea*', *Textual Practice*, 10 (1996), pp. 315–27

Ciolkowski, Laura E., 'Navigating the *Wide Sargasso Sea*: Colonial History, English Fiction, and British Empire', *Twentieth Century Literature*, 43 (1997), pp. 339–59

Creamer, Heidi, 'An Apple for the Teacher? Femininity, Coloniality, and Food in *Nervous Conditions*', *Kunapipi: Journal of Post-Colonial Writing*, 16 (1994), pp. 349–60

Dadzie, Stella, 'Searching for the Invisible Woman: Slavery and Resistance in Jamaica', *Race & Class: A Journal for Black and Third World Liberation*, 32 (Autumn 1990), pp. 21–38

Dangarembga, Tsitsi, *Nervous Conditions* (London: The Women's Press, 1997)

Donaldson, Laura E., 'The Miranda Complex: Colonialism and the Question of Feminist Reading', *Diacritics*, 18 (Autumn 1988), pp. 65–77

Dubey, Madhu, *Black Women Novelists and the Nationalist Aesthetic* (Bloomington and Indianapolis: Indiana University Press, 1994)

Dyer, Richard, *White* (London and New York: Routledge, 1997)

Eagleton, Terry, *Heathcliff and the Great Hunger: Studies in Irish Culture* (London and New York: Verso, 1995)

Equiano, Olaudah, *The Interesting Narrative of the Life of Olaudah Equiano, or Gustavus Vassa, the African. Written by Himself.*, in *The Interesting Narrative and Other Writings*, ed. and intro. Vincent Carretta (Harmondsworth: Penguin, 1995)

Erwin, Lee, '"Like in a Looking-Glass": History and Narrative in *Wide Sargasso Sea*', *Novel: A Forum on Fiction*, 22 (1989), pp. 143–58

Eze, Emmanuel Chukwudi, ed., *Race and the Enlightenment: A Reader* (Cambridge, MA and Oxford: Blackwell, 1997)

Fanon, Frantz, *Black Skin, White Masks*, trans. Charles Lam Markmann, Foreword by Homi K. Bhabha (London: Pluto Press, 1993)

——, *The Wretched of the Earth*, trans. Constance Farrington, Preface by Jean-Paul Sartre (Harmondsworth: Penguin, 1990)

Ferguson, Moira, *Colonialism and Gender Relations from Mary Wollstonecraft to Jamaica Kincaid: East Caribbean Connections* (New York: Columbia University Press, 1993)

Fichtelberg, Joseph, 'Word between Worlds: The Economy of Equiano's Narrative', *American Literary History*, 5 (1993), pp. 459–80

Fraiman, Susan, 'Jane Austen and Edward Said: Gender, Culture and Imperialism', *Critical Inquiry*, 21 (1995), pp. 805–21

Fuss, Diana, *Identification Papers* (New York and London: Routledge, 1995)

Gandhi, Leela, *Postcolonial Theory: A Critical Introduction* (Edinburgh: Edinburgh University Press, 1998)

Gates, Jr., Henry Louis, *The Signifying Monkey: A Theory of African-American Literary Criticism* (New York and Oxford: Oxford University Press, 1989)

Gerzina, Gretchen, *Black England: Life before Emancipation* (London: John Murray, 1995)

Gibbon, Frank, 'The Antiguan Connection: New Light on *Mansfield Park*', *Cambridge Quarterly*, 11 (1982), pp. 298–305

Gilbert, Sandra M. and Susan Gubar, *The Madwoman in the Attic: The Woman Writer and the Nineteenth-Century Literary Imagination* (New Haven and London: Yale University Press, 1979)

Gilman, Sander L., 'Black Bodies, White Bodies: Toward an Iconography of Female Sexuality in Late Nineteenth-Century Art, Medicine, and Literature', *Critical Inquiry*, 12 (1985), pp. 204–42

Gilroy, Paul, *The Black Atlantic: Modernity and Double Consciousness* (London and New York: Verso, 1993)

——, 'Diaspora and the Detours of Identity', in *Identity and Difference*, ed. Kathryn Woodward (London: Sage, 1997), pp. 299–343

——, *Small Acts: Thoughts on the Politics of Black Cultures* (London: Serpent's Tail, 1993)

Gregg, Veronica Marie, *Jean Rhys's Historical Imagination: Reading and Writing the Creole* (Chapel Hill and London: University of North Carolina Press, 1995)

Grewal, Gurleen, '"Laundering the Head of Whitewash": Mimicry and Resistance in *The Bluest Eye*', in *Approaches to Teaching the Novels of Toni Morrison*, ed. Nellie Y. McKay and Kathryn Earle (New York: Modern Language Association of America), pp. 118–27

Heward, Edward, *Lord Mansfield* (Chichester and London: Barry Rose, 1979)

Howells, Coral Ann, *Jean Rhys* (Hemel Hempstead: Harvester, 1991)

Huggan, Graham, 'A Tale of Two Parrots: Walcott, Rhys, and the Uses of Colonial Mimicry', *Contemporary Literature*, 35 (1994), pp. 643–58

Humm, Maggie, *Border Traffic: Strategies of Contemporary Women Writers* (Manchester: Manchester University Press, 1991)

Jacobs, Harriet A., *Incidents in the Life of A Slave Girl Written by Herself*, ed and intro. Jean Fagan Yellin (Cambridge, MA and London: Harvard University Press, 1987)

Johnson, Claudia L., 'Gender, Theory and Jane Austen Culture', in *Mansfield Park*, ed. and intro. Nigel Wood (Buckingham and Philadelphia: Open University Press, 1993), pp. 91–120

Kotzebue, August von, *Lovers' Vows*, adapt. Elizabeth Inchbald, ed. and intro. Jonathan Wordsworth (Oxford and New York: Woodstock, 1990)

——, *The Negro Slaves, A Dramatic-Historical Piece, in Three Acts, Translated from the German of the President de Kotzebue* (London: T. Cadell *et al.*, 1796)

Lacan, Jacques, *Écrits: A Selection*, trans. Alan Sheridan (London: Tavistock, 1980)

Lashgari, Deirdre, 'What Some Women Can't Swallow: Hunger as Protest in Charlotte Brontë's *Shirley*', in *Disorderly Eaters: Texts in Self-Empowerment*, ed. Lilian R. Furst and Peter W. Graham (Pennsylvania: The Pennsylvania State University Press, 1992), pp. 141–52

Litvak, Joseph, *Caught in the Act: Theatricality in the Nineteenth-Century English Novel* (Berkeley: University of California Press, 1992)

London, Bette, 'The Pleasures of Submission: *Jane Eyre* and the Production of the Text', *English Literary History*, 58 (1991), pp. 195–213

Loomba, Ania, *Colonialism/Postcolonialism* (London and New York: Routledge, 1998)

McClintock, Anne, 'The Angel of Progress: Pitfalls of the Term "Post-colonialism"', in Williams and Chrisman, pp. 291–304

Macherey, Pierre, *A Theory of Literary Production*, trans. Geoffrey Wall (London: Routledge & Kegan Paul, 1978)

Macleod, Christine, 'Black American Literature and the Postcolonial Debate', *Yearbook of English Studies*, 27 (1997), pp. 51–65

Malone, Maggie, 'Patriarchy and Slavery and the Problem of Fanny', *Essays in Poetics: Journal of the Neo-Formalist Circle*, 18. 2 (1993), pp. 28–41

Malson, Helen, *The Thin Woman: Feminism, Post-Structuralism and the Social Psychology of Anorexia Nervosa* (London and New York: Routledge, 1998)

Marren, Susan M., 'Between Slavery and Freedom: The Transgressive Self in Olaudah Equiano's Autobiography', *PMLA*, 108 (1993), pp. 94–105

Matus, Jill, *Toni Morrison* (Manchester and New York: Manchester University Press, 1998)

Meyer, Susan L. 'Colonialism and the Figurative Strategy of *Jane Eyre*', *Victorian Studies*, 33 (1990), pp. 247–68

——, *Imperialism at Home: Race and Victorian Women's Writing* (Ithaca, NY and London: Cornell University Press, 1996)

Michie, Elsie, 'From Simianized Irish to Oriental Despots: Heathcliff, Rochester and Racial Difference', *Novel*, 25 (1992), pp. 125–40

Middleton, Joyce Irene, 'Confronting the "Master Narrative": The Privilege of Orality in Toni Morrison's *The Bluest Eye*', *Cultural Studies*, 9 (1995), pp. 301–17

Moore-Gilbert, Bart, 'Crises of Identity? Current Problems and Possibilities in Postcolonial Criticism', *European English Messenger*, 6. 2 (1997), pp. 35–42

—— *et al.*, ed., *Postcolonial Criticism* (London and New York: Longman, 1997)

——, *Postcolonial Theory: Contexts, Practices, Politics* (London and New York: Verso, 1998)

Morrison, Toni, *The Bluest Eye*, with a new Afterword (London: Picador, 1994)

——, 'The Site of Memory', in *Inventing the Truth: The Art and Craft of Memoir*, ed. William Zinsser (Boston, MA: Houghton Mifflin, 1987), pp. 103–24

Mukherjee, Meenakshi, *Jane Austen* (Basingstoke and London: Macmillan, 1991)

Munafo, Giavanna, '"No Sign of Life" – Marble-Blue Eyes and Lakefront Houses in *The Bluest Eye*', *LIT: Literature Interpretation Theory*, 6 (1995), pp. 1–19

Nair, Supriya, 'Melancholic Women: The Intellectual Hysteric(s) in *Nervous Conditions*', *Research in African Literature*, 26. 2 (1996), pp. 130–9

Newman, Judie, *The Ballistic Bard: Postcolonial Fictions* (London: Edward Arnold, 1995)

Peach, Linden, *Toni Morrison* (Basingstoke and London: Macmillan, 1995)

Perera, Suvendrini, *Reaches of Empire: The English Novel from Edgeworth to Dickens* (New York: Columbia University Press, 1991)

Petersen, Kirsten Holst, 'Between Gender, Race and History: Kirsten Holst Petersen Interviews Tsitsi Dangarembga', *Kunapipi*, 16 (1994), pp. 345–8

Plasa, Carl and Betty J. Ring, ed. and intro., *The Discourse of Slavery: Aphra Behn to Toni Morrison*, Foreword by Isobel Armstrong (London and New York: Routledge, 1994)

Prince, Mary, *The History of Mary Prince, A West Indian Slave, Related by Herself*, ed. and intro. Moira Ferguson (Ann Arbor: University of Michigan Press, 1993)

Rhys, Jean, *Jean Rhys Letters, 1931–1966*, ed. Francis Wyndham and Diana Melly (London: André Deutsch, 1984)

——, *Wide Sargasso Sea*, ed. and intro. Angela Smith (Harmondsworth: Penguin, 1997)

Russell, Sandi, *Render Me My Song: African-American Women Writers from Slavery to the Present* (London: Pandora, 1990)

Rust, Marion, 'The Subaltern as Imperialist: Speaking of Olaudah Equiano', in *Passing and the Fictions of Identity*, ed. Elaine K. Ginsberg (Durham, NC and London: Duke University Press, 1996), pp. 21–36

Said, Edward W., *Culture and Imperialism* (London: Vintage, 1994)

Shakespeare, William, *Coriolanus*, ed. Philip Brockbank (London: Methuen, 1976)

——, *The Tempest*, ed. Frank Kermode (London and New York: Routledge, 1992)

Shelley, Mary, *Frankenstein*, ed. and intro. Marilyn Butler (London: Pickering, 1993)

Shohat, Ella, 'Notes on the "Post-colonial"', *Social Text*, 31/2 (1993), pp. 99–113

Spivak, Gayatri Chakravorty, 'Three Women's Texts and a Critique of Imperialism', *Critical Inquiry*, 12 (1985), pp. 243–61

Stewart, Maaja A., *Domestic Realities and Imperial Fictions: Jane Austen's Novels in Eighteenth-Century Contexts* (Athens, GA and London: University of Georgia Press, 1993)

Sugnet, Charles, 'Nervous Conditions: Dangarembga's Feminist Reinvention of Fanon', in *The Politics of (M)Othering: Womanhood, Identity, and Resistance in African Literature*, ed. Obioma Nnaemeka (London and New York: Routledge, 1997), pp. 33–49

Sutherland, Kathyrn, '*Jane Eyre*'s Literary History: The Case for *Mansfield Park*', *ELH*, 59 (1992), pp. 409–40

Thomas, Sue, 'Killing the Hysteric in the Colonized's House: Tsitsi Dangarembga's *Nervous Conditions*', *Journal of Commonwealth Literature*, 27. 1 (1992), pp. 26–36

Tiffin, Helen, 'Post-Colonial Literatures and Counter-Discourse', *Kunapipi*, 9 (1987), pp. 17–34

Vergès, Françoise, 'Creole Skin, Black Mask: Fanon and Disavowal', *Critical Inquiry*, 23 (1997), pp. 578–95

Vine, Steven, '"That Mild Beam": Enlightenment and Enslavement in William Blake's *Visions of the Daughters of Albion*', in Plasa and Ring, pp. 40–63

Vizzard, Michelle, '"Of Mimicry and Woman": Hysteria and Anticolonial Feminism in Tsitsi Dangarembga's *Nervous Conditions*', *SPAN: Journal of the South Pacific Association for Commonwealth Literature and Language Studies*, 36 (1993), pp. 202–10

Walvin, James, *Black Ivory: A History of British Slavery* (London: HarperCollins, 1992)

Williams, Carolyn, 'Closing the Book: The Intertextual End of *Jane Eyre*', in Jerome J. McGann, ed., *Victorian Connections* (Charlottesville: University Press of Virginia, 1989), pp. 60–87

Williams, Patrick and Laura Chrisman, ed. and intro., *Colonial Discourse and Post-Colonial Theory: A Reader* (Hemel Hempstead: Harvester, 1993)
Young, Robert J. C., *Colonial Desire: Hybridity in Theory, Culture and Race* (London and New York: Routledge, 1995)
——, *White Mythologies: Writing History and the West* (London and New York: Routledge, 1990)

Index